THE RACE CARD

POSTMILLENNIAL POP

General Editors: Karen Tongson and Henry Jenkins

Puro Arte: Filipinos on the Stages of Empire
Lucy Mae San Pablo Burns

Spreadable Media: Creating Value and Meaning in a Networked Culture
Henry Jenkins, Sam Ford, and Joshua Green

Media Franchising: Creative License and Collaboration in the Culture Industries
Derek Johnson

Your Ad Here: The Cool Sell of Guerrilla Marketing
Michael Serazio

Looking for Leroy: Illegible Black Masculinities
Mark Anthony Neal

From Bombay to Bollywood: The Making of a Global Media Industry
Aswin Punathambekar

A Race So Different: Performance and Law in Asian America
Joshua Takano Chambers-Letson

Surveillance Cinema
Catherine Zimmer

Modernity's Ear: Listening to Race and Gender in World Music
Roshanak Kheshti

The New Mutants: Superheroes and the Radical Imagination of American Comics
Ramzi Fawaz

Restricted Access: Media, Disability, and the Politics of Participation
Elizabeth Ellcessor

The Sonic Color-Line: Race and the Cultural Politics of Listening
Jennifer Lynn Stoever

Diversión: Play and Popular Culture in Cuban America
Albert Sergio Laguna

Antisocial Media: Anxious Labor in the Digital Economy
Greg Goldberg

Open TV: Innovation beyond Hollywood and the Rise of Web Television
Aymar Jean Christian

More Than Meets the Eye: Special Effects and the Fantastic Transmedia Franchise
Bob Rehak

Playing to the Crowd: Musicians, Audiences, and the Intimate Work of Connection
Nancy K. Baym

Old Futures: Speculative Fiction and Queer Possibility
Alexis Lothian

Anti-Fandom: Dislike and Hate in the Digital Age
Edited by Melissa A. Click

Social Media Entertainment: The New Industry at the Intersection of Hollywood and Silicon Valley
Stuart Cunningham and David Craig

Video Games Have Always Been Queer
Bonnie Ruberg

The Power of Sports: Media and Spectacle in American Culture
Michael Serazio

The Dark Fantastic: Race and the Imagination from Harry Potter to the Hunger Games
Ebony Elizabeth Thomas

The Race Card: From Gaming Technologies to Model Minorities
Tara Fickle

The Race Card

From Gaming Technologies to Model Minorities

Tara Fickle

NEW YORK UNIVERSITY PRESS
New York

NEW YORK UNIVERSITY PRESS
New York
www.nyupress.org

An earlier version of chapter 2 was previously published as Tara Fickle, "No-No Boy's Dilemma: Game Theory and Japanese American Internment Literature." *Modern Fiction Studies* 60.4 (Winter 2014): 740–66.

References to Internet websites (URLs) were accurate at the time of writing. Neither the author nor New York University Press is responsible for URLs that may have expired or changed since the manuscript was prepared.

Library of Congress Cataloging-in-Publication Data
Names: Fickle, Tara, author.
Title: The race card : from gaming technologies to model minorities / Tara Fickle.
Description: New York : New York University Press, 2018. | Series: Postmillennial pop | Includes bibliographical references and index.
Identifiers: LCCN 2018060476| ISBN 9781479868551 (cl : alk. paper) | ISBN 9781479805952 (pb : alk. paper)
Subjects: LCSH: Asian Americans—Social conditions. | Games—Social aspects—United States. | Asian Americans in popular culture. | Race discrimination—United States. | Game theory—Social aspects—United States.
Classification: LCC E184.A75 F45 2018 | DDC 305.895/073—dc23
LC record available at https://lccn.loc.gov/2018060476

New York University Press books are printed on acid-free paper, and their binding materials are chosen for strength and durability. We strive to use environmentally responsible suppliers and materials to the greatest extent possible in publishing our books.

Manufactured in the United States of America

10 9 8 7 6 5 4 3 2 1

Also available as an ebook

CONTENTS

List of Figures and Tables   vii

Introduction: Ludo-Orientalism and the Gamification of Race   1

PART I. GAMBLING ON THE AMERICAN DREAM

The Pitch: *Fair Play*

1. Evening the Odds through Chinese Exclusion   33

2. Just Deserts: A Game Theory of the Japanese
American Internment   47

The Catch: *The House Always Wins*

3. Against the Odds: From Model Minority to
Model Majority   79

PART II. MARCO POLO IN THE VIRTUAL WORLD

The Pitch: *Freeplay*

4. West of the Magic Circle: The Orientalist Origins of
Game Studies   113

5. Mobile Frontiers: *Pokémon* after Pearl Harbor   138

The Catch: *Free Labor*

6. Game Over? Internet Addiction, Gold Farming, and the
Race Card in a Post-Racial Age   177

Acknowledgments   199

Notes   203

Bibliography   231

Index   245

About the Author   257

FIGURES AND TABLES

I.1. Comics panel from Gene Yang and Thien Pham's *Level Up* (2011) and screenshot from *Pac-Man* (1980) — 18

1.1. Illustration of Bret Harte's "The Heathen Chinee" by Joseph Hull (1870) — 44

2.1. Political cartoon by Dr. Seuss, "Waiting for the Signal from Home . . ." (1942) — 48

3.1. *Newsweek* image of Japanese American Cub Scouts (1971) — 91

3.2. *New York Times Magazine* image of Chinese American boy in frontiersman costume (1957) — 93

3.3. *New York Times Magazine* image of Chinese American family (1957) — 96

4.1. Table of Roger Caillois's classification of games — 132

5.1. Screenshot of augmented reality technology in the mobile game *Pokémon GO* (2016) — 153

5.2. Screenshots of real-life locations as seen in Google Maps, the augmented reality mobile game *Ingress*, and *Pokémon GO* (2016) — 155

5.3. "My Location" feature in Google Maps and Apple Maps (2016) — 157

5.4. Map of *Pokémon GO* gyms in New York City (2016) — 163

5.5. Illustrated map of Greater East Asia Co-Prosperity Sphere from Japanese wartime propaganda booklet (1942) — 164

5.6. Screenshot of August 21, 2016, tweet depicting
Shinzō Abe as Mario   170

5.7. Screenshot from *South Park* "Chinpokomon" episode and
image of Shinzō Abe dressed as Mario (1999)   172

6.1. Comic panels from *In Real Life* (2014) depicting Anda's
first in-game encounter with Chinese gold farmers   185

6.2. Comic panels from *In Real Life* (2014) depicting Anda's
gold farmer avatar   195

Introduction

Ludo-Orientalism and the Gamification of Race

In the summer of 2016, *Pokémon GO*, an augmented reality (AR) mobile game based on the beloved 1990s Japanese franchise, took the United States by storm. Initially praised for promoting exercise and fostering new friendships, the game's novel lamination of virtual and real spaces soon exposed more insidious forms of social mapping. Minority players described being the target of suspicious glances while playing in predominantly white neighborhoods; suburban children were cautioned against straying into "bad" neighborhoods; an Asian American grandfather, the game's first casualty, was shot for alleged trespassing while playing near a Virginia country club. Many popular and social media commentators saw these incidents as evidence of the de facto segregation that still defines how race and space are delimited in the United States. They rued the fact that real-life inequality shattered the ludic illusion: that racism had spoiled the game by making it *too* real. For despite its cast of adorable, cartoonish "pocket monsters," *Pokémon GO* counterintuitively provided a disturbingly realistic approximation of the racial and economic schisms of everyday life. "Let's just go ahead and add *Pokémon GO* to the extremely long list of things white people can do without fear of being killed, while Black people have to realistically be wary," game designer Omari Akil concluded in his much-cited article "*Pokémon GO* Is a Death Sentence If You Are a Black Man."[1]

But was this unwanted intrusion of reality simply an unfortunate contamination, an inadvertent "glitch" of the game? Didn't *Pokémon GO*, by making distant travel a necessity for capturing Pokémon, in some sense actually *force* players into such boundary-crossing enterprises? Did it not, by making requisite such discomfort as might otherwise be avoided or at least anticipated in daily life, actively reify the abstract fact of inequality with an unpleasantly vivid material reality? Akil's observation that the very premise of the game "asks me to put my life in danger if I choose to play it as it is intended and with enthusiasm" suggests that *Pokémon GO* was not simply a reflection of existing white privilege, but an active participant in augmenting the "reality" of racial difference—that is, our sense of race as a socially meaningful sign of human difference—by extending it into the realm of play. If, as Friedrich Schiller famously remarked, "man only plays when in the full meaning of the word he is a man, and he is only completely a man when he plays," then in *Pokémon GO* nonwhite players encountered a "real-life" Pikachu and the fact of their own incomplete, "virtual" humanity in the very same moment.[2] For, like the Pokémon themselves, who only appeared on the game map when the player was within sufficiently close range, the social meaning of race "activated," was put into play, only once players traversed spatial borders and became aware of being "out of place," made to feel at once threatened and threatening.

If even a cute, seemingly "colorblind" game like *Pokémon GO* could be said to play a role in the way race acquires its meaning in everyday American life, grasping the implications of that kinship requires a radical revision of our current assumptions about games as innocent and fantastic escapes from the demands and toil of "real life." This book topples that myth by demonstrating how games have actively shaped Americans' thinking about race, progress, and inequality for over a century. To play a game, this book emphasizes, is not to free oneself from but rather to voluntarily subject oneself to arbitrary constraints. Although the nascent field of game studies has begun to attend more closely to the interpenetration of games and "real-world" political and economic relations, scholars have largely continued to challenge the notion of gameplay as racially free by focusing on the level of visual representation, such as the caricatures and stereotypes reproduced in video games like *Grand Theft Auto* or the number of skin shades available for avatars. Yet the overt "signs" of race that have historically constituted the horizons of our study of social politics in video games are epiphenomenal, on-screen symptoms of far more entrenched racial fictions encoded within. In a non-anthropocentric game like *Pokémon GO*, there are virtually no visible signs of race—at least, not in the limited way we have come to think of that term through corporeal qualities like skin color, hair, body type, accent, and so forth, and especially from within a black-white binary. *The Race Card* extends our purview of games and play beyond that artificial binary, and below the surface, by examining the infrastructure of gaming as itself a raced project. In this respect, it builds on more syncretic "second wave" discussions of gaming representation that have emerged to resist the tendency to view representation as "pure content" separable from game mechanics, thereby loosening the grip of equally artificial binaries of aesthetics versus mechanics, image versus code, story versus game.[3]

The book focuses specifically on the experience of Asian Americans and the longer history of what I call ludo-Orientalism, wherein the design, marketing, and rhetoric of games shape how Asians as well as East-West relations are imagined and where notions of foreignness and racial hierarchies get reinforced. *The Race Card* argues that ludo-Orientalism has informed a range of social processes and policies that readers may not even think of as related to play, from the Japanese American internment to the globalization of Asian labor, while offering a window into the bigger picture of how race is played out both in and through games. That it was not a black man but an Asian American one who ultimately fulfilled Akil's prophetic warning of *Pokémon GO*'s lethal consequences for nonwhite players is itself illustrative of this dynamic. For it is through the enduring Asian American experience of being made to feel like a "perpetual foreigner" regardless of birthplace or citizenship, of constantly being asked, "Where are you from?" that blackness and racial difference more broadly came to signify in *Pokémon GO* as a disorienting experience of spatial dislocation.[4] Asian Americanness, that is, provided a model for the way minority players as a whole were made to experience their Otherness, even as the fact of the *game's* Asian Otherness—its Japanese origins—receded to effective irrelevance. Such moments of doubled and occluded racial perception, in which Asianness becomes at once the most visible and the most attenuated sign of the convergence of racial and ludic fictions, constitute this book's major sites of intervention.

Asians have had a long and equivocal intimacy with gaming in the American imagination, stereotyped on the one hand as humorless workaholics afflicted by a racial allergy to all things fun and frivolous and yet, on the other, harboring a peerless global proclivity for gambling and games of chance.[5] Framed as both the hardest of workers and the most hardcore of players, play for the archetypal Asian is never "just" play: they practice violin until their fingers swell; play *StarCraft* until they drop dead in the middle of the internet café; consistently take home the gold, silver, and bronze at every eSports (professional video gaming) championship—and sometimes at the Olympics, too. Indeed, these ludo-racial dualities get at the very heart of what it means to be Asian in America, to be at once yellow peril and model minority, to be constantly misread through stereotypes of "all Asians looking alike." Asian Americans and Asians are, obviously, not identical: it is, however, in being seen as interchangeable that the two labels, and the two processes of Asian American racialization and Orientalism, as Colleen Lye points out, have served similar epistemological functions, shaping the way Asian Americans are in turn made sense of at the level of both national and racial difference. Recognizing these contradictions thus requires acknowledging that they both exist as part of what Lye calls a single racial form, the coherence of which, I suggest, is itself dependent on a subtended ludic logic.[6] At the same time, this book's transnational focus underscores how deeply the fortunes and perceptions of Asians and Asian Americans are intertwined, and the extent to which U.S.-Asian relations shape what it has historically meant and continues to mean to be Asian in America.

Race more broadly is indisputably and multifariously at play in today's video and computer gaming cultures. Indeed, as a growing body of scholars in game studies has aptly demonstrated, there is hardly an aspect of the digital game industry in which race—functioning intersectionally with gender, sexuality, class, and other categories—does not play a crucial role. It shapes the form and content of on-screen representations, online player interactions (e.g., on Xbox Live), and game modifications; the dynamics of professional game tournaments, fan communities, and player-generated artifacts; the outsourced labor of global production and the privileged position of leisurely consumption; and the historical positioning of video games as the province of white heterosexual masculinity, what Ed Chang calls their "technonormativity."[7] *The Race Card* contributes to such scholarly conversations, particularly part II's readings of specific video games and labor politics, in order to advance our understanding of games as, in David Leonard's terms, a racial compass.[8] At the same time, the book demonstrates that this phenomenon is neither limited to nor the product of video games, but rather has a long and important prehistory. While remaining attuned to N. Katherine Hayles's dictum of medium-specific analysis, this book emphasizes the striking points of ludo-racial continuity between today's video games and yesterday's parlor games by situating these cultural artifacts within a long century of ludic euphemisms and Orientalist fantasies.[9]

One of the most important and long-running of those euphemisms is that of life as a game. In his influential work *Gamer Theory*, equal parts manifesto and meta-commentary on digital games, McKenzie Wark describes the modern world as the quintessential "gamespace." In Wark's view, video games are not so much new as newly revelatory of the extent to which social reality resembles—but ultimately fails to produce the satisfaction and live up to the promises of—a massive game: "The digital game plays up everything that gamespace merely pretends to be: a fair fight, a level playing field, unfettered competition."[10] Lisa Nakamura further observes that since "the algorithms or set of rules that many Americans believe have governed access to the 'good life'— defined as job security, a comfortable retirement, the right to be safe and secure and free from violence—have proven themselves broken, games appeal all the more because they embody this very promise."[11] In the afterword to the recent anthology *Gaming Representation*, Nakamura offers a fascinating discussion of this "cruelly optimistic" discourse of "procedural meritocracy" in digital games. The popular belief that players who suffer in-game discrimination or bias, particularly women and minorities, can "earn the right to question or change the rules by excelling at the game . . . leverag[ing] the mechanics of the game to create a win-condition for themselves and by implication for their gender, race, and sexuality," is a deeply troubling replay of the model minority logic that has long characterized attitudes about Asian Americans. Indeed, it is no coincidence that Nakamura dubs such idealized players the "gamic model minority." As Nakamura argues, "Believing in meritocratic play as the path to acceptance and respectability for minorities and women in sexist and racist gaming cultures is the cruelest kind of optimism . . . meritocratic ways of thinking about freedom from racism and sexism within games that make these things seem not rights at all, but rather privileges to be earned."[12] In other words, by carefully and critically reading today's video games, we are able to discern the "reality" of the "real world": its truths as well as its falsities.[13]

Examining how Asian Americans have been variously vilified and celebrated not only within games but in racial discourses about "fair play" and meritocracy thus illustrates how games and play are instrumental to the social engineering of race relations. Asian Americans make visible the fact that games are a double-edged sword. They can be used to advocate for the equality of opportunity absent in the real world, but also to justify the inequality of outcome in which it is already abundant. Scholars of race in both the social sciences and the humanities have rightly noted how foundational racial thinking has been to contemporary neoliberalism's ability to naturalize economic and other structural inequalities by making them appear fair. Yet, as this book demonstrates, the ludic plays as significant a role in this process as the racial, for it provides the very definition of fairness that neoliberalism cleaves to: wherein an individual's or group's position can be seen as "deserved" in the same way that the winner and loser of a footrace can be said to deserve their respective lots so long as they both started at the same line. It is precisely because Asian Americans' emergence as a "model minority" is an embodiment of this logic—with the group's economic success being offered as proof of race's irrelevance to one's ability to compete—that they offer a particularly privileged terrain through which to undertake a systematic examination of American society as what sociologist Georg Simmel pithily called "the game in which one 'does as if' all were equal."[14]

The point of this book is thus less that we need to take games seriously than that we need to recognize how serious a role they already play as a cultural episteme, in the Foucauldian sense of a general "politics of truth" for a particular epoch—and, further, to understand how games' metaphorical saturation of every realm of "serious" social relations, from the game of warfare to romance to education to electoral politics, has, through the counterintuitive logic of cliché, allowed us to instead see them as inherently unserious, apolitical, and colorblind. For it is this tendency to overlook games that has also obscured the fact that gaming and racialization are already closely intertwined. For example, *Pokémon GO*'s use of GPS and AR technology is in some sense simply a digital version of a racial episteme that has served the objectives of conquest and exploitation for centuries. Colonial discourses have long interpellated nonwhite subjects through a programmatic logic that Charles Mills describes as a "circular indictment: You are what you are in part because you originate from a certain kind of space, and that space has those properties in part because it is inhabited by creatures like yourself."[15] Such is an uncannily apt description of the logic underlying the *Pokémon GO* universe itself. The 841 pocket monsters are divided into elemental types, each of which tend to "spawn" in specific areas or "biomes." One has a much higher chance of encountering a Water-type Pokémon like Poliwag (a tadpole-like creature) near lakes and oceans, while a Steel-type Pokémon like Magnemite (a cycloptic metal sphere that "feeds" on electricity) can often be found near skyscrapers and railway stations. There is, in other words, an important and overlooked symmetry between the *racial* logic that undergirds spatialized systems of oppression and exploitation and the *ludic* logic crucial to securing our perception of games *as* games—that is, as a fantastic virtual world that is Other than the real world—and vice versa. Indeed, racialization itself might be understood as an analogously location-based technology that has been seamlessly automated into the interface of everyday life.

Pokémon GO, in short, does not so much represent race as model its run-time behavior. Race functions here as what Ian Bogost has described as the "procedural logic" of video games, whereby the algorithms that make up the game's software "[enforce] rules to generate some kind of representation, rather than authoring the representation itself."[16] This means more than just that racialization involves the imposition of rules about where people racially and spatially belong. While all games arguably have rules, not everything with rules is a game. It is, instead, the *difference* between the rules of the game and the rules governing other, non-gamespaces that matters. Mills reminds us that "in entering these (dark) spaces, one is entering a region normatively discontinuous with white political space, where *the rules are different* in ways ranging from differential funding (school resources, garbage collection, infrastructural repair) to the absence of police protection."[17] The rules of both "dark" and "white" spaces, in other words, do not simply impose different degrees of freedom or unequal resource allocation; they differentiate the spaces themselves *as* "dark" or "white." The specific content of those rule systems is in some sense less important than the way that rules as such are functioning as an instrument for boundary making, securing the borders and hence the identity of each space. The game's rules—its ludic logic—themselves become a discursive tool: a means not simply of specifying different procedures but of interpreting difference and validating conclusions about the value of that difference.

By focusing on racialization in terms of its underlying ludic logic—the technologies that transform an imagined fiction into a social reality, a chance combination of alleles into a deterministic life course—*The Race Card* explains how arbitrary typologies of human difference are made to feel not only real but justified in the contemporary epoch.[18] For the democratic fantasy of perfectly equal opportunity we pursue within games has its counterpart in the way we use the discourse of gaming to shore up national fictions about the United States as a "level playing field." Indeed, gaming's recent amelioration from social problem to social panacea—its rehabilitation from antisocial waste of time to the antidote for a "broken" reality—is only the latest example of Americans' invocation of the ludic as a rhetorical tool to grapple with the anxieties and contradictions instigated by broader shifts in the structure of the economy and the relations among social groups within it. From the "gospel of play" used to shore up a fading Protestant work ethic in the late nineteenth century to the "fair play" of twenty-first-century neo-liberalism, Americans have found in games and gaming discourse a powerful vehicle for resolving as well as exposing paradoxical cultural conceptions about the value of hard work as the key to class mobility as well as racial uplift.[19]

Ludo-Orientalism and Techno-Orientalism

This book's notion of ludo-Orientalism is related but not reducible to the more well-known concept of techno-Orientalism, which has in recent years been capaciously deployed to address the fetishized, commodified intersection between technology and Asianness across a very wide range of phenomena. Scholars have used the term to explore the generic conventions of late twentieth-century science fiction or cyberpunk (and more recently, speculative and dystopian) literature; the literal mechanization of Asian bodies as cyborgs or machines; the development and manufacture of technology by Asian bodies and minds; and everything in between. In Asian American studies in particular, one finds a rich set of transnational, transmedial topics and concerns, such as those collected in the recent *Techno-Orientalism: Imagining Asia in Speculative Fiction, History, and Media* and in contemporaneous work on science and speculative fiction, cinema, and even video games.[20] Scholars like Vit Šisler, Philipp Reichmuth, and Stefan Werning have rigorously documented video games' exotifying, functionalized representations of East Asia and the Middle East, particularly as they reflect the so-called military entertainment complex's vision of a post-9/11 world order. Christopher B. Patterson profitably expands our understanding of techno-Orientalism as both transnational and "transethnic" while raising the visibility of Asian American game studies in a recent entry in the *Oxford Research Encyclopedia of Asian American Literature and Culture*.[21] Steve Choe and Se Young Kim have analyzed American and European responses to the chilling phenomenon of "Asian gamer death"—players who die as a result of addiction to, and in many cases at the very controls of, online games—as an example of the "discursive powers of techno-Orientalism" and its adaptive ability to quell anxieties about the perils of virtual escapism. Takeo Rivera has deployed an "erotohistoriographic" lens to productively examine how the "vicious techno-Orientalist representations" in video game franchises like *Deus Ex: Human Revolution* "[invoke] fears of dystopian transhumanism through a violent interplay of Asian bodies and cybernetics," a trend made familiar through film productions like *Blade Runner* yet made especially problematic, Rivera notes, given that Asian American gamers constitute a significant (yet largely invisible) proportion of the online gaming community.[22] These are just a few examples of the emergent, interdisciplinary scholarship building around the topological, transnational phenomenon this book refers to as ludo-Orientalism.

However, to be clear, what is meant by the "gaming technologies" of this book's subtitle is not simply the computational medium or mechanics of video games as techno-Orientalist interfaces. Rather, *The Race Card* brings those insights to bear on the way that gaming, both digital and analog, is *used* in everyday life to provide alternative logics and modes of sense making, particularly as a means of justifying racial fictions and other arbitrary human typologies. Wendy Hui Kyong Chun has drawn our attention to the way that race signifies not only through but as technology, "a technique that one uses, even as one is used by it—a carefully crafted, historically inflected system of tools, mediation, or enframing that builds history and identity."[23] This definition of technology usefully broadens the scope of the term beyond the digital media of the contemporary moment. Gaming technologies—whether a game controller, a pair of dice, or even a metaphor like a "stacked deck"—all function as stand-alone "operating systems" that allow, and quite often require, users to operate the meaning-making machine in question without possessing detailed knowledge of its inner workings.[24]

This is why I bring together, under a single rubric, games like *Pokémon GO*, poker, and mahjong; representations *of* such games in literary fiction; social attitudes *about* games in various historical moments; and, finally, gaming metaphors and idioms. There has been strikingly little overlap between these cultural forms in existing game studies scholarship, partly due to contentious debates in the early 2000s between "ludologists" and "narratologists" over games' uniqueness and their autonomy from literature and other media. Despite compelling arguments by scholars like Henry Jenkins, Espen Aarseth, and critics of interactive fiction and role-playing games more broadly, the reigning methodological approach in game studies has involved treating gaming rhetoric as distinct from "real" games and to view play, representation, and storytelling as distinct, or even antagonistic, concerns.[25]

Yet the embedded mechanics of video games and the overlooked predominance of game tropes in national culture—as the two ends of the spectrum of gaming technologies—share a far greater ideological and historical intimacy than has been acknowledged. Just as the visual, on-screen representations of race in video games are epiphenomenal to their embedded, programmatic logic, the "freedoms" that games allow us in play are only meaningful when understood in relation to what we can't do—or rather, will not risk doing—outside of play due to socially and legally imposed constraints. Games are escapes not because they are more free, but because they are differently constrained: their rules provide a substitute for existing relations of power and systems of valorization, swapping out one set of rules for another. It is, in fact, precisely the fictions about games that we cleave to—the fantasy that games are a liberatory "exodus" from daily life rather than a "more radical simulacrum" of it, to invoke the claims of Edward Castronova and

Jean Baudrillard, respectively—and the social contradictions we subsequently use the language of games to resolve that provide some of the most compelling evidence for the necessity of a more capacious definition of the term "game."[26]

Such capaciousness counterintuitively offers a means of resolving certain contradictions inherent to game studies, where scholars have for decades struggled to find a precise definition for gaming. As Roger Caillois, one of the founding fathers of game studies, lamented in 1958, "The multitude and infinite variety of games at first causes one to despair of discovering a principle of classification capable of subsuming them under a small number of well-defined categories."[27] The ludic taxonomy he proposed—a four-part matrix of games divided into competition, chance, mimicry, and vertigo, which is discussed in detail in chapter 4—is instructive not only for its content but for what it reveals about the precariousness of the venture itself: for, as Jacques Ehrmann has noted, Caillois consistently falls "victim [to] his own categories" from the very moment he articulates them, forced to gloss over the contradictions and aporias they are founded on.[28]

The problem is not restricted to the academic study of games, which is distinguished mainly in its recognizing *as* a problem the broader cultural ease with which we almost as a matter of instinct are able to recognize "games" when we see them, and accordingly invoke the term to describe a dizzying variety of activities, behavioral patterns, and systems ranging from the material to the virtual, the stylistic to the conceptual, the wholesome to the illicit. The definition Dutch historian Johan Huizinga, and later Caillois, arrived at was of games as voluntary, rule-bound, undetermined (i.e., with uncertain outcome), economically disinterested activities set apart from "ordinary life." As useful as this definition continues to be, it does not change the fact that games are, in the end, simply those things that people call games. "Game" itself, from that perspective, is essentially a classification system, a way of categorizing human activities and expressions according to the (equally nebulous) binary of "serious" and "playful." And, like the equally artificial classification system of race with which it is intertwined—which categorizes human beings, at the broadest level, into the binary of "white" and "nonwhite" (and more specifically, "black")—such ludic distinctions are neither natural nor neutral.

Rather they are, in implicit ways we are often entirely unconscious of, a means of creating hierarchies and differential systems of value, and of disciplining and legitimizing precarious and arbitrary divisions. Asian Americans' liminality within a black-white binary—their falling, as simultaneous "model minorities" and "honorary whites," out of bounds of the constructed color line—is, in fact, part of why the ludic has figured so prominently in their characterization.[29] And it is also, I suggest, why Asian American writers and literary scholars have repeatedly seized on the critical potential of the ludic to destabilize that larger system and expose its exceptions.[30] For the literary representation of Asian American bodies is inextricable from issues of their racial representation in the American body politic as well as in the national imagination—a formal entanglement that mirrors, and is mirrored by, the ludic multiplicity we have been discussing.

The Game of Representation

"Asian American," like "game," is a precarious fiction: an "openly catachrestic" category, in Colleen Lye's words, that not only amalgamates a massive range of ethnic, linguistic, class, and generational differences but is problematically intertwined with externally imposed stereotypes of Asians all looking alike.[31] As Frank Chin candidly put the problem, "What if all the whites were to vanish from the American hemisphere, right now? . . . What do we Asian Americans, Chinese Americans, Japanese Americans, Indo-Chinese, and Korean Americans have to hold us together? What is 'Asian America,' 'Chinese America,' and 'Japanese America'?"[32]

Chin's answer to this question? Aiiieeeee!—not coincidentally, the name of the Asian American literary anthology he co-edited and in which this commentary appears. For Asian American literature has long been the site through which these difficult questions have surfaced and been struggled with: the place, in other words, where "Aiiieeeee!" as a racist media representation of Asian American voices becomes intertwined with the Asian American authorial voice and the representational burdens of "authenticity" and stereotype busting with which these writers are encumbered. It is also where, in an effort to articulate the paradoxes and tensions of strategic essentialism—where "Asian American" becomes a category at once potentially liberating and constraining—we also find the ludic being explicitly invoked.

Take, for example, Mark Chiang's compelling description of Asian American literary and political identity as moves in what he calls the "game of representation":[33]

> For Asian Americans, it is not the represented who choose the representatives but the representatives who choose one another and themselves, through a process of mutual recognition and contestation. In other words, anyone can declare himself or herself to be an Asian American and thus a representative, but that person becomes a representative only when recognized as such. This recognition typically takes the form of identifying someone as either an ally or an opponent in the struggle over representative legitimacy, for disputing one's claim as a representative also implies recognition that *one is in the game and must be taken seriously*. The indeterminacy of this situation is compounded for those outside the game who lack the means of recognition and are therefore incapable of distinguishing among various claims to representative status.[34]

Here we have a very different understanding of racialization as itself a game of representation, rather than as the product of in-game representation that video game scholars have tended to see it as.[35] Chiang brings Pierre Bourdieu's insights into the competitive games we play in everyday life for the prize of social and cultural capital in conversation with Louis Althusser's famous example of interpellation to emphasize how, as Chiang puts it, "the subject is not simply an effect of ideology but (re)produces ideology by playing the game."[36] "Asian American," in short, functions as both an immaterial form of capital—one inextricable from "real" economic capital—and a form of ideological (re)production, a means of putting race into play.

In other words, if Asian American representation is itself a game, then the ludic here becomes a way of representing the problematics of representation in the first place: that is, by giving it expression in the form of a game. Here, as in so many other places, the term "game" is one we tend to read over or through, as a throwaway metaphor meant merely to connote a sense of conflict, competition, and strategy. Yet, as we will see throughout this book, such a perception limits our ability to recognize the critical potential, as well as the disciplinary perils, of gaming discourse. Indeed, the very fact that we so effortlessly gloss over a phrase like the "game of representation" is itself, like our ability to effortlessly deploy the word "game," a peculiar and important phenomenon. After all, as anyone who has tried to apply traditional interpretative frameworks to decode a term like the "race card" quickly discovers, it does not, in fact, function very well at all as a metaphor, in the sense that we are stymied when posing queries like "Is race like a joker or a deuce?" or "What does the rest of the deck look like?" And yet, such questions and hence contradictions rarely arise: not because we are "lazy" readers or speakers, but because these ludic idioms make a kind of inherent *sense* to us. We respond to a phrase like the "race card" as we do to anything we call a game, immediately grasping—or at least thinking we are grasping—the intended meaning. It seems like a "logical" connection.

And it is: but only because games are wholly guided by their self-determined, self-enclosed, absolute logic. Hence their sense cannot be adequately expressed through the language of other logical systems: this is why the "race card" looks like *nonsense* by the general standards of figurative language use.[37] And it is also part of what makes ludic logic so powerful as a conceptual technology. It allows us to make sense out of what looks like nonsense, but also to render meaningless what might normally be considered highly deterministic aspects of a situation: for example, the difference between a chess piece made of gold and one made of wood, or a recent Chinese immigrant and a sansei (third-generation Japanese American). For it is these same "rules of irrelevance," to use Erving Goffman's phrase, which make racial representation, Asian American or otherwise, not simply a contest or a feud but a game.[38] The game of strategic essentialism, of which Asian American representation is one particular version, works by flattening particular differences between individuals and reifying other, arguably equally arbitrary, similarities in order to ideationally construct the sense of coherence crucial for making meaningful political moves, for getting into the game.[39] To speak of the game of representation, then, is not merely to observe the similar ways in which political representation and games work: it is to recognize that games provide the logic that allows a fiction like "Asian American" to function as a politically meaningful category in the first place.

Reading the Magic Circle

The perception of Asian Americans as inherently "unplayful" has effectively migrated from cultural stereotype to a methodological injunction in Asian Americanist scholarship, where, with few exceptions, sociological and humanistic accounts of Asian American racial formation have focused exclusively on the realms of labor and law. This association with labor is certainly not without basis. But we need to better understand what work is being constructed against and through—particularly as the perceived antithesis of play and leisure. In doing so, we discover how variable and complex are the representational meanings of both work *and* play. This complexity becomes visible once we augment the political and economic stakes of the game of representation to include its literary stakes—to shift, that is, from the particular kinds of fictions that gaming technologies license to the way they teach us how to *read* those fictions. For if material games license immersive fictions for their players, representing something *as* a game—"gamifying" it—can also imbue the representation with certain essential features that games are understood to possess.

Among these is the ludic integrity and sanctity known as the "magic circle," a term Johan Huizinga described as a membrane that encloses in-game activities and distinguishes them from out-of-game ones, as "forbidden spots, isolated, hedged round, hallowed, within which special rules obtain."[40] In this book, I use the term "magic circle" to refer both to the physically isolated, dedicated locations of many games, and to the metaphysical frame enclosing them: the invisible contextual scaffolding that allows in-game actions, as sociologist Gregory Bateson observed, to mean something other than what they would signify in daily reality. This conversion is most often made visible as shifts in language—in blackjack, to say "hit me" is not to invite a physical assault—or in legality—the actions performed on the on-screen football field or within games like *Grand Theft Auto* are the same that, if conducted in real life, would lead to a charge of battery or worse. The magic circle of the playground or the video game is thus intended to function as what Bateson calls a meta-communicative message, tacitly informing the players (and spectator) that what is occurring is play rather than "real" life.[41]

The message "this is play," whether explicitly stated or instead implicitly communicated through, for example, a puppy's playful nip as opposed to a bite, is not only descriptive but also didactic. It provides the receiver with instructions for how to understand the events occurring inside the magic circle—just as a picture frame, in Bateson's example, "tells the viewer that he is not to use the same sort of thinking in interpreting the picture that he might use in interpreting the wallpaper outside of the frame."[42] That it seems strange to speak of "interpreting" wallpaper is in part the point: the frame, in other words, differentiates picture from wallpaper by placing the former in the realm of interpretation and the latter in the instrumentalized realm of what we might call "social fact." This phrase comes from Colleen Lye's critique of Asian American literary studies and its tendency toward reading practices that have elsewhere been described as "historical instrumentalism." That is, as Jinqi Ling and Sau-ling Wong (who pioneered the concept of the "Asian American *Homo Ludens*") have cogently noted, we too often instrumentalize Asian American texts in terms of necessity and extravagance (a dyad Wong draws from Maxine Hong Kingston's *The Woman Warrior*), limiting the bulk of critical discussion to only "the useful parts" of such scenes, particularly in terms of their perceived authenticity and historical "realism."[43] In short, we reduce such texts to the status of wallpaper rather than picture, subordinating the work of interpretation to that of fact-checking.

The public outcry that followed the 2011 publication of Amy Chua's *Battle Hymn of the Tiger Mother* suggests that the perception of Asian American writers as always already outside the magic circle has profoundly shaped the way these texts are read by Americans as a whole. For it is precisely the inclination to "believe in" Asian American texts—to regard them as "real," nonfiction stories—that has led reviewers to praise an explicitly fictional work like *Woman Warrior* for its "authenticity" and "honesty"—or to reprimand one like *Tiger Mother* for its "misleading" portrayal of Asian parenting and its putative "endorsement" of child abuse. Chua responded to critics' subsequent excoriation of these "Chinese" parenting practices—which included threatening to burn her daughters' stuffed animals and never allowing them to "attend a sleepover" or "get any grade less than an A"—by insisting that *Tiger Mother* was a "satirical memoir. It's intentionally self-incriminating. . . . [It's] supposed to be funny, partly self-parody." Yet Chua's reframing of the issue as a "genre problem" utterly failed to satisfy critics' skepticism, which, as Chua herself observed, boiled down to the question "When we read your book, how do we know what to believe and what not to believe?"[44]

The magic circle Bateson and Huizinga described as the result of a straightforward, almost automatic boundary-drawing exercise is, as Chua's fruitless requests for playful consideration suggest, itself a representational privilege of the non-racialized. This is, once again, a ludic site where what it means to represent and be read as a representative of "Asian America" models the way such circumscribed ways of reading afflict minority expression as a whole.[45] For if magic circles, in Huizinga's account, are "temporary worlds within the ordinary world, dedicated to the performance of an act apart," then what it means to be Asian American, in classic works like Kingston's *The Woman Warrior* and John Okada's *No-No Boy*, is to struggle to map the difference between these two worlds, to, as Kingston put it, "figure out how the invisible world the emigrants built around our childhoods fits in solid America."[46] The magic circle has traditionally been regarded as a liberating, pleasurable demonstration of the extent to which fictional narratives can feel real despite the fact—or more properly, because of the fact—that they are fabricated or imaginary. But there is an Other side to this story. For Kingston's narrator and so many others, being Asian American is inextricable from the maddening incapacity to tell fact from fiction: to distinguish, as she puts it, between "real" and "made-up" stories, to be able to "tell a joke from real life."[47] Life becomes a game one plays at playing: in the words of Chinese American author Jade Snow Wong, "a constant puzzle" that "no one ever troubled to explain," a guessing game with all the breath-holding tension of Hasbro's Operation where "you figure out what you got hit for and don't do it again if you figured correctly."[48] One is not provided with the rules beforehand but forced, as one often is in contemporary video games, to deduce the rules through the very act of playing. The connection is made even more explicit in recent works like Gene Yang and Thien Pham's graphic novel *Level Up*, where the arcade

 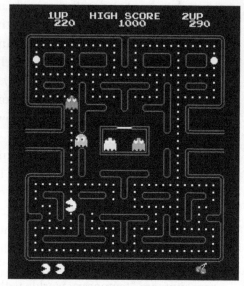

Figure I.1. Ghosts chasing the Asian American protagonist of *Level Up* (A) in imitation of the Japanese classic arcade game *Pac-Man* (NAMCO, 1980) (B). From *Level Up* © 2011 by Gene Luen Yang. Illustrations © 2011 by Thien Pham. Reprinted by permission of First Second, an imprint of Roaring Brook Press, a division of Holtzbrinck Publishing Holdings Limited Partnership. All rights reserved.

classic *Pac-Man* is used to represent the quintessential Asian American experience of being "a little yellow man running through a maze," chased by ghosts (fig. I.1).[49]

Non-Playing Characters

While playful figures like the confidence man, the trickster, or the "signifying monkey" have greatly shaped the ways we read, teach, and evaluate American literature, particularly the genres of Native American and African American literature, this has definitely not been the case for Asian American literature. In that sense, examining games in Asian American literature allows us not simply to contest false assumptions about the "non-playing characters" of the Asian American canon but to reevaluate what it means for ethnic bodies and texts to be seen as "playful" in the first place. That is, literary critics like Henry Louis Gates Jr. have compellingly illustrated how play in African American texts can function as a means of escaping one's liminality—or more properly, exploiting the blind spots it creates—by "gaming" the system. Insofar as these subversive games have themselves subsequently been read as representative of an African American literary tradition, however, they risk being once again reduced to the status of wallpaper. Indeed, we might understand the comparatively instrumentalist ways in which games in Anglophone literature have historically been read as pure allegories—I am thinking here of the famous chess scene in Thomas Middleton's *Women Beware Women*, or the poker game in William Faulkner's short story "Was"—as part of a similarly reductive racializing logic, one that both writers clearly grasped in their strategic use of parlor games to represent the constrained agency created by race, class, and gender dynamics.

In short, literature is a crucial site to examine ludo-racial dynamics. Stuart Moulthrop recently observed of contemporary game studies that "it has become unfashionable to speak of antipathy between games and stories, after some defining schoolyard moments in which early ludologists faced down their literary harassers, winning a grudgingly respectful truce."[50] Although it is now acceptable to speak of games as stories, one is struck by the unaffected status of games *in* stories. Literary representations of games have never engendered analogous territorial disputes, with both parties evidently perceiving them as the rightful and obvious province of literary studies.[51] Yet the games found in stories, even more than the stories found in games, constitute a kind of semi-autonomous borderland between ludology and narratology, resembling "real" games in their dynamics but literature in their execution. This formal problematic of being both-yet-neither is arguably part of why games feature so prominently in Asian American literature as expressions of racial liminality.

Games in Asian American literature are where the "invisibles" of race and culture become especially apprehensible to both character and reader. They serve a narrative function analogous to the ¶ function button in word processing software (currently called "Show Invisibles" in Apple Pages or "Show Editing Marks" in Microsoft Word), rendering visible the white spaces that we generally perceive simply as the absence between words, but which in fact lend structure and hence sense toachaoticundifferentiatedseriesofletters. Yet this in-text "activation" of race by way of games is, as we saw in *Pokémon GO*, a profoundly disorienting experience, making it difficult to read the forest for the trees. Indeed, Asian American writers consistently draw our attention to games as sites where racial, cultural, linguistic, and economic differences are not erased but magnified: and which, not coincidentally, tend to crop up in these texts precisely at the moments where the characters' interpretive faculties are most compromised.

The use of the playground as the stage for racialized trauma—the dramatic revelation of being "Asian Americanized"—found in Jade Snow Wong's *Fifth Chinese Daughter*, one of the earliest and most influential Asian American works of the mid-twentieth century, is a convention found throughout Asian American bildungsromans. In the book, Jade Snow's earliest inklings of being "different" are a direct result of her aberrant relationship to normative notions of American child's play. Relegated to the sidelines at an after-school game of softball—"Jade Snow did not do well in such games because Mama always discouraged physically active games as unbecoming for girls"—Jade Snow is struck by a stray ball.[52] Her teacher, a young Caucasian American woman, rushes to hug the injured girl, who is dumbstruck by the unfamiliar physical intimacy, for her own parents "never embraced her impulsively when she required consolation." The "wonderful comfort" of the teacher's arms, however, soon turns to "embarrassment" and then to "panic"; fleeing the ball field, Jade Snow returns home weighted with the newfound burden of consciousness that "'foreign' American ways were not only generally and vaguely different from their Chinese ways, but that they were specifically different, and the specific differences would involve a choice of action."[53]

This zero-sum conception of Asian and "foreign" American practices—and of the effect they have on the way one plays—is further dramatized in Amy Tan's *The Joy Luck Club*, when one of the Chinese immigrant women scoffs at her American-born niece's claim to know how to play mahjong from having been taught by Jewish friends:

"Entirely different kind of playing," [Lindo] said in her English explanation voice. "Jewish mah jong, they watch only for their own tile, play only with their own eyes."

Then she switched to Chinese: "Chinese mah jong, you must play using your head, very tricky. You must watch what everybody else throws away and keep that in your head as well. And if nobody plays well, then the game becomes like Jewish mah jong. Why play? There's no strategy."[54]

When Lindo's own daughter, Waverly, is learning to play chess and confounds her brother with constant questioning of the rules—"But why do [pawns] go crossways to take other men? Why aren't there any women and children?"—the ludic logic of Asian American assimilation is made unmistakable:

My mother patted the flour off her hands. "Let me see book," she said quietly. She scanned the pages quickly, not reading the foreign English symbols, seeming to search deliberately for nothing in particular.

"This American rules," she concluded at last. "Every time people come out from foreign country, must know rules. You not know, judge say, too bad, go back. They not telling you why so you can use their way go forward. They say, don't know why, you find out yourself. But they knowing all the time. Better you take it, find out why yourself." She tossed her head back with a satisfied smile.[55]

It is precisely through scenes like these, where Asian American writers' representations of games constitute a doubling of the game of Asian American representation, that we can begin to discern the "American rules" that keep the race card in play.

Operating System

The Race Card's organization formally mirrors the critical analysis developed in its chapters, emphasizing how ludo-Orientalism functions as a nation-building discourse which defines the United States and the "West" in relation to abstract game ideals of fairness and freedom; as a racializing discourse that makes Asian difference meaningful by characterizing it in gaming terms, and that Asian American artists, activists, and game designers also play with and at times subvert; and as a contingent, protean discourse that produces different outcomes for different ethnic, temporal, spatial, and generic configurations.

The book's structure is guided by the formally playful, ludic logic of a six-sided die. The opposing faces of modern dice, as a rule, add up to seven: that is, 1 and 6 are arranged on opposite sides, as are 2 and 5, and 3 and 4. Thus, on the single-step progression of numerical sequence (1, 2, 3, etc.) we have a secondary ordered coherence created by a common sum (1+6 = 7, 2+5 = 7, 3+4 = 7).

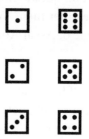

Such is the oppositional yet complementary coherence implicitly at play in this book: chapter 1 examines the intersection of racialized play and labor in the context of nineteenth-century Chinese American gold miners; chapter 6, in the context of twenty-first-century gold farmers, players of *World of Warcraft* who make a living acquiring in-game virtual currency and selling it for real money to (mostly Western) players looking to accelerate the tedious "grind" of the leveling-up process.

Chapter 1, "Evening the Odds through Asian Exclusion," uncovers the influential role of gambling in the passage of late nineteenth-century immigration laws barring Asian laborers. Although historians have long treated Asian American gambling as a minor phenomenon or exaggerated stereotype, gambling was a significant source of recreation and revenue for Chinese American communities and, further, took center stage in exclusion debates. Exclusionists depicted Chinese Americans as "inveterate gamblers" and dissolute cheaters whose "cheap labor" constituted not only unfair competition for other immigrant laborers but an affront to the "fair play" on which U.S. democracy was ostensibly founded. This chapter analyzes the congressional and literary record of these debates to show how ludo-Orientalist rhetoric crucially elevated economic arguments to the transcendent realm of ethics and ideals. By aligning (white) American values with ludic ideals and Asian immigrants with the degradation of these ideals, exclusionist rhetoric weaponized Asian Americans' association with gambling, a process made possible in part through the "misreading" of satirical works like Bret Harte's "The Heathen Chinee." This first chapter also sets the stage for the rest of the book by showing how Orientalist fictions about Asiatic threats are inextricable from national fictions about the United States as an idealized gamespace.

Chapter 6, "Game Over? Internet Addiction, Gold Farming, and the Race Card in a Post-Racial Age," shows how the recent gold farming controversy revived "cheap play" as a tool for condemning Chinese "cheap labor," powerfully informing how internet gaming addiction is itself culturally and spatially represented in popular and psychiatric discourse. Twenty-first-century American anxieties about ludic immersion, compounded by the nation's own destabilized position in the global economy, have led American game developers as well as medical professionals to pathologize gold farming as exclusionists had Chinese gambling: symptomatic of an "Asian" psychosis that fails to respect normative boundaries between play and work, virtual and real world.

Chapters 2 and 5, in turn, examine the mid-century ludic discourses and twenty-first-century traces of World War II and the Japanese bombing of Pearl Harbor through the game-theoretical logic underlying Japanese American internment narratives and the atomic history underlying the Japanese *Pokémon* franchise. Chapter 2, "Just Deserts: A Game Theory of the Japanese American Internment," argues that the lay understanding of games as fair and unbiased allowed World War II military officials to invoke game theory to resolve the thorny contradictions of imprisoning American citizens on racial grounds. A branch of applied mathematics that would eventually form the backbone of 1950s U.S. foreign policy as a "scientific" means of predicting enemy behavior, game theory has often been considered a defining discourse of Cold War America. Juxtaposing internment-era novels and military correspondence alongside game theory textbooks and popular media accounts, this chapter reveals, however, that a decade before it was applied to the "red menace," game theory amplified and then neutralized the threat posed by the "inscrutable intentions" of one hundred thousand Japanese Americans by reframing their fervent claims of U.S. loyalty as little more than a bluff.

I read the literary works in chapter 2 alongside the military documents because, first, they illustrate the symmetry of the problem that

Asian racial difference created for both the U.S. government and Japanese Americans even before the internment and the loyalty questionnaire: that of a zero-sum conception of Asian and American identity. And second, because they show how that problem, although it seemed to be one of military necessity or of conscience, was from a formal perspective about issues of representing or accounting authentically for the interiority of Asian individuals, and in particular the role of race as chance (how to "read" or represent it). In other words, game theory was a response not just to a military threat but to a literary problem with which Asian American writers (and readers of Asian American fiction) have also struggled.

Chapter 5, "Mobile Frontiers: *Pokémon* after Pearl Harbor," reveals the unacknowledged legacy of Japanese racial ideologies, imperialist ambitions, and wartime losses that lurk beneath the game screen. Whereas U.S. military officials during World War II rationalized internment on the basis of an imagined transnationality linking Japanese Americans to imperial Japan, Japanese video game developers like Nintendo have developed sophisticated marketing and aesthetic strategies to erase signs of any Japanese "cultural odor" from their products. The illusion of ahistorical universality crucially buttressed the fantasy of *Pokémon GO* as a truly "free" game, masking the invasive and dehumanizing data mining structures that make it enormously profitable for its developers. At the same time, *Pokémon* and other "cute" character franchises have become instrumental ambassadors in soft power efforts to increase the value of Japan's "global domestic cool" in the international (and especially Western) eye through a series of national branding campaigns.

Finally, Chapters 3 and 4 function as the bridge connecting the two parts of the book.[56] At issue in both chapters are how Asian Americans and East Asia, respectively, served as ludic models closely associated with games of chance. Chapter 3, "Against the Odds: From Model Minority to Model Majority," uses games of chance to illustrate the overlooked kinship between the appeal that hardworking Asian Americans held for white sociologists and the appeal that gambling held for Asian Americans. In other words, the chapter emphasizes again the formal symmetry between the way both parties were using gambling to try to rationalize larger paradoxes in cultural theories of race and economic mobility by reframing immigration and social mobility as risk-taking opportunities.

Gambling served an ideational narrative function, which is made clear through its representations in both literary and journalistic fictions: to gamble is not just to wager money on an uncertain outcome, but to tell a story to yourself about what *could* happen ("What would I do if I won the lottery?"), or to explain why something *did* happen ("It was bad luck," or conversely, "The game is fixed!"). The model minority myth, from that perspective, was essentially a racialized version of the gambling narrative, wherein Asian Americans modeled a new way of representing and explaining the relationship between past and future, merit and heredity.

In model minority discourse, Asian Americans were held up as heroic gamblers in order to discipline other minorities as well as working-class whites. In the foundational ludic theories examined in chapter 4—namely Johan Huizinga's *Homo Ludens* and Roger Caillois's *Man, Play, and Games*—Orientalist notions of the mystical East and rational West profoundly structured the way Huizinga conceptualized the relation between "play" and "ordinary life," and Caillois the taxonomic division of games into the binary of competition (*agon*) and chance (*alea*). Chapters 3 and 4 thus both, individually, revise our understanding of the foundational narratives that have become the bedrock of Asian American studies and game studies, respectively. Chapter 3 leverages the theoretical potential of ludo-Orientalism to upend the reigning assumption that the model minority myth involved the banishment of Asian associations with gambling in favor of hard work; and chapter 4, to upend similarly entrenched assumptions about game theories (and games) as inherently disinterested, universal intellectual inquiries having nothing at all to do with race and culture.

Reorienting our perception of signal moments in modern U.S. race relations, *The Race Card* develops a new set of critical terms for understanding the literature as well as the legislation that emerged from these agonistic struggles. The book offers a pointedly new approach to both Asian American racialization and the "gamified" discourses of daily life, going beyond the explicitly visual and textual stereotypes through which people have traditionally challenged the idea of gameplay as racially free as well as exposed the "techno-Orientalist" intersection between Asian and machine.

In attending to race as it becomes automated and algorithmic rather than visually expressed, *The Race Card* not only redresses game studies' traditional focus on visual representations by disaggregating inequality's on-screen symptoms from the racial ideologies encoded within, but contributes to a broader conversation in social and cultural studies about media as a doubling or "modalization" of the world carried on through the literary formalist approaches of Mark Seltzer's *The Official World* and N. Katherine Hayles's *How We Became Posthuman*.[57] At the same time, it offers a corrective to the implicit assumption that the overwhelming amount of data we all produce and consume on a daily basis is somehow, in its "rawness" or virtuality, free from the concrete inequalities and highly stratified social systems through which these streams of zeroes and ones flow. The book thus charts a new course in game scholarship, directing our focus away from games as empowering vehicles that allow people to inhabit new identities, and toward how games themselves are used as instruments of "soft power" to advance political agendas and discipline national subjects.

But what of the reader who does not read the foregoing pages and who will, therefore, remain ignorant of the intricate ludic logic underlying its structure? What will they miss—and what, in turn, is the reward for those who have taken the time to read these pages? The same thing lost or gained by those who know that the opposite sides of a die add up to seven. That knowledge is, from one perspective, meaningless: it has no effect on a player's ability to roll dice or the dice's ability to generate random numbers. This is because dice are like the ludic and racial technologies this book looks at as a whole: operating systems that obviate the need (and, in many cases, the ability) for the user to understand the system's internal workings. That is precisely how such systems are able to function semiautonomously, to "autocorrect" and update, to endure so long as the hardware allows. To be ignorant of a die's (or this book's) formal organization is thus, in that sense, simply to allow these systems to perform their disciplinary work as quietly and invisibly as they always have.

To be aware of a die's underlying logic, on the other hand, is to be counterintuitively drawn further into the game, seduced by a rationale that seems objective and inevitable: of course that makes sense, we think; the numbers *must* be arranged that way, otherwise they would not add up to seven. The internal consistency created by the system itself, in other words, comes to signify as evidence of its nonarbitrariness. This is the ludo-Orientalist dynamic we will see repeated throughout this book: in the "obvious" kinship between Asian Americans and Asian nationals; the perception of Occident and Orient as antithetical yet complementary cultures; and, of course, in the way the book itself draws our attention to the overlooked symmetry between seemingly divergent cultural forms. The payoff, then, lies in recognizing *all* of these as equally arbitrary discursive fictions that nonetheless powerfully shape the way we think about race and games. Even more, they reveal how gamification and racialization work in tandem as mutually constitutive ways of orienting ourselves to and through difference. These are the technologies we use to make things add up, seem equal, and otherwise distribute value across the borders of the magic circle.

PART I

Gambling on the American Dream

The Pitch

Fair Play

1

Evening the Odds through Chinese Exclusion

Does any one suppose the Geary bill, prohibiting Chinese immigration, would ever have passed into law had the Mongolians taken kindly to poker? It was not fear of the introduction of idolatry by these heathens that impelled the congress of the United States to set up a fence against them. To be sure, that was the alleged reason, but members of congress . . . afterwards confessed that they had been spurred to action mainly by the assertion of the lobbyists that unless Chinese immigration was speedily checked, "fan-tan" would inevitably supplant our national game.

And hence the Geary law . . . stands as a sort of notice to the world that immigration which might retard the growth of our poker industry, is not wanted in this free country.
—Garret Brown, *How to Win at Poker*

The above passage, taken from Garrett Brown's enormously popular *How to Win at Poker* (1899), is facetious but not entirely fallacious.[1] In the late nineteenth-century United States, Chinese immigrants' affinity for games of chance rendered them not only alien but an active threat to U.S. identity and destiny. Indeed, in the years leading up to the 1882 Exclusion Act—the first in a series of federal laws that barred the immigration of Chinese laborers and denied Chinese Americans naturalization rights—it would be difficult to overestimate the frequency with which the trope of Chinese immigrants as "inveterate gamblers" was invoked in magazine articles, newspaper op-eds, literary fiction, and even official legislation. For example, in the 1877 report of a joint congressional committee convened specifically to investigate "the character, extent, and effect of Chinese immigration into this country," and whose findings directly contributed to the successful passage of the Exclusion Act, witness after witness testified to the Chinese's "natural passion" for gambling—an "incurable" addiction, the committee concluded, unmatched by any except the "darker races," specifically Mexicans and Indians, from whom East Asians, as "Mongolians," had been distinguished in scientific and popular racial taxonomies since the eighteenth century.[2]

It was not simply Chinese immigrants' pursuit of games of chance, but the *foreignness* of the particular games they played, which became additional evidence of their alien status. From fan tan (番攤) to pai gow (牌九) to baak-gap-piu (白鴿票, later called keno), such ludic alienness could be used not only to support arguments for Chinese exclusion, but, interestingly, to argue for the ideological inclusion of other, non-Asian minorities. Such, in fact, was Brown's broader intent in the passage quoted above, in using the "Chinese question" as a contrast to an equally irreverent meditation on what, in the postbellum United States, had come to be called the "Negro question." "If anything were lacking to show the negro's adaptability to American citizenship," Brown mused, "his innate love of poker would settle the question. Too much praise can not be bestowed upon those negroes who have progressed from abject slavery to 'craps' to complete emancipation by poker."[3] Emancipation by poker is at once as absurd and as cogent as Exclusion by fan tan; for, as this book reveals, games of chance and racial legislation share a far greater intimacy than we might expect, and one that extends far beyond the nineteenth century. Particularly noteworthy in the Brown example, however, is that Asian Americans' penchant for "foreign" rather than American games turns them into the illegitimate, negative analogue to African Americans, whose "patriotic" embrace of poker can be used to argue for their fitness to be free and full American citizens.[4] The triangulation of black, Asian, and white, then, was in fact one crucial way gaming rhetoric was shaped by, and in turn sought to subtly critique, the broader political and social terrain of U.S. race relations.

Scholars in Asian American studies have been somewhat too quick to assume that the consistent invocation of the Chinese as "inveterate gamblers" was as baseless as it was racist, and to dismiss it in favor of focusing on racialized labor as the primary issue in exclusion debates. Yet gambling was minor neither to early Chinese American experience nor to debates over immigration and exclusion. In 1878, San Francisco alone boasted forty exclusively Chinese-run and -patronized gambling houses. In Fiddletown, California, a trading center for mining camps with one of the largest Chinese American communities in the state, a full 10 percent of Chinese residents in 1880 reported their occupations as related to gambling or lottery.[5] In addition to gambling houses, lotteries were popular and familiar enough that even in smaller Chinatowns drawings were made twice daily, and the winning numbers posted at all major Chinatown restaurants and storefronts.[6] Although, for obvious reasons, the exact number of Chinese American gamblers is difficult to obtain, the industry was sufficiently large and profitable enough to engender specialized Chinese "Gamblers Unions"[7] with a roll of dues-paying members and extensive tong protection networks.

While the prevalence of Chinese American gambling was in part the inevitable outcome of bachelor societies comprising young, unattached men with a limited number of recreational outlets, it was also a regular and even expected pastime in the frontier communities in which they resided. Elaine Zorbas reminds us that "everybody gambled in California in the gold rush days"; in 1849, the state even officially recognized gambling as a legitimate profession.[8] As one witness before the joint congressional committee remarked, "California was originally settled by gamblers, and this early passion has continued to the present day, till we may almost say today that our population is composed of gamblers!"[9] Why, then, given gambling's widespread cross-racial popularity, was it yet, as Stewart Culin noted in 1891, "often looked upon as one of the distinctive traits of the Chinese, and as such is almost invariably commented upon when any reference is made to them in casual speech"?[10] Why, too, given gambling's legitimization as a productive occupation in California and other frontier communities, would the practice be seized on by white exclusionists in these same communities as definitive evidence of the Chinese's dangerously immoral influence on American youth?

The answers to these questions lie in pejorative shifts in American attitudes toward gambling and toward Chinese immigrants between the 1850s and the 1880s. During this period, as Ann Fabian notes, "the moral values of a world based on production and productive labor gave way before the miraculous fertility of speculative capitalism."[11] Even the *San Francisco Illustrated Wasp*, arguably the most virulent anti-Chinese publication of the day, saw Chinese gambling as part of a broader social ill stemming from such shifts in economic and social relations. In 1879, the *Wasp* published a fictionalized letter from a Chinese American laborer to his love back in China. "Ah Fong," as he was called, was introduced in the paper not simply as "a Love-Lorn Chinaman" but "an Observant Critic" on American social dynamics. Having recently bribed his way out of jail on charges of gambling, he reflected on the injustice of both the charge and his release: "in this country," he tells his beloved, "I smack justice on each eye with a piece of gold and she becomes blind." But while he surmises that "in this country I shall always be the debtor and never the creditor," he yet notes that the very notion of gambling's criminalization is equally bankrupt:

> Why the sages and wise men have declared gaming to be, socially, an evil I am at a loss to know. Life, everywhere, and in this country, perhaps, more than any other, is a risk, a gamble, a chance. . . . What is called business is but a game of chance. The merchant sends off his ship full of merchandise to where he thinks there will be a good market; if there is not a good market, he loses; if there is a good market, he wins. What is that? The stock speculator buys his securities in the hope of a rise; upon exactly the same principle that the gambler backs a horse in the hope that he will win the race. Where is the difference? Even the very solons who have pronounced against gambling hold their own positions as the result of a successful game of chance—an election.[12]

As this unexpectedly sympathetic portrayal of the Chinese American dilemma suggests, the perceived linkage between the age's "most reviled vice" and the age's most reviled immigrant group was reflective not merely of regional racial anxieties about Asian Americans in particular, but of national anxieties about broader sea changes in material and ideological economies of the period. Gambling was, until well into the century, understood less as a moral failing than an economic boon: lotteries were regularly used to fund state and city projects. It was not until the 1870s—when even California followed other states in criminalizing house games—that it acquired a uniquely vilified status on economic grounds as a parasitic scourge, embodied by the growing numbers of late-century stock and commodities traders who "brought nothing to market and . . . offered no real exchange for the profits they made."[13]

So, too, with early Chinese immigrants, who in the mid-1800s were, if not celebrated, at least tolerated in mining camps and in the United States as a whole—in part for their tax contributions during economic depression.[14] It was also not until the 1870s that exclusion grew from a concern of the Western states—which, due to frontier industries like gold mining, had the highest concentration of Chinese immigrants—to a galvanizing issue nationwide.[15] Now, their "heathenness," association with vices like gambling, opium, and prostitution, and "cheap" labor were all marshaled by exclusion proponents as evidence of Chinese immigrants' unassimilability and their unfitness to be (and to compete with) American citizens. Like stock traders, Chinese workers were then framed as economic parasites, undercutting American laborers' efforts to secure fair pay and funneling the profits of American industry back to China rather than reinvesting them in the national economy. In short, exclusionists framed Chinese Americans as the embodiment of the moral as well as economic ills of gambling.

Historians of nineteenth-century U.S. culture have identified gambling and games of chance as central sites through which these tensions—and hence U.S. identity—were articulated throughout the second half of the century. Jackson Lears, for example, has suggested that gambling debates revealed the "fundamental fault lines in American character," counterposing two distinct yet equally influential narratives and images through which the United States had historically defined itself. The first account

> puts the big gamble at the center of American life: from the earliest English settlements at Jamestown and Massachusetts Bay, risky ventures in real estate (and other less palpable commodities) power the progress of a fluid, mobile democracy. The speculative confidence man is the hero of this tale—the man (almost always he is male) with his eye on the Main Chance rather than the Moral Imperative. The other narrative exalts a different sort of hero—a disciplined self-made man, whose success comes through careful cultivation of (implicitly Protestant) virtues in cooperation with a Providential plan.[16]

Given that the very decades in which these struggles over the meaning of gambling were being waged were the same in which the status of Chinese immigrants was most hotly contested, it is striking to note the almost total absence of scholarly consideration given to that group—as either workers or gamblers—in historical accounts. While one frequently finds an entire chapter devoted to African American gaming in studies of nineteenth-century gaming, there are rarely sufficient mentions of Asian Americans to warrant even an index entry.[17] Such an omission not only gives the false impression that Asian American gambling was irrelevant or historically minor during these years, but reinforces the tendency to understand gambling, and American race relations more broadly, as an exclusively black-and-white affair.

Work Cheap, Play Cheap

The difference between us and other pioneers, we did not come here for the gold streets. We came to play. And we'll play again. Yes, John Chinaman means to enjoy himself all the while.
—Maxine Hong Kingston, *Tripmaster Monkey*

The competition over the meaning of gambling as legitimate occupation or criminal enterprise was no more a purely moral debate divorced from economic realities than was the criminalization of Chinese labor immigration purely an economic debate in which gambling served merely as sensationalist fodder. Although gambling was certainly used as ammunition in arguments about Chinese immorality, ultimately its most efficacious role was as a rhetorical vehicle used to influence debates specifically over Chinese *labor* practices. As one witness noted in his testimony before Congress, "To object to Chinamen because they 'labor too well' or because they are 'cheap, reliable, and industrious laborers' is void of reason or humanity. . . . The Chinamen are the first people treated as criminal or objected to because they were 'reliable, industrious, or economical. With all other people those qualities are considered virtues.'"[18] Gambling, as we will see, provided the crucial vehicle that allowed such arguments to transcend "reason or humanity" and successfully rewrite Chinese labor from economic virtue to racial vice.

Although games are popularly understood to be the antithesis to labor, in fact, as Ann Fabian and others have compellingly demonstrated, games of chance were sites through which the ideological and economic tension between contrasting labor systems was materially and rhetorically reconciled in nineteenth-century national culture. The ludic theories of Huizinga and Caillois, discussed at length in chapter 4, defined games as "magic circles" isolated from economic reality. As Michael Oriard observes, however, gaming is more accurately seen as existing along a continuum of work and play, marking "the meeting of 'play' and 'work' in the social world. A game is paradoxically a workful expression of the play spirit," or, conversely, "a playful kind of work."[19]

And as the nature of work fundamentally changed with the onset of industrialization in nineteenth-century America, it was accompanied by equally seismic shifts in the meaning of work. As work became "just work," as sociologist C. Wright Mills put it, the leisure sphere—and the concept of the ludic as pure creativity and invigorating self-expression—took on the responsibility for the measure of a meaningful life.[20] Scholars like William Gleason have argued that this shift was catalyzed by declining faith in the Protestant work ethic. As factory labor "bankrupted" the Protestant work ethic, Americans increasingly turned to nonwork forms for the sense of fulfillment once ostensibly provided by the "gospel of work."[21] Many nineteenth-century play theorists accordingly sought to make work more meaningful by making it more "joyful" or by encouraging fitness and exercise as a form of "productive" leisure. The result, beginning in the late nineteenth-century and culminating in the years following World War II, was a rise in the cultural significance of play that labor sociologists in the postwar period would call a "leisure ethic." Mills and others, however, rued the fact that "now work itself is judged in terms of leisure values. The sphere of leisure provides the standards by which work is judged; it lends to work such meanings as work has. . . . It becomes the center of character-forming influences, of identification models: it is what one man has in common with another; it is a continuous interest."[22]

This tension between work and play crystallized in debates over Chinese exclusion. Games of chance provided both language and logic for nineteenth-century Americans to articulate the benefits and costs of ostensibly "free" competition and Chinese "cheap" labor—a phrase popularized, although not invented, by Bret Harte's infamous 1870 poem "The Heathen Chinee." "Cheapness" here had a double meaning. In a literal sense, it referred to the fact that Chinese immigrants tended to be willing to work for lower wages than their American counterparts. While immigrant populations in general, including those hailing from eastern Europe, were a primary source of "cheap labor," Chinese cheap labor in particular was seen as threatening because of its perceived "unfree," indentured, "coolie" status. Although in truth only a fraction of Chinese immigrant laborers were coolies, exclusionists painted all Chinese workers as essentially slave labor, whose ability to survive on starvation wages, thrive in the most deplorable living conditions, and be satiated by the meagerest of rations threatened to reduce all Americans to an equally "degraded" condition.[23] According to such commentators, the deck was stacked against the "honest" white workingman: if given free competition, they complained, "John Chinaman" would win every time.[24] For their part, proponents of Chinese immigration—including Harte himself, as we shall see—defined justice in ludo-Orientalist terms, framing exclusionists as poor sports hiding behind the excuse of racial prejudice. Chinese immigrants' improbable success, in this view, was the most compelling evidence of all that the game was fair.

While opponents to exclusion praised Chinese cheap labor as a testament to the colorblind justice of supply and demand, exclusionists put the language of gambling to equally dubious ludo-Orientalist use to contest such celebratory narratives, suggesting that the never-ending "hordes" of Chinese laborers arriving (and lingering) on American shores was the result not of economic rationality but its opposite. In one "expert" witness testimony or anti-Chinese op-ed after another, white tailors, miners, and merchants testified to the "well-known" fact that in China, both women and men were regularly forced to immigrate as prostitutes or coolies as a result of "runners" coercing them into accruing significant gambling debts, for which the victims were forced to sign an extended labor contract.[25] Gambling, in this version of the story, was not merely a problematic by-product of Chinese immigration, but a driving factor in that immigration's continuation; some "experts" even claimed that stopping gambling would effectively end immigration from the supply side.

Ann Fabian wryly notes that "just as gambling enabled some of small means to speculate in financial matters, debates about gambling enabled some, who might otherwise have hesitated to address economic issues, to speculate on financial matters."[26] While this was certainly the case for some of the above self-declared authorities, more remarkable was that such speculation was not limited to sham experts. George Duffield, a policeman and Chinese "special"[27] who was one of the few non-Chinese with extensive insider knowledge of the workings of Chinatown gambling (such houses were usually not open to whites), spoke at length on everything from the rules of fan tan to the average Chinese laborer's cost of living—a major point used by anti-Chinese elements to emphasize their driving down cost of fair wages:

> CHAIRMAN: What is the general result with Chinamen who work [for those wages]? Do they lay up money? Do they accumulate?
>
> DUFFIELD: Hardly. You may find a few in the washing business here who may accumulate a little money, but gambling is such an inveterate passion with them that it nearly all goes that way. Very rarely will you find any of them who can raise any considerable amount of money . . .
>
> BROOKS: Then the laboring class, according to your idea, do not send much money out of the country.
>
> DUFFIELD: I do not think they do.[28]

The matter-of-factness of his answers conceals the radicalness of their content. Duffield's statements bluntly, and seemingly unintentionally, upend the reigning historical understanding of anti-Chinese sentiment—as motivated largely by the "parasitic" nature of Chinese sojourners whose wages were whisked away back to China—that has defined our current understanding of the "yellow peril" and its relation to the model minority. Duffield's comments, in short, undercut one of the most entrenched assumptions about nineteenth-century Chinese labor and immigration. Here, Chinese American gamblers are cast not as inscrutable, scheming parasites but as victims of their own violent passions and, further, as the *hosts* for unscrupulous intra-ethnic parasites who bleed them of their money. Stewart Culin, whose 1891 book *The Gambling Games of the Chinese in America* reveals both significant research knowledge and sympathy for Chinese immigrants and the "vulgar prejudice" leveled against them, underscored Duffield's claims in observing that significant gambling losses were regularly incurred by Chinese laborers, most of whom, "from their youth and lack of money, if for no other reason, were quite unaccustomed to hazard their earnings in the manner that is almost universal among the Chinese in the United States effectively."[29] Becoming easy marks for the gambling house proprietors—who, in Culin's account, were the only ones who "reap the benefit" of Chinese labor and, as true sojourners, "return with competencies to China"—these poor saps were "compelled to stay on far beyond the time they would otherwise remain in this country," thus lending "permanency to their settlements."[30]

The Chinese American exclusion debates showcase the capaciousness and flexibility of a ludo-Orientalist rhetoric that is capable of at once buttressing and critiquing competing arguments. As gambling could be used to explode the sojourner myth, so it was also used by other "experts" to counter the foundational myth that the majority of immigrants were coolies: thus, as Giles Gray, an attorney and surveyor of the Port of San Francisco pointed out, not only had his twenty years of dealing with court cases involving Chinese immigrants convinced him, "most positively, that the Chinese do not come here slaves to any person nor to any company"; the very fact of their gambling provided the most indisputable proof of it. For "if they were all slaves," Gray argued, then "their masters would hardly allow them to spend their earnings in gambling, as many now do." The very "voluntariness" of gameplay, which Huizinga and Caillois identified as the ludic's most essential characteristic, here becomes a means of asserting the non-coerced status of Chinese labor.

Gambling allowed both sides of the exclusion debate to discuss work and play not only as cause and effect, but as a two sides of the same racial character trait. For exclusionists, this meant linking, as one witness put it in a separate congressional inquiry, the idea of the Chinese as both "cheap labor" and "cheap men." In arguing that "the Chinaman could live longer without food than without lying or cheating,"[31] exclusionists implied that their "cheapness" in a ludic sense—of playing "dishonorably"—was the psychological analogue to the bland and meager rice that made up their diet and ensured their unfair competition against those who "lived on beef."[32]

"The Heathen Chinee"

For all their adaptability, gaming tropes and allegories often prove to be as risky as games of chance themselves; the very flexibility of meaning and possibility that gaming allows means the gap between intention and interpretation is significant. The same game can look very different from the perspective of one player to another, or, in the case of "The Heathen Chinee," author and reader. In September 1870, a largely unknown American writer named Bret Harte penned a poem that became, nearly overnight, not only "one of the most popular poems ever published" but, by many accounts, did more than "any other writer" had to shape "the popular conception of the Chinese" in the United States during the period.[33] Originally titled "Plain Language from Truthful James," the poem was soon circulating as the more familiar "The Heathen Chinee." It dramatizes a game of euchre[34] played between the eponymous Irish American narrator, his compatriot Bill Nye (no apparent relation to the scientist), and a Chinese immigrant named Ah Sin. "Truthful James," while initially "grieve[d]" upon discovering Bill's intent to cheat the "childlike and bland" Ah Sin, is soon consumed by a more "frightful" revelation: Ah Sin is an even more skillful cheat than Bill, ultimately trouncing the two Irish cardsharps at a game he initially professed not "to understand." In response, an outraged Bill lets loose an exceptionally strange war cry—"We are ruined by Chinese cheap labor"—and falls on Ah Sin, revealing "twenty-four jacks" concealed in the latter's voluminous sleeves and, staining his long fingernails, the wax he had been using to mark cards.[35]

Within days the poem had been reprinted in dozens of newspapers and magazines, and soon emerged as a virtual motto for anti-Chinese labor organizations—adapted into speeches, read before meetings, and even presented on the floor of Congress—all despite Harte's emphatic protests that the poem was intended to be a "satiric attack on race prejudice," not an endorsement of it. Although contemporary scholars have echoed Harte's own protestations, they have mainly attributed the poem's "misappropriation" by its intended targets to the "ambiguity" of the work itself, comparing it to a Rorschach test, in which one could see any pattern, and could thus put it toward any purpose.[36] The assumption, then, has been that the poem's obliqueness was largely a product

Figure 1.1. Illustrated versions of "The Heathen Chinee," often vividly depicting the violence visited on Ah Sin, were common. Illustration by Joseph Hull. "The Heathen Chinee," unauthorized printing, Chicago Western News Company, 1870.

of its genre and thus, like all satires, fully reliant on the reader to enact an ironic reading rather than a literal one; that it contributed to an especially hostile and charged debate topic simply compounded the likelihood of it being read as anti-Chinese. Yet the irony of the anti-Chinese movement co-opting Harte's poem lay less in their misreading than in Harte himself unintentionally giving rhyme and reason to the conflation of work and play that had already been implicit in the movement itself. Harte's poem became the perfect narrative instrument for translating Chinese labor from economic virtue to moral vice, for seeing it as not simply "cheap" but as a form of "cheating."

Although one can easily read Bill Nye's outburst about being "ruined by Chinese cheap labor" as a Freudian slip, revealing his desire to work out within the magic circle of the card table the violent frustrations he had long wished to physically unleash beyond it, Nye's semantic conflation of Ah Sin's gaming habits and labor practices was, as we have seen, also giving voice to a long-developing intimacy between "cheap" labor and "cheap" play. The poem allowed exclusionists to frame the Chinese laborer as a cheat by reframing labor itself as a different sort of game: one guided less by the rules and logic of what Roger Caillois called *agon* (competition) or the "economic rationality" of supply and demand, and instead by *alea* (chance) and the abstract virtues of honor and absolute, instantaneous justice.

To cheat at a game is to transform honesty from a fact to an illusion: indeed, what appears most honest becomes most suspect, and gives the game much of its dynamic excitement, as with bluffing in poker. So, too, did exclusionists use Harte's poem to render Chinese honest labor only a bluff, a deliberate deception for the race's actual "dark ways." The metaphor of a chance-based card game had further rhetorical and ideological uses, many of which Harte likely did not even intend. Caillois observed that "recourse to chance helps people tolerate competition that is unfair or too rugged. At the same time, it leaves hope in the dispossessed that free competition is still possible in the lowly stations in life. . . . Anyone can win. This illusory expectation encourages the lowly to be more tolerant of a mediocre status that they have no practical means of ever improving. Extraordinary luck—a miracle—would be needed. It is the function of *alea* to always hold out hope of such a miracle."[37] To cheat at a game of chance is accordingly to cheapen the game itself and the ideals it stands for, absolute fairness and equal opportunity chief among them. Ah Sin's cheating, then, could be seen (and was, at least by James, Nye, and their real-life counterparts) as not simply a personal affront, but, like the parasitic stock investors, an affront to the very honor of virtuous free labor. In short, it robbed white workingmen of their necessary fantasies.

As "cheap" laborers, Chinese immigrants, Colleen Lye has noted, "represent[ed] a paradoxical condition of 'willing slavery,'" such that "Asiatic racial form emerged as an historical expression of the actual unfreedom of free wage labor."[38] As "cheap" players, Chinese immigrants further translated that economic system's unfreedom into an expression of its unfairness. Through the invocation of aleatory tropes and logic, exclusion was reframed as an effort to level the playing field, an imposition of restrictive rules that made it, like all game rules, at once less free and more fair. Decreasing the freeplay of the market, exclusionists argued, allowed for greater abstract freedom as a national ideal.[39] Conceived in this way, white workingmen like Nye and James were absolved of moral responsibility. For while Harte may have intended to rationalize Ah Sin's cheating as a prudent response to Bill Nye's own, it could easily be—and indeed was—read the other way around: Bill Nye might even be said to have been forced to cheat in order to compete with the cheating Ah Sin. In seeking to abolish Chinese labor, one could even argue that the Bill Nyes of the nation were simply seeking, through cheating, to redeem themselves from the depths of moral depravity into which that labor would force them as helpless victims: for it was inevitable that Chinese labor, claimed numerous witnesses before the Canadian Royal Commission on Chinese immigration, would "degrade and dishonor labor."[40] Such an argument might seem especially bereft of "logic or humanity"; but, as with all gaming discourse, the meaning of "cheating" is itself quite flexible. As critics like Mia Consalvo and Josh Bycer have noted of contemporary video game culture, "cheating" is frequently distinguished by players (and some designers) from "exploitation," the latter defined as the use of existing mechanics in unintended ways, the former as going "outside the game" to "alter, modify or change the experience of the game from the developer's original intent."[41] Even when cheating is recognized as cheating, Consalvo notes, moral opprobrium does not always follow; such actions can even be perceived positively, a means for an outmatched player to "turn the tables" or "even the odds."

For all his authorially intended ignorance and awkward verses, then, it is Truthful James who ultimately emerges as perhaps the most skilled cheater of all; for beneath the clumsy stanzas lies a sophisticated series of "rhetorical contortions" that produced a version of the truth that Harte's exclusionist readers found more than sound. In this, they were not so different from some of their enemies. Just as Eastern investors and speculators framed themselves as virtuous producers instead of immoral gamesmen, so did this scene of euchre provide sufficiently elastic material for white workingmen to refashion themselves as moral authorities. By the very logic according to which Harte launched his satire—the justice of being cheated by a superior cheater—so was the anti-Chinese movement able to turn the tables on his message in the name of fair play—or more precisely, fair pay.

2

Just Deserts

A Game Theory of the Japanese American Internment

In the wake of Japan's surprise attack on Pearl Harbor on December 7, 1941, the long-standing stereotype of the "inscrutable Oriental" acquired newly threatening—and peculiarly ludic—resonances. According to the Roosevelt administration, the 120,000 Americans of Japanese descent who called the West Coast home were problematic because their "inscrutability" constituted the ultimate poker face, making it impossible, as Dillon S. Myer, director of the War Relocation Authority, would complain, to tell whether they were thinking "what we think they are thinking."[1] Which meant, after Pearl Harbor, that their outward declarations of loyalty to the United States might be nothing more than strategic bluffs to conceal their subversive intentions. While mainstream media outlets (fallaciously) reported on the growing strength of a "fifth column" of Japanese American saboteurs ready to blow up military bases and burn down the Golden Gate Bridge (fig. 2.1), government officials publicly despaired of distinguishing loyal Japanese Americans from "enemy aliens." Insisted Commanding General John L. DeWitt, the man behind the relocation plan, "It [is] impossible to separate the sheep from the goats."[2]

Thus we find future Supreme Court chief justice Earl Warren, then attorney general of California, recommending the mass incarceration of Japanese Americans not by referring to the physical menace that their bodies supposedly posed to national security, but to the far more galling problem of their "hearts and minds": "When we are dealing with the Caucasian race, we have methods that will test the loyalty of them, and we believe that we can, in dealing with the Germans and Italians, arrive at some fairly sound conclusions. . . . But when we deal with the Japanese we are in an entirely different field and we cannot form any opinion that we believe to be sound."[3] Like Dillon Myer, Warren essentially defined

Figure 2.1. Propagandistic images of Japanese Americans as saboteurs flooded the American media, including this one by popular children's author Dr. Seuss, "Waiting for the Signal from Home . . . ," *PM Magazine*, February 13, 1942. Image courtesy of the UC San Diego Special Collections & Archives.

whiteness as a "tell" that need only be "read" correctly in order to decode a person's intentions—or at least, to make "some fairly sound conclusions" about where their allegiances lay. But, also like Myer, Warren is ultimately forced to admit that the nation's investment in a particular set of racial assumptions had produced its own paradox—making race, for non-Caucasians in general and Asian Americans in particular, into a kind of "anti-tell."

Race, according to this logic, did not categorically ensure one's loyalty or disloyalty—for how then to explain white American traitors?—but rather determined the trustworthiness of one's outward assertions of loyalty. Japanese Americans were not disloyal *because* they were Japanese; rather, it was because they were Japanese that their loyalty could not be determined.[4] Hence the justification of internment as a "military necessity," an argument here rehearsed by Secretary of War Henry Stimson in a 1943 report: "While it was believed that some [Japanese Americans] were loyal, it was known that many were not. To complicate the situation no ready means existed for determining the loyal and the disloyal with any degree of safety. It was necessary to face the realities—a positive determination could not have been made."[5] Whereas nineteenth-century exclusion discourse drew on games as tropological vehicles for their racializing aims, here we see a subtler version of ludo-Orientalism that uses the logic rather than the language of games to achieve analogous ends. That is, Stimson, Warren, Myer, and DeWitt all characterized Japanese American loyalty as a contingent assertion of the sort with which we are well versed from a whole genre of "bluffing" games like poker, I doubt it (a.k.a. BS), or detective (various iterations include murder, mafia, and lonely ghost). While, as shown in the previous chapter, exclusionists (emblematized by Harte's Bill Nye) used the rhetoric of fair play to calibrate economic and national ideals of equal opportunity and "honest" labor, internment advocates argued that the relocation order was, if not entirely just, at least entirely justified, because conducted according to impartial rules and strategic considerations. Indeed, as we will see, it was precisely by conceptualizing the situation as a rule-governed, zero-sum competition between the United States, on the one side, and Japanese Americans and imperial Japan, on the other, that the government was able to defend internment—and internees, their responses to it.

The aptness of this ludic model to the internment would seem to lie in effectively capturing how Japanese American loyalty was at once contingent—conceivably but not necessarily true, or, to use Stimson's terms, "believed" but not positively "known"—as well as strategic, a "move" intended to advance a personal agenda. But we could also reverse the picture. We might say that games were not simply an apposite vehicle for internment advocates to communicate an emergent racial theory, but that gaming helped to ratify claims of "military necessity" by shoring up their dubious fictions and tenuous connection to material reality. After all, there is no way to categorically determine in advance whether your opponent in poker is bluffing; what little evidence you might gather from their mannerisms or probability theory is by definition insufficient for a positive determination. By framing loyalty as the analogue to a game bluff, and Asian inscrutability to a "poker face," state-sponsored discourses hit on a compelling and putatively color-blind justification for internment that subordinated the role of evidence or military intelligence to that of imagination and "expert" intuition. If separating "the sheep from the goats" was a game in form even if not in name, that meant, like all games, it could be won—through a gambit called "relocation."

Seen in this light, the internment aligns with Cold War America's subsequent embrace of what Steven Belletto has recently dubbed the "game theory narrative." A branch of applied mathematics, game theory would become the explicit basis of the Eisenhower administration's foreign policy, most evident in its response to the U.S.-Soviet nuclear conflict. Yet, as Belletto points out, game theory simultaneously functioned as a *domestic* discourse of "scientific" risk management, reassuring Americans that it was now possible to "prevent nuclear exchange by conceptualizing the cold war as a game, and by playing this game according to specific rational strategies."[6] While Cold War culture may have been the first to give this procedural schema a succinct appellation, "game theory" is not simply a schematic that can be retroactively applied to understand the internment: more than that, it formally parallels how this military conflict was already conceptualized *as* a dilemma.

Most often associated with mathematician John von Neumann, game theory emerged from his conviction that there was something decidedly "untrivial" about games like poker, bridge, and even baseball; for him, such games were scale models of real-life conflict, and, working with German-born economist Oskar Morgenstern, he set about translating their logic to economic, and eventually military, applications. "Real life consists of bluffing, of little tactics of deception, of asking yourself what is the other man going to think I mean to do," von Neumann observed, "and that is what games are about in my theory."[7] And that, I suggest, is also what they were about during the internment years. Neither veteran military commanders like DeWitt nor Japanese American writers and ex-internees like John Okada (author of *No-No Boy*) and Hiroshi Nakamura (author of *Treadmill*) would explicitly invoke the term "game theory." Yet their Manichean approach to the internment and the explicitly self-reflexive language they used to describe the loyalty issue—not to mention the novelists' extensive uses of contests like poker, bridge, boxing, and craps to thematize that dilemma—shared von Neumann's interest in defining international (and interpersonal) conflict as a high-stakes parlor game being played out in real time.

Indeed, what is even more striking than the ludic parallels between the way the United States negotiated the threat of "death from above" during the Cold War and of "death from within" by Japanese American saboteurs during the decidedly hot war that preceded it, is the way internees themselves internalized this game-theoretical lens. As Peter Suzuki rightly notes of *Treadmill*, an "underlying theme [of the novel] is that, despite the seemingly clear-cut nature of many War Relocation Authority policies, there were always two sides to each of them. . . . They required great thought and deliberation on the part of the people in deciding which to follow, and when, ultimately, choices were made. . . . There were no satisfying solutions as the choices themselves generated unanticipated situations and problems. As a consequence, the incarcerated were forever facing dilemmas."[8] This chapter accordingly takes seriously literary depictions of the internment as a game "played with an intensity that was fearful to watch," one in which "we cheated, we lied, we were honest, we were brave, we stood on the hot burning sands and made our decisions, each according to his own conscience."[9] Doing so reveals an unexpected and overlooked symmetry between the way both American military officials and Japanese Americans made sense of the arbitrary, incomprehensible events and zero-sum decisions that followed Pearl Harbor. This approach supplements our focus on game theory as a prescriptive tool for managing the contingencies of international warfare by attending to it as a descriptive portrait of the national imagination, wherein ludic perceptions of loyalty as an all-or-nothing choice were the product of racial assumptions about Asian American "inscrutability" and "un-Americanness." It demonstrates, in short, how games provided, and continue to provide, a calculus for negotiating modern problematics of racial identity formation.

Theoretical Humanism

Despite the title of von Neumann and Morgenstern's weighty 1944 treatise on the subject—*A Theory of Games and Economic Behavior*—game theory was from the outset not envisioned as a theory *about* games, but rather a theory of human behavior that used the lens and language *of* games. As Roger McCain put it, "the game is to game theory as the experiment is to experimental science," the latter being "not about experiments" but rather about "understanding the natural world" through the aid of experiments.[10] Of course, insofar as the medium shapes the message, neither experimental science nor game theory can be fully divorced from its vehicles; indeed, as will become clear by the end of this book, theories that *use* games (game theory) and theories *about* games (the field of game studies), despite being seen as disparate entities, are, like "real" and metaphorical games, necessarily related in practice. Nonetheless, in theory, beginning with von Neumann and Morgenstern's, games served as a model for human decision making, specifically in relation to the economic choices we make in an effort to maximize our gains and minimize our losses. Von Neumann sought to establish whether there was always a rational way to play a game—which is to say, a way of choosing an optimal strategy given an inherent amount of uncertainty about the other players' intentions.[11] The question game theory set out to answer was thus a version of the one Dillon Myer posed as the problem of figuring out whether Japanese Americans were thinking what he thought they were thinking.

The answer, according to von Neumann, was yes, at least in the case of zero-sum games of strategy between two or more "rational but distrusting beings."[12] This meant that the situation to be modeled must be characterized by opposing interests—that is, the parties are at complete cross-purposes—and a state of partial agency and knowledge. That is, each party must be able to exert some degree of control over the situation, and possesses some knowledge or information about it (e.g., the contents of one's own hand in poker). However, such control must be incomplete—often as a result of chance and the rules, which in poker determine both one's own hand and curtail one's ability to see others', but do not, for example, forbid bluffing. Given these minimum requirements, innumerable "games," whether played for fun, money, or life and death, could, at least theoretically, and with sufficient computing power, be successfully "solved"—that is, the optimal strategy for each party determined—using the formulas first developed by von Neumann and Morgenstern (and, later, broadened and refined by John Nash and other game theorists).

Since the 1950s, and especially over the last decade or so, critics in the humanities in particular have taken game theory to task for its ostensibly dehumanizing mechanisms, its ability to foreclose the real-life complexity of decision making—and the equally real and complex facets of race, gender, and class—by overemphasizing conflict's purely "rational" dimensions. These critics' readings of influential postwar American works like Philip K. Dick's *Solar Lottery*, Joseph Heller's *Catch-22*, and Stanley Kubrick's *Dr. Strangelove* thus tend to treat such cultural productions as categorical denunciations of game theory as a "deterministic model of behavior that evacuates human agency."[13] Such readings have in turn served as the basis for larger arguments about Cold War America's embrace of game theory within a broader framework of psychic and structural fragmentation that is understood to characterize an inherently "postmodern" sensibility.[14]

While there is no denying that authors like Dick, by their own admission, wanted to critique the nation's overreliance on game theory (and on "science" more generally), my response to those very valid concerns, like those regarding the prudence of applying such a "dehumanizing" theory to an indisputably anthropocentric field like Asian American studies, is to point to game theory's inherent affinity with secular humanist discourses more broadly. Game theory was not, despite prevailing critical arguments to the contrary, primarily an attempt to use binary logic as a substitute for human complexity, nor did its axiomatic assumptions about the rationality of its players preclude their inherent humanity. Far from it: being rational, for von Neumann, was part of being human. Rationality is what allows us to foresee the consequences of our decisions; it is also what lets us weigh the various "human" factors inherent in those choices—and hence allows us to make decisions (and play games) in the first place. As Oskar Morgenstern put it, "Rational behavior is not an assumption of [game] theory; rather, its identification is one of its outcomes."[15]

Game theory thus need not be seen as an anti-humanist bogeyman, but offers a nuanced account of what it *means* to be human in an era characterized by rapid technological development and the increasing globalization of conflict. For if game theory has been "misunderstood" as being about "real" games rather than interactive decision making, critiques of its "dehumanizing" representation of human behavior have simultaneously mischaracterized this as a failing of the theory rather than evidence of its utility. For game theory captures with disturbing precision the equally dehumanizing representation of Asian Americans as enemy aliens and the internment's rationalization of racist action in the purely pragmatic language of national strategy. Indeed, looking backward from Cold War culture to internment culture allows us to re-frame dehumanization as a prerequisite for, rather than an outcome of, game-theoretical modeling.

Such historicizing, read from the other direction, also reveals an unexpectedly "rational"—but no less problematic—element at work in the seemingly illogical racism of internment discourse. In "Appli-cation of Theory of Games to the Identification of Friend and Foe," a working paper published in 1949, three RAND scientists embarked on an early quest to translate game theory's mathematical insights to the military context. "An important problem in warfare has always been the identification of friend and foe," it began.[16] "A current example of this problem is the 'loyalty oath,'" the purpose of which, as the paper's title suggests, "is to separate friend from foe."[17] The oath the authors were referring to is not, however, a binding document which an individual signs his name to or ceremoniously reads aloud; rather, they define the oath as "one of two signals: (F) or (E)," through which some given tar-get, encountering an observer (O), represents itself as either friend (F) or enemy (E).[18] This signal could refer to any number of oral, written, or even physical communications: a Morse code transmission, a sworn statement of fidelity, the raising of a particular flag. Game theory's in-genuity lay in reducing those various expressions to a binary model, and in understanding the interaction between observer and target as a game in which four payoffs are possible, which the paper defines as "1) if O identifies F as F; 2) if O identifies F as E; 3) if O identifies E as E; 4) if O identifies E as F."[19] The question then becomes: how should the observer respond to the signal "friend" (F)?

The authors' grim conclusion is, in fact, the same one the Roosevelt administration arrived at regarding Japanese denizens after Pearl Har-bor. In lieu of a code or password known only to the observer and his friends, the observer's optimal course of action is to treat *every* signal as an enemy signal; one can't, in other words, be too careful. But this is more than a mathematical justification for the trampling of civil rights;

it tells us something rather more interesting about the way game theory is bound up with what Niklas Luhmann has called second-order observations. As Mark Seltzer puts it, these are complex games "in which we move against opponents whose intentions, or what look like them (bluffs), enter into the form of the game."[20] In other words, the way that O interacts with an incoming signal depends less on the actual content of the signal (whether F or E)—or, for that matter, on whether the signaler is actually F or E—than on the fact that O treats it as a *signal*, which is to say, as the form of intentionality itself.

The RAND authors' decision to name an observer—rather than an interpreter, a decoder, or a reader—makes sense precisely because O's observations are not synonymous with identifications: the latter defines the target, as Luhmann considers first-order observations to do, "as that which is," whereas the former incorporates the recognition that it could, in fact, be otherwise.[21] The distinction between observation and identification, in other words, is like the distinction between the game's payoffs and its moves; the payoffs are not that O makes a "correct" identification, but correspond to the contingent outcomes of those identifications. The point is not merely that modernity, as Luhmann points out, is defined by contingency—that which is "neither necessary nor impossible"—but that such contingency is what makes our choices as modern subjects look more like game moves and less like grocery shopping. As Luhmann expresses it, "Second-order observations offer a *choice* . . . whether certain designations are to be attributed to the observed observer, thereby characterizing him, or seen as characteristics of what he observes."[22]

This insight into how the issue of choice collides with multiple forms of constraint in turn sheds light on the equivocal forms of agency produced at the nexus of loyalty and race during internment. Racial difference had long meant a contingent relationship to national belonging for the racialized, legally ratified in the United States through racial restrictions on citizenship, immigration, property ownership, miscegenation, and the like. America's entrance into World War II, however, saw the concept of national loyalty newly defined as racially contingent in ways that overrode distinctions of citizenship or birthplace; thus were European Americans hailing from Axis nations able to escape, on the basis of their common whiteness, the loyalty accusations leveled at Japanese Americans, even those born U.S. citizens. That this latter group constituted the majority of potential internees—some 62 percent, or nearly seventy thousand people—meant, however, that some other, less overtly racist explanation had to be provided to justify the internment's unconstitutional imprisonment of American citizens, nearly half of them children, with no proof of their having committed any crime. We accordingly find the concept of loyalty not only invoked but redefined in the wake of Pearl Harbor, from an established character trait denoting the kind of person someone is based on past actions ("a loyal friend"), to a concealed, even subconscious algorithm determining how an individual would act in a given situation—in short, what *move* a friend or enemy would make.[23]

Inscrutable Loyalties

The impact of this racially contingent conception of national loyalty is eloquently captured by Hiroshi Nakamura's often-overlooked novel *Treadmill*, which further documents how the state's reductive attempts to determine Japanese American loyalty were often unexpectedly reproduced by the internees' own decision-making strategies. "Inscrutability," in other words, became a problem not only for the American government, but for the "inscrutable" internees themselves.

Hiroshi Nakamura was born in Gilroy, California, in 1915 to immigrant parents from Hiroshima, Japan. Following the internment order, he was incarcerated at Salinas Assembly Center before being moved to internment camps in Poston, Arizona, and eventually Tule Lake, California. After the war, Nakamura and his wife moved to Los Angeles; he sent the manuscript of *Treadmill* to several publishers but, despite their recognition of its merits, the rampantly anti-Japanese postwar environment led them to decline. A copy of the manuscript did, however, find its way to the National Archives in Washington, DC, where it was discovered in 1974 by anthropologist Peter Suzuki (mere months after Nakamura had died) and eventually published by Mosaic Press in 1996.

Treadmill is a unique book, being the only known novel to be written during the internment itself. The immediacy of the experience partially accounts for its vivid, detailed descriptions of camp life, which according to Nakamura's widow, Mary, are based on a combination of first-hand experience and careful observation. Although the book is not a memoir—instead it is narrated through the perspective of Teru Nogu-chi, a young nisei (second-generation Japanese American) woman—the characters are not entirely fictional creations. According to Mary Naka-mura, many of them, particularly the members of the Noguchi family, are "composites of persons [Hiroshi] had known, met, or heard about"; it is a testament to what Suzuki calls Nakamura's "keen ethnographic eye" that the author was able to transform even thirdhand knowledge into such compelling, lively portraits. We meet the Noguchi family on the eve of internment; the book traces their difficult journey along the same route Nakamura himself took, beginning in Salinas, California and ending, just after the war, in Tule Lake, where Teru, her parents, and younger brother await repatriation to Japan.

Treadmill is on every level a narrative about interdependent, strategic decision-making. At times, it uses literal games to dramatize this process, and the novel is shot through with scenes of characters playing bridge, baseball, and go.[24] But just as often, it documents the far more nuanced games the characters play through the complex cognitive and affective strategies they develop to combat the ever-present uncertainty and insta-bility that define their daily existence. True to its title, the novel dwells on one of the most arbitrary and absurd of these trials: the Leave Clearance form, more commonly known as the "loyalty questionnaire." This docu-ment was developed by the Army and the Office of Naval Intelligence "to determine the likelihood that a U.S.-born Nisei being considered for military service would be loyal to the United States or to Japan."[25] Dis-tributed in 1943 to adult nisei men and later, following minor modifica-tions, to all internees over the age of seventeen, the loyalty questionnaire has become one of the most defining moments in both the internment experience and its critical appraisal. The controversy that subsequently erupted in the camps was over two specific questions:

27. Are you willing to serve in the armed forces of the United States on combat duty wherever ordered?
28. Will you swear unqualified allegiance to the United States of America and faithfully defend the United States from any or all attacks by for-eign or domestic forces, and forswear any form of allegiance or obe-dience to the Japanese emperor, or any other foreign government, power, or organization?

One's answers determined whether one was labeled "loyal" or "disloyal"—or, in game theory terms, friend or foe. For males eligible for military service, two yes answers often resulted in being sent to the front in a segregated combat unit to fight for the very country that imprisoned them, and one or more no responses, to jail as a draft dodger for refusing to do so (such individuals were known as "no-noes" or "no-no boys," as referenced in the title of Okada's novel).

What is especially fascinating about Nakamura's novel is what it reveals about the "real" reasons behind individual responses to the loyalty questionnaire and the strategy, rather than merely the injustice, that characterized these decision-making processes. While political convictions, ethical principles, and cultural values are all offered as possible motivations for answering in a particular way, most of the characters wind up answering the reverse of their desires, guided far more often by their attempts to respond based on how they think the other internees will respond, or on what they think the government expects them to say. Indeed, the novel masterfully captures the growing feeling of paranoid skepticism among internees about just what kind of game the American government is playing with the loyalty hearings. The first half of the book is largely occupied by conversations and debates within the camp community about whether, for instance, the state's repatriation offer "was simply a trick of the American government to secure what amounted to an outright expression of loyalty to Japan and thus lay open the road to prosecution."[26] Similarly, the first round of loyalty hearings (internees were later offered an opportunity to change their noes to yeses) leads to a widespread anxiety that the questionnaire is actually an elaborate attempt to ensnare traitors and thus justify the internment program—although, as Mr. Noguchi himself suggests, echoing General DeWitt's own protests against the loyalty questionnaire, "What an asinine question. Who is going to put down in writing that he intends to break laws?"[27] But after the second round of loyalty hearings commences, the American government, as well as Teru's voice, recedes into the background, replaced for an extended period by an unspecified omniscient narrator and a shift in the perspective of the players, too. Having been involuntary forced into the game and to accept its arbitrary rules, they now seek to make the best of a stacked deck, endlessly speculating and strategizing in an effort to predict what other internees, rather than the state, are planning to do in response to the questionnaire.

Thus we encounter anecdotes like this one, offered by a nisei woman Teru meets on the train to Tule Lake, the internment camp in which no-noes were segregated: "My husband, he's *Issei* [a first-generation Japanese immigrant], so we went on the same day to register and I went and answered no-no. Then I came home and find he's answered yes. It was funny because I'd expected him to answer no from the way he's been talking and he thought I'd answer yes because I always used to fight with him about it."[28] Crucially lacking here is any reference to the moral or ideological factors guiding the wife's decision; rather, the operative phrases are "I'd expected him to answer no" and "he thought I'd answer yes." What is "funny" about this scene is precisely its absurd irony, in which each spouse's attempts to answer as they expect the other to leads both to adopt positions that directly oppose their own convictions; moreover, their desire to use rational logic to arrive at the *same* answer is precisely what leads to their divergence. If this sounds like the plot of a Shakespearean comedy—or, to cite the literary example von Neumann himself used to illustrate game logic, like a passage lifted from a Sherlock Holmes novel[29]—a number of other vignettes reveal the equally reflexive but far more tragic consequences for those internees who were, similarly, trying to "take comfort in having done what the others had done" by "doing what they were expected to do."[30] On the same train to Tule Lake, a scuffle breaks out in a nearby car between Kurisu, a former leader of the pro-Japanese camp riots, and Bob Santo, one of his most loyal followers. Teru's friend Ichiro explains the cause of the fight: "Kurisu advised Bob and the rest of his group to answer no-no. . . . Bob had a lot of faith in his judgment; and so, he did as he was advised, satisfied that *they were all in the same boat together.* However, at the last moment, Kurisu's son changed his answer and now Kurisu isn't coming to Tule lake [sic] with us. Bob feels that he's been double crossed and is quite upset as you can see."[31] Bob's faith in one set of ideals—those of solidarity among the oppressed—has turned him into a martyr who has not only lost his rights as an American citizen but, just as important, has fallen victim to the shifty tactics of his treasonous mentor. "You with your fine talk about Japanese spirit," he screams at Kurisu. "Well, I'll show you who's the true Japanese." The irony, once again, is that Bob is in fact revealing precisely those "Japanese" characteristics that DeWitt and his office used to rationalize the internment, particularly the latter's assertion that the members of this "unassimilated, tightly knit racial group" were entirely incapable of independent thought and autonomous action.[32]

What is especially disturbing about this scene is Ichiro's, and indeed the novel's, tendency to blame Bob for his own wretched fate. The narrative voice depicts him as a petulant child who throws a temper tantrum for being "double crossed"—"hitching up his pants truculently" as he advances on Kurisu, fists raised—rather than sympathizing with his entirely admirable (and, as game theory would suggest, completely rational) decision to choose a cooperative course of action by throwing his lot in with a political movement that might lead to actual social change.[33] The final injustice in *Treadmill*, then, is not the indignity of being imprisoned by one's own government, but rather the shame of being betrayed by the very people who are most intimately connected to one's plight.

Games become a way to represent as well as rationalize the gap between assertion and intention, to explain why one's responses to the loyalty questionnaire did not necessarily match up to personal feeling, but instead constituted a strategic move intended to advance an endgame objective. The game that the novel seems most interested in, then, is a social dilemma known colloquially as the stag hunt. Variously called a "trust dilemma," "coordination game," "or assurance game" in game theory literature, the stag hunt—a term drawn from Jean-Jacques Rousseau's *A Discourse on Inequality*—has also been discussed as a peculiarity of atomic logic. Essentially, it is a group game in which each player's desire to "catch a stag"—to cooperatively bring down a quarry that is impossible for a lone individual to subdue—is constantly threatened by her temptation to "defect," as game theory calls it: to leave her post and pursue a single hare that has happened by, a prey she can easily catch by herself. Despite the fact that bringing down a stag, rather than several individual hares, constitutes the most advantageous outcome for the group as a whole (as game theorist John Nash proved through the equilibrium theorem that bears his name), the fact remains that mutual cooperation remains as elusive as the noble stag. What *Treadmill* reveals is not merely that self-interest trumps common interest during the internment, but that even the most admirable attempts at political solidarity and coalition building are constantly threatened by their own internal contradictions—a sobering reminder, we might also add, that the distinction between the "irrationality" of the American government's decision to intern its citizens and the internees' own decision-making processes is not as clear-cut as we might want to assume.

Treadmill adds further complexity to its account of the controversy by using gender as a vehicle to explore questions of national loyalty and assimilation. Because women were ineligible to be drafted into the U.S. Army, female internees' decisions to answer yes or no on the loyalty questionnaire have often been historically eclipsed by men's, or seen in comparison as a largely symbolic political act. "Women don't count so they may as well answer yes-yes," one young man remarks, while another suggests that women should simply answer "the same way as their men folk" so as not to be separated.[34] When, after Teru answers yes-yes, her employer gives her an opportunity to leave camp for a secretarial job in Cleveland, she consults her father for permission. Calling together the family, Mr. Noguchi (who has decided to leave the United States and be repatriated to Japan) informs his three children that, while he and his wife have decided to take their teenage son Tadao back to Japan, Teru and her sister may make their own decisions: not simply because they are of a legal age to do so, but because they are female. As he puts it, "I regard relocation and marriage in the same light. Your mother and I have known, as all parents know, that we must steel ourselves against an eventual way of parting while at the same time we daily tighten the bonds. It is difficult. In a Japanese family it is considered a disgrace for a married daughter to return home. Her decision is an important one."[35] Teru's choice to answer yes constitutes an abandonment of her parents and her symbolic "motherland" (Japan), but one which, because she is female, is viewed as natural and indeed inevitable.

In having Mr. Noguchi liken a female yes on the loyalty questionnaire to an acceptance of a marriage proposal, Nakamura brilliantly brings full circle the metaphorical connections between love and loyalty that are developed throughout the novel. This extended metaphor is introduced first through the evolving romantic relationship between Teru and another nisei, George Motoyama, whose "white teeth, squarish jaw, [and] clean cut" appearance, like his English first name, clearly make him the "all-American" choice for Teru.[36] When George proposes to Teru just before internment, her indecisiveness rehearses her equally ambivalent feelings toward the nation he represents and anticipates the loyalty oath it will soon demand. For "Teru had expected [the proposal] but not so abruptly," and she can say no more than "I don't know" in response to George's pleading "Why not? Don't you love me?"[37]

Nakamura further nuances this gendered dilemma of marriage and national loyalty by including the perspective of issei women in camp, many of whom were "picture brides" who often first encountered their new husbands and their new country in the same moment. As Teru muses, becoming "American," for her mother and the many women like her, was synonymous with becoming a wife: immigration itself involves the women's metaphorical consummation with a foreign nation which, like their new husbands, "they'd known of . . . only through hearsay," still "strangers when they'd gotten on the train that carried them to . . . a nuptial bed."[38] Teru's ultimate decision to change her answers to no-no—to join her family in repatriation to Japan—reflects her symbolic decision to become a "picture bride" in the opposite direction, bound for a country she has never seen and a future with her new beau, the no-no boy Jiro Nishikawa.

Strategic Filiality

While the Japanese population of Hawaii was never interned—largely due to its crucial role in the plantation economy—the resonances between *Treadmill*'s portrait of zero-sum familial and national loyalty and that which Milton Murayama paints of early twentieth-century Hawaiian plantation life in *All I Asking for Is My Body* (1975) suggests the broader significance of games and game theory to mid-century Japanese American literature as a whole. Indeed, the way the novel defines "Japaneseness" as a deterministic mechanism that powerfully shapes—or is imagined to shape—Japanese American decision making offers insight into the culturally "foreign," rather than ludically familiar, models on which Cold War game theory drew for its authority.

Although contemporary cultural artifacts like *A Beautiful Mind*—a 2001 biopic of John Nash—portray game theory as the hallowed province of prodigies, professors, and military intelligence, the mid-century saw a concerted effort to make game theory accessible and applicable to Americans of all walks of life. Beyond the many journalistic features on the topic in publications like *Fortune* magazine, books like J. D. Williams's *The Compleat Strategyst: Being a Primer on the Theory of Games of Strategy* were extremely popular. The goal, as Williams wrote, was to "bridge the gap between the priestly mathematical activity of the professional scientist and the . . . intelligent layman": an endeavor that, interestingly, was conceived of as mutually beneficial. Beyond showing readers how to "formulate and solve simple problems according to the principles of Game Theory," the primer was an early effort at crowdsourcing. It encouraged readers to "suggest applications [of game theory] to problems selected from those they encounter"; this "data in the field of human interaction" would allow researchers, in turn, to "improve the bases of abstraction" and hence the scope of game theory.[39]

This quasi-anthropological framing of game theory takes on especial relevance when considering the foreign "encounters" that texts like *The Compleat Strategyst* and William Poundstone's best-selling *Prisoner's Dilemma* (1992) used to illustrate the applications of game theory to lay readers. Consider, for example, the opening lines of Poundstone's book: "A man was crossing a river with his wife and mother. A giraffe appeared on the opposite bank. The man drew his gun on the beast, and the giraffe said, 'If you shoot, your mother will die. If you don't shoot, your wife will die.' What should the man do?"[40] This is not, Poundstone readily admits, a story of his own invention, but a traditional African "dilemma tale," told by the Popo of Dahomey. It seems a curious choice for the inaugural example in a book billed as both a biography of von Neumann and a social history of game theory—unless we view it as part of a much longer tradition of "foreign" folkloric traditions being, as Poundstone himself observes, "appropriated by Western writers and philosophers." For "appropriation" certainly is at work in the way Poundstone is using the dilemma tale: not as the didactic moral tool the Popo ostensibly use it for, but rather as a quasi-scientific proof demonstrating the inadequacy of ethics as a decision-making system.

Poundstone's subsequent characterization of himself as an ethnographer or translator suggests something more than merely the continuation of a "Western" humanistic tradition, however. Rather, it serves a strategic function akin to Williams's earlier self-portrait in *The Compleat Strategyst* as an apostle bringing the word of game theory to the masses. Indeed, both books might be said to constitute a kind of textual indoctrination, one that functions as the "soft power" counterpart to game theory's use by RAND military researchers to develop more effective ways of waging war against America's enemies. By using the Popo tale, Poundstone effectively frames game theory as a solution to, rather than an instigator of, such life-and-death conflicts. The reader is obviously intended to identify with the man—even though, insofar as game theory has proven to be a powerful and effective military weapon, he might do better to recognize himself in the giraffe. Yet that potential recognition is even more fully foreclosed in Poundstone's translation of the folktale into "more Western and technological terms":

> You, your spouse, and your mother are kidnapped by mad scientists and placed in a room with a strange machine. All three of you are bound immobile to chairs. In front of you is a push button within reach. A machine gun looms in front of your spouse and mother, and a menacing clock ticks away on the wall. One of the scientists announces that if you push the button the mechanism will aim the gun at your mother and shoot her dead. If you don't push it within sixty seconds it will aim and fire at your spouse. You have examined the machine and satisfied yourself that its remorseless clockwork will perform as stated. What do you do?[41]

In this version, the talking giraffe is replaced by mad scientists, and the man's pistol by a remote-controlled machine gun—both of which, one is supposed to realize, are even less open to reasonable negotiation than an anthropomorphic ungulate might be. Hence the need for game theory.

The problem is that game theory isn't actually much help against such irrational enemies. Although the giraffe or mad scientist may derive some perverse ludic pleasure from the problem box[42] nature of the situation, it is not a very good "game" at all: not to the man and his loved ones, certainly, but also not even for game theory. For a one-person, two-strategy "game" like this, whose outcome is determined solely by one individual (or, if one is splitting hairs, by one individual's choice *or* by the passage of time), with no significant element of chance or competition, is, as even Williams acknowledges, "uninteresting, from the Game

Theory point of view."[43] This is because game theory's recommendation in such a situation is essentially that of your moral compass's, simply put in more coldly rational terms: "Select the course of action that yields the most and do it." In other words, if you think your mother's life has more value—put in game-theoretical terms, if her being alive has greater utility to you than your spouse doing so, and you therefore assign this outcome a greater payoff—then you do nothing; if the reverse is true, you push the button. If the payoffs are exactly equal, flip a coin; if none is handy, use another chance device. For example, note the time—you do have a clock, after all. If the second hand is on an even number, push the button; if odd, do nothing.

Although it may not be a good illustration of what game theory actually does, this example remains quite instructive insofar as it reveals what Poundstone (and hence his readers) *thinks* game theory can do: essentially, eliminate the sense of guilt and responsibility associated with making a difficult decision. The dilemma tale demonstrates the power of game theory as rhetoric, even and perhaps especially when it is of limited use as a mathematical model. For it appears to allow individuals to forego the uncertainties associated with emotion and thought in favor of swift and decisive action, reducing complex situations to binary decisions that can be made despite moral ambiguities—and, at least in theory, without the burden of a guilty conscience.

Poundstone's use of the dilemma tale is also a valuable artifact in the sense that, despite the numerous changes he makes to create his "Western" translation, what does not change is the nature of the family relationships (self, spouse, and parent) under threat. Although Poundstone changes "wife" to "spouse" in an effort to be more inclusive, he does not do the same with the mother. What does this tell us about the specific value of the maternal—rather than generally parental—role, and its ostensibly zero-sum yet symmetrical relation to the spousal? Why, for that matter, might the most agonizing human dilemma of all be represented as the choice between wife and mother—rather than, say, mother and father, parent and child, spouse and offspring, and so forth?

Treadmill offers a compelling explanation to the first question in likening Teru's experience as a Japanese American woman answering yes on the loyalty questionnaire to choosing one's husband and "host" country (the United States) over one's parents and "home" country (Japan).

Murayama's internment-era bildungsroman *All I Asking for Is My Body*, however, suggests that even before Pearl Harbor racial loyalty was similarly conceived of by many Japanese Americans. Like Mr. and Mrs. Noguchi, the Japanese Hawaiian immigrants in young Kiyo Oyama's life narrate the relation between the United States and Japan in terms of domestic kinship and marital/parental conflict. Yet the novel's depiction of that agonizing decision-making process is a far cry from the melancholy but inevitable "giving away of the bride" Mr. Noguchi describes in *Treadmill*. It is rather a violent, even sadistic event of the Popo dilemma tale variety, as voiced by the teacher Mr. Takemoto: "'Don't bring any shame to the Japanese race. Don't shame your family name and your parents. . . .' In my eighth grade class he'd said, 'If your mother and wife were drowning and you could save only one of them, which would you save?' . . . 'There's no doubt that the white man would save his wife. But what would you do? You have only one mother, you can have only one mother . . .'"[44] Here, the question "What would you do?" is entirely rhetorical, because race works to make independent thought both unnecessary and undesirable: if one is white, one saves one's wife; if Japanese, one's mother. Race, in other words, takes the place of both moral compass and the coin flip or clock. Indeed, it turns the "game" into a one-person, one-strategy exercise, in the game theory sense of "strategy" as "a complete description of a particular way to play a game, [one which] must prescribe actions so thoroughly that you never have to make a decision in following it."[45]

What this means, in *All I Asking for Is My Body*, is that affect has no effect; national loyalty is not a feeling, it is a choice—although one that race can serve to obviate. Mr. Takemoto accordingly downplays the transformative effects of immigration and assimilation by aligning racial, cultural, and national values, using the dilemma tale to draw a didactic line that yokes the nation-state to its diasporic communities. Dedicated "to the family," Murayama's novella as a whole is particularly interesting because it constructs, even while it critiques, Mr. Takemoto's vision of a narratively coherent Japanese "transnation" by foregrounding the same rhetorical strategies General DeWitt had himself deployed to justify the internment.[46] "In the war in which we are now engaged racial affinities are not severed by migration," DeWitt insisted. "To conclude otherwise is to expect that children born of white parents on Japanese soil sever all racial affinity and become loyal Japanese subjects, ready . . .

if necessary, to die for Japan in a war against the nation of their parents."[47] (Of course, as we saw earlier, figures like Earl Warren and Henry Stimson *had* concluded otherwise. DeWitt's claim, in fact, directly contradicts Warren's foundational justification for interning Japanese Americans but not Italian or German Americans on the basis of the latter's racially noncontingent assertions of loyalty.)

That the parent-child relation would serve as a metonym for the nation-subject relation is certainly nothing new, but its formal, rather than affective, centrality to the novel is worth emphasizing. *All I Asking for Is My Body* draws an explicit parallel between filial piety and national loyalty, suggesting that the same cultural values of obligation, obedience, and reciprocity underwrite and mutually reinforce one another. The primary conflict in the book, after all, is between Kiyo's parents and his older brother Tosh: as the eldest son in a family besieged with a $6,000 debt accumulated by previous generations, Tosh is required to surrender not only his educational aspirations and then his wages, but, as the novel's title implies, his very body to the voracious demands of his familial and national obligations.

Mr. Snook, another of Kiyo's teachers, becomes the novel's official mouthpiece for lodging a Marxist critique against the Hawaiian plantation hierarchy, explicitly using Japanese "filiality" and other cultural values to explain the group's "passive" acceptance of their place at the bottom of the social structure. Tosh serves, in more ways than one, to translate that discourse into an impassioned rallying cry that, like the pidgin English of the title, seeks to unify the oppressed across racial and linguistic divides by literally taking back the means of production: the body. The plea for autonomy, for "my body," becomes, however, a simultaneous plea to allow that body to keep for itself not simply the fruits of its labor but those derived from its sportive play. After getting his hands on a series of Jimmy DeForest's "How to Box" pamphlets, Tosh becomes obsessed with boxing, a pastime that disturbs his parents not only because it takes time away from his familial obligations, but because it threatens to turn his oratory skills—"You punch with words," Kiyo berates him—into threatening physical advantages. And indeed, it isn't long before the Oyama supper table becomes a boxing ring and, while Kiyo looks on, Tosh "thr[ows] a left hook to father's solar plexus, as Jimmy DeForest called it."[48]

We might be tempted to read this "unthinkable" martial confrontation between Tosh and Mr. Oyama as a blunt analogy for the struggle between youthful American "individuality" and patriarchal Japanese "groupthink." That Murayama sets this scene on the eve of Pearl Harbor, however, reframes the difference between punches thrown to defeat a matched opponent in play and those aimed in earnest at an unsuspecting victim into a subtle distinction between war and surprise attack. For Kiyo, war's similarity to a game—"Everything, even wars, had certain basic rules"—makes it, like Tosh's boxing, an inherently "noble" pursuit despite its casualties; whereas the Japanese military strike, like Tosh's attack on his aged father, seems not only "criminal," but evidence of the Japanese nation's unsportsmanlike "cowardice."[49]

Recognizing, suddenly, the pragmatism of Tosh's depiction of their father as "the guy that holds all the cards," Kiyo rebels simultaneously against his parents' and the Japanese nation's refusal to "play fair" by deciding to volunteer for the American draft. This narrative strategy allows Murayama to critique the hypocrisies of American exceptionalism while remaining fully aware of its captivating appeal to the national subject who finds opportunities for self-determination within those elisions. Just as boxing allows Tosh to find a more acceptable physical outlet for his psychic and emotional aggression, enlisting allows Kiyo to reclaim his body for himself—though he remains seemingly unaware of the irony that he can only do so by offering that body up as a sacrifice to an equally oppressive set of national ideals. Here we see the fantasy of escaping one's circumstances, a theme that runs through so many immigrant narratives, getting translated from labor to sport to war. Mr. and Mrs. Oyama's failed attempts to realize the American dream through immigration engender Tosh's alternative strategy to win fame and fortune through boxing; when he gets knocked out after just a few match-ups, his brother Kiyo trades fighting games for war games, believing, like Tosh, that "once you fought, you earned the right to complain and participate, you earned a right to a future."[50]

For a novel that is resolutely realist—which, as Jinqi Ling has noted, takes advantage of that mode's transformative rather than homogenizing potential to capture the complexity of its subject matter—the last four pages of All I Asking for Is My Body, which detail Kiyo's actions after enlisting, seem almost to mock the book's painstaking portrayal of each character's inability to escape the entrenched institutional constraints placed on him.[51] While sporting games provide Murayama with both metaphor and means to lodge a critique of Japanese American social and cultural conditions in early twentieth-century Hawaii, those games ultimately produce little more than moral victories for Tosh and Kiyo; as they, and the reader, are constantly reminded, boxing has done nothing to ameliorate the $6,000 debt that plagues the family like a terminal illness. How, then, are we to read the novel's closing section, in which Kiyo enters the army with $25 in his pocket, starts joining craps games, discovers a way to "padroll" (increase the odds of a particular roll by picking the dice up in certain combinations), and in less than forty-eight hours wins enough to mail a $6,000 check back home with instructions to "pay up all the debt"?[52]

Given the novel's explicit use of boxing as a means of cleaving together "war" and "game," it seems reasonable to read Kiyo's actions within his own framework for understanding Tosh's attack on Mr. Oyama and Japan's attack on Pearl Harbor—which is to say, as cowardly perversions of the game's noble ideals. After his craps victory, Kiyo is haunted by the unspoken charge of "playing dirty," of robbing his unsuspecting fellow soldiers—"Thank God they were strangers!"[53]—by feigning unfamiliarity with the game. Although this strategy serves Kiyo better than it did Bret Harte's Ah Sin, the success of the deception necessitates its own rhetorical sleight of hand. "It wasn't really cheating," Kiyo tells himself. "It was dog eat dog, every dog was after something for nothing, you never gave a dog an even break."[54] It is difficult as a reader to recognize amid this newfound callousness the same young boy who decried the dehumanizing machinery of the plantation system a mere fifty pages earlier. Indeed, what is especially disturbing about his victory is that it becomes "too easy" for Kiyo to slip into the mind-set of Mr. Nelson, the plantation boss: "It was their fault if they couldn't spot it," he declares of his now-impoverished fellow players. "Besides, if I didn't take their money, another padroller would've."[55]

The point here is not that game theory, as a scientific model of human decision making, negates the question of moral responsibility or quantitatively justifies its abuses; but rather that, as a rhetorical instrument of racialization, it can be used to produce precisely that perception. For most of the novel, the game-theoretical framing of "Japaneseness" effectively calibrates Kiyo's transnational value system. But after Pearl Harbor, when imperial Japan adopts an entirely different strategy—what Mr. Takemoto labels "pragmatism," arguing that "nations act on a pragmatic basis, they do what they think is best for the moment"[56]—Kiyo, too, opts for a policy of self-interest: what we might call a choice of wife over mother. From this perspective, the craps game offers a syncretic account of filial piety, national loyalty, *and* capitalist accumulation. Kiyo's inherent faith in the opportunities, rather than limits, of that game— "Believe in the odds. That's the only way" becomes his mantra—means that his victory is also a victory for the structural inequalities on which such American dreams rely.

Rational Irrationality

The calibration of multiple value systems—economic, familial, national, cultural—that we saw in *All I Asking for Is My Body* is in John Okada's novel *No-No Boy* enacted at the level of form as well as content. Thus the titular character Ichiro Yamada equates his no-no response on the loyalty questionnaire to "turn[ing] his back on the army and the country and the world and his own self."[57] Such repetitive syntax, which in fact becomes the novel's most enduring stylistic hallmark, is, as we have seen, essentially the form that internment logic takes: for internees, certainly, there was no difference between the army and the country, because one could only secure his American citizenship if he agreed to enlist. There was, in other words, no maybe, just a "life-giving yes," an "and" that coordinates the individual with the nation and with reality; or, for Ichiro, an "empty no," a "total rejection" of one and hence all of those terms.[58]

For Kiyo, as for Mr. Takemoto, General DeWitt, William Poundstone, and even John von Neumann, game theory provided a means of justifying the rationality and hence fairness of one's decisions. For Ichiro, it allows him the possibility of resolving the tortuous self-loathing and rejection that has resulted from his no-no response. *No-No Boy* drives home the counterintuitive truth that being able to "see through" a game—to see it *as* a game—is not a deterrent but a prerequisite to being able to successfully play it. As Mark Seltzer puts it, "If one does not see, and see through, the rules one cannot play by the rules; seeing through the game is part of it. That is to say, *in order for self-determinations to count as self-determinations, they have to be seen as such.*"[59] Hence the novel's (and Ichiro's) protracted struggle to rehabilitate the postwar Japanese American self into one that is able to retroactively see its responses to the loyalty oath as self-determinations, just as internees in *Treadmill* were made to feel that those choices "counted."

For Ichiro, this rehabilitation can also be read as a kind of historical revisionism. For the loyalty questionnaire was, as we have already seen, largely a Hobson's choice, an illusory "take it or leave it" decision. While, for issei like Mr. and Mrs. Noguchi, or Ichiro's parents, a yes answer would have left them as stateless persons with no citizenship rights in either Japan or America, answering yes as a draftable nisei man like Ichiro essentially constituted a tacit pledge to "prove that [one] deserved to enjoy those rights which should rightfully have been his."[60] Despite the obvious injustice of the situation and the obviously victimized position internees occupied, however, critics have struggled to move beyond psychoanalytic explanations for why internees in literature as well as real life frequently maintained a postwar silence about their experience that seemed more befitting of a shameful family secret than an unconstitutional national travesty. That is, *No-No Boy*'s nominal acceptance into the postwar American literary canon has allowed a greater number of readers to understand and sympathize with the psychic fragmentation that resulted from Japanese Americans' forceful exclusion from the American body politic and the Hobson's choice created by the loyalty questionnaire. Yet seeing internees as helpless victims targeted by a racist state makes it more difficult to account for one of the defining aspects of this foundational Asian American text, which is the way that Ichiro continues to berate himself for making the "wrong" choice even after he fully recognizes that it was really "no choice at all."

For Ichiro's rehabilitation in the novel depends on his being able to see it as a "real" choice. Which is to say, as something like a game move: first, a rational choice rather than one made "in a frightening moment of insanity"; and second, as a self-determined, autonomous decision rather than a response coerced by the government or, what is even worse in Ichiro's mind, by his Japanese immigrant mother.[61] The two concepts—filiality and national loyalty—become as inextricable in Okada's account as they do in Nakamura's and Murayama's. Indeed, it is through the same wife/mother dyad we saw in the previous section that Ichiro is at least psychically, if not legally, able to retroactively change his answer from no to yes by transferring his loyalty from mother to lover.

Indeed, Ichiro's redemption, and his masochistic compulsion to take personal responsibility for the nation's wrongs, unfolds through an explicitly sexualized and gendered register. Critics have rightly attended to the psychoanalytic resonances of Ichiro's postwar identity quest from fragmented liminality to "wholeness," a transition mediated by the analogously "damaged" characters of Kenji, a nisei war veteran with a gangrenous leg; Emi, a young nisei woman effectively abandoned by her soldier husband; and, of course, Mrs. Yamada, whose refusal to believe that Japan has lost the war makes it very clear to the reader and to Ichiro that she is "not all there."[62] Much has been made, especially, of Kenji's role in redeeming Ichiro's masculinity by having the latter serve as the impotent veteran's sexual prosthesis in a series of liaisons with Emi. In another oft-cited scene, Kenji and Ichiro compare the former's "eleven inches" of remaining leg with the latter's psychic and legal war wounds to determine "whose is bigger."[63]

Kenji's leg, like Ichiro's sense of guilt, is "eating away at him"; as critics have pointed out, the wooden prosthesis that Kenji wears becomes an explicit reminder of America's hollow ideals. It is his continually festering stump, however—a wound which eventually kills him—that anticipates Ichiro's revelation of the "sickness" that plagues the Japanese American community as a whole. The "madness" Ichiro initially presumes is confined to his mother and a handful of like-minded "crazy" issei—who believe the victorious Japanese fleet will soon be arriving to reward the loyal no-noes—is ultimately revealed by Kenji as a kind of mass psychotic break afflicting yes-yeses as well. In a sobering parallelism of the sort we have become familiar with in internment discourse, Kenji echoes General DeWitt's infamous pronouncement—"A Jap's a Jap whether he's an American citizen or not"—in his scorn for nisei veterans who have been harassing Ichiro: "They think just because they went and packed a rifle they're different but they aren't and they know it. They're still Japs."[64]

The maternal "madness" that Ichiro initially sees as his filial inheritance thus unexpectedly serves as an opportunity to recognize his mother's—and hence reclaim his own—comparative rationality: "Was it she who was wrong and crazy not to have found in herself the capacity to accept a country which repeatedly refused to accept her or her sons un-questioningly, or was it the others who were being deluded, the ones, like Kenji, who fought and gave their lives to protect this country where they could still not rate as first-class citizens because of the unseen walls?"[65] Here, as with game-theoretical thinking more broadly, rationality is meaningful not merely as the psychological but the *mathematical* antith-esis of insanity. Thus, once again, we find Ichiro reclaiming his rationality and his masculinity in the same gesture. Seeking to resume the college engineering degree his incarceration had interrupted, he fondly recalls happier days commuting to the university and "the slide rule with the leather case which hung from his belt like the sword of learning which it was."[66] The racialized, unmistakably phallic image of a "finely calculated white sword" reframes internment as an act not only of insanity but of castration—which makes his no-no response, by extension, the ultimate act of irrationality, guided neither by brain nor by penis. "Where was the shaft of exacting and thrilling discovery when I needed it most?" he asks himself. "If only I had pictured it and felt it in my hands, I might well have made the right decision." The slide rule becomes the analogue to Kenji's amputated leg, producing in Ichiro a phantasmagoric sexual impotency that only reveals itself as a psychosomatic condition after mul-tiple encounters with Emi.[67]

Ichiro's sexual relations with Emi can be figured not simply as a masculinity-redeeming consummation, but as a choice in the game the-ory sense. That is, we can read Ichiro's mother and his no-no-boy status as mutually constitutive not merely because, as many critics have noted, Ichiro considers himself "not strong enough to fight" her and thus too weak to fight *for* America. Rather, like the princess in Frank Stockton's short story "The Lady, or the Tiger?" (an oft-cited example in game the-ory), whose attempt to signal to and thus sway the protagonist's choice of doors makes her a threat equal to the as-yet-unseen tiger, Mrs. Yamada's status as friend or foe remains unknowable until Ichiro opens the door to which she points and discovers what lies behind it.[68] Okada's novel, of course, makes it painfully clear that in this dilemma there is no lady, only two tigers—one that leads to Ichiro's psychic disembowelment; the other, symbolized by Kenji, to literal amputation and death. Ichiro's "mistake," then, lies not in his decision to answer no; rather, what he comes to regret far more is blindly following his mother's pointing finger—or, as he puts it, to "think for himself."[69] Emi and Mrs. Yamada, like so many female characters in internment literature, become powerful not because they predetermine other characters' decisions, but because they engender, as we saw in the dilemma tales, the very need to make decisions, thereby reifying the contradictory impulses and competing loyalties that define the strategic games I have been discussing. Ichiro's loyalty to lover or to mother is not simply a choice between two people, but instead represents his valuation of the concept of choice itself: as Mr. Takemoto implied, one's mother, like one's race, is specifically the woman that one cannot choose; one's wife, on the other hand, is the woman that one can.

Thus, if sexual intercourse with Emi offers Ichiro an opportunity to symbolically change his answer to a "life-giving yes," Ichiro, as an extension of Kenji, ostensibly plays an equally heroic role in rescuing her from symbolic death by nominal widowhood. In "saving" this potential wife (the future of their relationship remains unsettled by the book's close), Ichiro thus also symbolically abandons his mother to death. Upon her son's return from prison, Mrs. Yamada praising his choice, vehemently agreeing with her friend that, had Ichiro "gone in the American army to fight Japan, I would have killed myself with shame."[70] And so we find the woman's eventual suicide—seemingly a result of insanity or unfortunate accident—occurring, not coincidentally, in the wake of Ichiro's deepening and disapproved-of relationship with Emi.

Modern Fictions

If Ichiro's experience in *No-No Boy* illustrates the lasting impact of game-theoretical thinking as the United States entered the Cold War, the book's subsequent "rescue" by Asian American writers in the 1970s speaks to the schema's protracted afterlife in the late twentieth and early twenty-first centuries. For *No-No Boy*, in its republished, 1976 form (courtesy of the University of Washington Press), is a story about post-internment Japanese American rehabilitation bookended by two accounts of its own rehabilitation. The text is preceded by Lawson Fusao Inada's preface—a Kerouacian description of the road trip he took with Frank Chin to Seattle to meet Okada's widow—and immediately followed by Frank Chin's retelling of the same story in the afterword. Whereas Inada's effusive introduction, particularly the poet's exuberant declaration that the book is all about "love," anticipates the novel's own optimistic conclusion, Chin's trademark anger and acerbic tone in the afterword might be said to draw analogous inspiration from the cynical rage that epitomizes Ichiro's early internal monologues. The material and emotional distance separating Inada's and Chin's narratives thus reflect Ichiro's own evolution within the novel, and especially his shifting perspective on his mother. Consider Chin's and Inada's radically divergent attitudes toward Dorothy Okada, who upon their arrival informs them that she has just finished burning all of her late husband's personal effects, including a partially completed manuscript. Inada's reaction to this revelation: "It hurt." Chin's response: "I wanted to kick her ass around the block."

Like the two doors in "The Lady, or the Tiger?" which are as likely to lead to the male protagonist's delight as to his dismemberment, these two rhetorical extremes present a dilemma to the critical reader of *No-No Boy* which, like Ichiro's own, is inextricably tied to the figure of the Japanese American female. The Asian American woman becomes a powerful site of contestation within both the novel and Asian American studies writ large not simply because she disrupts the coherence of a militant Asian American masculinity, or stands in for the "feminizing" American discourse historically used to deny the possibility of Asian masculinity in the first place. Rather, she provides a crucial opportunity for her male counterparts to vocalize their own political or cultural agency by categorizing her as either friend or foe to his particular "cause." In this case, such a binaristic vision becomes the rudimentary foundations of a Manichean critical paradigm for assessing Asian American literature as either "real" or "fake," a dichotomy that would reach its apex in *The Big Aiiieeeee!*'s reverent endorsement of works like Okada's and its excoriation of (mainly female) authors like Maxine Hong Kingston, Jade Snow Wong, and Amy Tan.

While the fiction of Philip K. Dick and Joseph Heller illustrates how game theory has shaped the way postwar American literature is written, works like *No-No Boy* and *Treadmill* reveal how game theory has further shaped the way that literature is read. Indeed, internment discourse's game-theoretical framing of Japanese Americans' "inscrutable" intentions was understood as a simultaneously racial and literary problem. That is, the way internment advocates represented the inscrutable Asian face as a text to be read, and its hidden loyalties disclosed, strikingly resembles the

New Critical concept of the "intentional fallacy," introduced by American scholars W. K. Wimsatt and Monroe Beardsley in 1946, which recommended that extratextual evidence, whether explicit authorial assertions or readers' affective responses, be metaphorically interned in order to maintain the integrity of critical practice.[71] Too, the way Wimsatt and Beardsley framed the dilemma created by "intentionalism" would certainly have captured the sympathies of DeWitt and Stimson: "One must ask how a critic expects to get an answer to the question about intention. How is he to find out what the poet [was trying] to do?"[72]

Aesthetic interpretation, Wimsatt and Beardsley argued, must be based on the work itself. But this "internal evidence" of authorial intent could only be truly discerned, and the success or failure of the work truly decided, by the expertise of the critic.[73] Subordinating the author's explicitly stated intention for a work to the critic's interpretation of it further suggested that what counted as "evidence" was itself largely a matter of critical opinion; indeed, making such a determination was, from this perspective, the critic's right as well as his responsibility. What we have, in other words, is an aesthetic theory whose relation to literature is like that of games to game theory: the claims being made are as much about the problem of reading people as reading books, as much about representational authority as authorial representation. These are, in short, *political* theories, what German sociologists Christopher Daase and Oliver Kessler eloquently describe as "cognitive frame[s] for political practice."[74] Insofar as these frames offer new ways of reading internment literature, that literature also allows us to recognize the enduring but often overlooked presence of such frames as they have shaped American military conflicts not only past but present. Indeed, no great expertise is required to detect the "internal evidence" of internment's game-theoretical legacy in comments like those made by Secretary of Defense Donald Rumsfeld, here arguing for the 2003 invasion of Iraq despite a paucity of evidence that the latter was supplying weapons of mass destruction to terrorist groups: "As we know, there are known knowns; there are things we know we know. We also know there are known unknowns; that is to say we know there are some things we do not know. But there are also unknown unknowns—the ones we don't know we don't know. . . . Simply because you do not have evidence that something exists does not mean that you have evidence that it doesn't exist."[75]

The Catch

The House Always Wins

3

Against the Odds

From Model Minority to Model Majority

No one could suspect that times were coming . . . when the
man who did not gamble would lose all the time, even more
surely than he who gambled.
—Charles Peguy, *The Portal of the Mystery of Hope*

Chance is not merely sought out but carved out.
—Erving Goffman, "Where the Action Is"

While parlor games offered Americans a theoretical model to rationalize wartime racism as fair play, gambling games allowed them to make
sense of the increasingly un-level playing field that defined postwar life.
In the face of a fading Protestant work ethic and a stratified and mechanized post-Fordist labor economy, Americans turned in droves to games
and leisure as both pastime and perspective to give life renewed meaning. The enchantment with games was simultaneously a response to and
an expressive vehicle for the nation's disenchanted perception of success as "an accidental and irrational event," as sociologist Leo Lowenthal
put it, and hence with social mobility more broadly as the product of
a "ridiculous game of chance."[1] In describing life "as a game, a sort of
lottery," sociologist C. Wright Mills's influential 1951 study of "white-
collar" class dynamics likewise captured a mid-century sense of gaming
not as an escape from, but rather as the very definition of, real life.[2] The
ludic, in other words, was used not only as a metaphor to emphasize
the analogous role of chance in lotteries and in real life, but as a model
to explain—to rationalize—the maddening irrationality of modern life.
"Just as the 'lucky stroke' magically bolsters hope in an increasingly limited structure of opportunity," Mills wrote, "so the idea of the 'bad break'
softens feelings of individual failure."[3]

The intervening decades have seen the full-blown institutionalization of such ludic rhetoric, as the language of luck and lottery has given
way to more official-sounding euphemisms like "equal opportunity"
and strenuous debates over "affirmative action." The lack of correlation
Lowenthal in 1944 described between "ambition and possibilities"—
between input and output, effort and reward—is recapitulated in 2006
by Walter Benn Michaels as a fundamental contradiction of neoliberalism, defined by a national discourse that espouses a "simultaneous
commitment to the importance of hard work and ability (making your
money) . . . and to the irrelevance of hard work and ability (inheriting
it)."[4] While, for Lowenthal, the mid-century outpouring of popular biographies of athletes, actors, and other "heroes" of the entertainment
industry were key to making the whole "ridiculous game of chance," if
not wholly agreeable, at least more palatable to middle-class readers,
for Michaels, it is the "American love affair with race"—as opposed to
class—which serves that function in the age of neoliberalism.[5] "Diversity," in this view, is "at best a distraction and at worst an essentially reac-
tionary position," one that not only "obscures the fundamental problem
of economic inequality" but perversely allows us to "celebrate economic
difference by pretending that it is cultural difference"—by treating class,
that is, as itself a kind of "racial" identity.[6]

Understanding race and class in such antipodal terms recalls the
similar tendency we have already begun to see surrounding the framing of work and play as diametrically opposed rather than dialectically
inextricable.[7] A number of critics have stridently challenged arguments
like Michaels's and those that posit race as epiphenomenal to class,
highlighting the tendency of such "class-reductionist" arguments, as
Chris Chen has described them, to "reduce structural exploitation to
distributive inequalities in wealth" and thereby produce racial difference and identity politics as a ready straw man for Marxist critiques of
neoliberalism.[8] It is little surprise that many of these counter-discourses
have arisen among scholars working in or proximate to Asian American studies, given that Asian Americans have been the group most
often sighted in Michaels's crosshairs for their crimes against class
consciousness.[9] Indeed, for Michaels, the celebratory rhetoric of Asian
Americans as high-achieving, law-abiding model minorities has been
exemplary of this obfuscating process whereby, in his view, "issues of

class" are transmuted and reduced to "issues of culture."[10] This familiar rehabilitation narrative has historically been traced back to the 1950s, when Asian Americans were ostensibly spirited, Cinderella-like, from their yellow peril–era disgrace as parasitic "cheaters" and "inscrutable" threats to be praised, instead, as economic and moral paragons. This chapter also takes up that Cold War moment as an opportunity to emphasize not the discontinuity between but the triangulational intimacy of the moral, racial, and economic discourses that collectively produced the figure of the model minority.

Model minority discourse was unquestionably, as critical consensus holds, a "narrative of national racial progress premised on the distinction between 'good' and 'bad' minorities."[11] Asian Americans' spectacular redemption as modern-day Horatio Alger protagonists created a rhetorical vacancy that was readily filled by other minorities, specifically African Americans, who were now cast as "welfare bums" gaming the system. The Asian American "success story" was, in that sense, as strategic as it was celebratory, as economic as it was racial—and as compelling as it was coercive. Numerous stakeholders, including parts of the community itself, conscripted Asian Americans to serve as the face of U.S. racial democracy in a geopolitical PR campaign for a new world order and, on the home front, as a rhetorical fire hose in the domestic damage control effort to curtail the burgeoning civil rights movement.[12]

Yet, as this chapter demonstrates, that narrative served as significant a role in naturalizing class as racial inequality—and not merely for minorities, but for the majority of white Americans as well. Indeed, if the implicit targets of what David Palumbo-Liu has dubbed the "model minority thesis" were blacks and other "problem minorities," the intended audience was imagined to be the white majority, and more specifically the white middle class.[13] The innumerable news items responsible for constructing the resulting "model minority myth" satisfied not only white readers' prejudicial assumptions about African Americans but also their voracious and well-established appetite for celebrity biographies and the "mythology of success" such stories perpetuated. Media representation of the "magazine heroes" and "mass idols" of the mid-twentieth century, as Lowenthal observed, deftly subordinated the deterministic role of hard work to that of random chance: to lucky breaks, fortuitous timing, and other "freakish" turns of events.[14] Such randomness, indeed, played a crucial role in the framing of Asian American success as what articles variously described as an "against all odds" victory over racism and a "spectacular comeback" from internment's devastating losses.[15]

The model minority myth has maintained its power in the interceding decades despite strenuous critical and community efforts to debunk it by demonstrating the gap between fiction and statistical reality—for example, the high poverty rates of many Southeast Asian American communities, or the wage gap separating Asian Americans and whites of equivalent educational levels. Reframing the model minority myth as a narrative about Asian Americans not merely as hard workers but as heroic underdogs—catapulted from fortune's fools to her favorites in the blink of an eye—offers an equally novel and compelling means of accounting for what Ellen Wu rightly describes as the remarkable "success of this success story" in the American imagination.[16] It allows us, that is, to recognize the model minority narrative as, like gambling itself, a deeply seductive discourse. For if, as a disciplinary model for other minorities, the model minority obscured the structural racism that made failure a near inevitability for nonwhites, as an aspirational model for the white majority it obscured the economic mechanisms that made class mobility into an analogously improbable event. This has been especially true in the neoliberal era, wherein, as Michaels observes, the impersonal sorting mechanism of the market ostensibly produces a "neoliberal utopia where all the irrelevant grounds for inequality (your identity) have been eliminated and whatever inequalities are left are therefore legitimated."[17] In such a setting, the fantastic and seductive nature of the Asian American success story even more closely resembles that of the celebrities Lowenthal described. As comedian Bo Burnham cogently quipped, "Taylor Swift telling you to follow your dreams is like a lottery winner telling you, 'Liquidize your assets, buy Powerball tickets, it works!'"[18]

To liken the model minority to a Powerball winner—to emphasize success's aleatory prerequisites over its meritorious ones—is in no way to diminish the significance of Asian American achievement. It is, instead, to elevate the comparatively insignificant role that gambling and concepts like chance and risk have played in existing critical assessments of the model minority, where focus on law or labor has to date left largely unconsidered the role of ludo-Orientalism as a vehicle for model minority discourse and as a point of continuity with earlier yellow peril stereotypes. Yet, insofar as Colleen Lye's contention that "yellow peril and model minority are best understood as two aspects of the same, long-running racial form" holds true, the model minority's rehabilitation of Asian Americans involved not banishing the specter of the "inveterate gambler" but simply its pejorative connotations.[19] Just as nineteenth-century commodity traders rhetorically transformed their gambling from parasitic vice to "virtuous production," engineers of the model minority myth transformed Asian racial difference from "stigma to multiculturalist virtue."[20] And they did so, as we will see, in remarkably similar ways, deftly refashioning the sojourning coolie's inhuman tolerance for the trials and deprivation of Gold Mountain life into the heroic gambler's appetite for the sizable risks and uncertain rewards of the American dream.[21]

While critics of the model minority have historically attended to the language of hard work over hard play, we must consider how the concept of chance has been equally foundational to their own interventions. Myth-busting efforts, as mentioned above, have almost always used quantitative approaches and the baselines of statistical probability to demonstrate that, in Frank Wu's account, "the Asian-ness of Asian Americans offers only sketchy explanations of the data"—in this case, the fact that 42 percent of Asian Americans had attained a college degree as compared with 25 percent of the general population, and made up nearly 20 percent of the entering class at Ivy League colleges despite constituting less than 3 percent of the general population.[22] "Sophisticated statistical analysis," however, revealed "only faint correlations between race itself and academic success": factors like parental education, teacher feedback, peer support, and study habits were shown to be far more influential in determining student success. The point, for Wu and innumerable other critics, is that race's "influence is scarcely more than the effects of random chance": if luck is involved, it lies in being born to well-educated parents and a supportive community.[23] By this logic, then, Asian Americans are not "racially" better equipped for success than non-Asians, but neither are their achievements purely the result of hard work: random chance, instead, takes the place of racial determinism. Thus, if the model minority myth itself drew a positive correlation between Asian American race and success, and critics have in turn replaced "race" with "random chance," the result is an even stronger sense of the model minority as, in fact, the model majority: as exemplary, that is, of the perception held by the general population, of living in "a world governed more by chance and luck" than fair competition.[24]

To understand the success of the model minority myth, and why the most exhaustive and well-researched efforts have failed to effect a change in racial perception, is also to understand why an analogous lack of correlation between effort expended and reward reaped has failed to effect significant political change. And it involves recognizing how both of these successful failures—from the perspective of "the house"—are in turn inextricable from the question of why Americans led the world in losing nearly $117 billion last year on gambling games such as lotteries, casinos, and sports betting (China, Macau, and Hong Kong combined came in a distant second place at some $62 billion).[25] In short, it is to recognize the formal similarities between gambling at casinos and "gambling" in life decisions. As discussed above, the latter is not merely a metaphor, because gambling is not merely a recreational alternative to work—a way of spending one's money—but a way to make a living (as with stockbrokers) and, more broadly, a way of viewing life in terms of its expected value, its potential "payoffs." As Jackson Lears reminds us, debates about gambling are "never just about gambling [but] about different ways of being in the world."[26] Indeed, gambling need not involve money at all; to gamble is simply to "risk anything of value on the outcome of an event involving a large degree of chance or uncertainty . . . in the hope of gaining some advantage, benefit, or success."[27] Such, as we will see, is the concept at the heart of the model minority myth—which, as a "success story," is ultimately as much about the moral triumph of American speculative capitalism as the assimilative victories of Asian Americans. For the same seductive "illusion of control" that gambling provides—what psychologists who have begun to study the neurological bases for gambling addiction define as "the belief that the gambler can exert skill over an outcome that is actually defined by chance"—is found in the neoliberalist illusion that hard work and ability supersede the role of luck: that America is, in short, a level playing field, not just a "ridiculous game of chance."[28]

This chapter deepens our knowledge of the origins and the stakes of the model minority myth, augmenting the established recognition of its disciplinary function aimed at shaming other minority groups by attending to its oft-overlooked function as an aspirational model for white Americans. The analysis accordingly shifts our focus from the coercive political ends served by the discourse to the ludo-Orientalist means through which it unfolded, beginning with the steady stream of mainstream media representations of postwar Chinese and Japanese Americans as heroic risk-takers reaping the rewards of an all-American life, domesticating the nineteenth century's most reviled vice and immigrant group into the twentieth century's most virtuous Americans. I examine how these domesticating narratives became a springboard for, first, a series of nostalgic portraits of Asian American family life as a scale model of a bygone American golden age lost in the crass consumerism of modern life, and later, for far less celebratory portraits of the evacuated agency of post-internment life painted by Asian American writers like Hisaye Yamamoto and Wakako Yamauchi in their short stories "Las Vegas Charley" and "The Sensei."

Model Americans

The reigning assumption has been that the model minority stereotype involved a rhetorical erasure of the "Asian" affinity for gambling and the other moral vices invoked during the yellow peril era, celebrating instead the group's penchant for hard work and frugality. Yet gambling was not abolished but rather domesticated in model minority discourse, where it functioned as a sort of crucible for the emergence of this new, "model" Asian American. Early model minority narratives suggested, at times explicitly, that Asian Americans' against all odds economic success was the result not simply of hard work but serious play, of an unparalleled willingness to risk everything in pursuit of the American dream, even when racial injustice transformed what should have been a level playing field into a stacked deck. Certainly the very act of immigrating—abandoning the familiar to seek one's fortunes in a new and foreign country, at great personal risk—could be (and was) viewed as initial evidence of such a proclivity. Studies of Asian American mental health have even recently begun to explore a direct neurological correlation between Asian immigration and other high-risk behaviors. In a striking echo of yellow peril claims of "inveterate gambling," Timothy

Fong, an assistant professor of psychiatry at UCLA, explicitly links the material and metaphorical connotations of gambling in summarizing his study's findings: "[Asian immigrants] who . . . take a chance and come to America are more likely to gamble because immigrating to America from your homeland is a huge gamble in and of itself. . . . Most likely they have some kind of biological predisposition to gambling in general, in life."[29]

If a gambling "spirit" could be seen to motivate first-generation Asian immigrants, so too has the aleatory fantasy of the United States as a nation where, as a character in Amy Tan's *The Joy Luck Club* puts it, "anybody can become anything" provided an equally compelling narrative. Modern accounts of economic capital—even those, à la Pierre Bourdieu, that acknowledge its immaterial forms—have a habit of treating games of chance as the antithesis to the complex real-world machinations of capitalism and the "serious" forms of wage labor it rests on. Thus, according to Bourdieu, in stark contrast to "capital, which . . . takes time to accumulate and . . . contains a tendency to persist in its being," games like roulette, his seminal example, constitute "an imaginary universe of perfect competition or perfect equality of opportunity, a world . . . without heredity or acquired properties, in which . . . every prize can be attained, instantaneously, by everyone."[30] While, for Bourdieu, these "simple games of chance" were mere fantasy, and the antithesis of the complex mechanisms of the "economic game" that drove real-world capitalism, their status as "imaginary" is perhaps precisely why they have historically occupied such a central place in Asian American immigration narratives.[31]

Such a racially coded gambling spirit seems entirely antithetical to the hard work and frugality we now think of as *the* defining traits of the model minority. Yet gambling is, from another perspective, the crucial vehicle through which the discourse's shoring up of the attendant fantasy of the United States as a level playing field could be pursued in the first place. The work ethic was of limited utility in explaining Asian American success for the same reasons that work itself had decreased in motivational power. For C. Wright Mills and many others, the decline of the Protestant work ethic—the culmination of a century-long transition from "a nation of small capitalists into a nation of hired employees"— had bankrupted the power of the "old middle class work ethic": "The gospel of work has been central to the historical tradition of America, to its image of itself, and to the images the rest of the world has of America. The crisis and decline of that gospel are of wide and deep meaning. When work becomes just work, activity undertaken only for reason of subsistence, the spirit which fired our nation to its present greatness has died to a spark."[32] Gambling, however, was not the antithesis of hard work but in fact the prerequisite to making that work meaningful: not by guaranteeing success, but rather by making it into a possibility. The nineteenth-century figure of the "confidence man" had already amply demonstrated the profitability of such logic, which makes the very potential for change contingent on an investment unlikely to see fruits: the illogical but irresistible perception, in the famous words of hockey legend Wayne Gretzky, that "you miss 100 percent of the shots you don't take." (To which Friedrich Nietzsche would surely counter, "Hope in reality is the worst of all evils because it prolongs the torments of man.") Certainly one's success rate of shots is contingent on one's skill and training, but such training and skill is irrelevant unless one first takes the chance—the gamble—to make a shot despite the fear of failure.

As counterintuitive as it might at first appear, it is thus ultimately unsurprising to find this inclination to take risks among those Asian American traits most emphasized and admired by the earliest proponents of the model minority myth. In January 1966, the *New York Times Magazine* published "Success Story, Japanese-American Style," a six-page article by sociologist William Petersen frequently (but incorrectly) cited as the original source of the term "model minority." The article, like the book into which it was eventually expanded, is riddled with gambling metaphors. Time and again, Petersen marveled at Japanese Americans' ability to succeed despite the "overwhelming odds against them." To have "bet their lives, determined to win in even a crooked game," sent their children to school to "avidly prepare . . . for that one chance in a thousand" of white-collar employment: in short, to have, barely two decades after their utter economic and social ruin during internment, and by "their own almost totally unaided effort," managed to achieve middle-class status.[33]

What made for a feel-good story to readers, however, also presented a sizeable challenge to Petersen and other sociologists as a phenomenon that defied not only popular expectation but also scholarly explanation. Whereas other minorities had been unable to transcend the "visible stigma" of race in either economic or social condition, Japanese Americans had "climb[ed] over the highest barriers our racists could fashion" and risen "above even prejudiced criticism." Whereas other "nonwhite" communities were riddled with poverty, crime, inferior educational levels, and lower life expectancies, Japanese Americans were "exceptionally law-abiding," possessed a median of 12.2 years of schooling, and enjoyed an average life expectancy of 81.2 years (females) and 74.5 (males). Whereas "problem minorities"—specifically African Americans—were forced to rely on the welfare system, Japanese Americans had assiduously avoided public assistance, even after having their entire net worth (an estimated $200 million) wiped out by internment—a crime for which the government did not compensate them until 1965, and even then at the rate of around "30 or 40 cents on the dollar."[34]

This latter devastation—a financial loss predicated on a preemptive racial identification and instantiated by an unconstitutional deprivation of legal protection as American citizens—is a key moment of triangulation through which the model minority established itself as a racial, economic, and moral discourse. Critic Randy Martin has cogently traced the neoliberal entanglement of moral and political economies through what he dubs the "financialization of daily life," attending in particular to how terms like "risk management" and "preemption" have semantically bridged the realms of finance capital and national security. As Martin observes, the meanings of financial risk, referring to an expected return on one's investment, and of security risk, referring to a contingent safety threat posed by others, now "readily slide into one another."[35] Military policy and fiscal policy become co-constitutive—and this phenomenon is both unmistakably clear in, and indeed helps to explain, the difference between yellow peril–esque internment-era discourses and Cold War model minority discourses. Whereas, as we saw in the arguments made by military officials and members of the judicial branch in the last chapter, Japanese Americans were initially framed as security risks and "enemy aliens," in model minority discourse we see that risk being transvalued into a positive racial attribute. Now, it is Japanese Americans' voluntary embrace of risk, in the form of a carefully self-managed, shrewdly speculative market sensibility, that is presumed to be responsible for transforming financial losses into middle-class comforts. As Martin points out, "Risk is not unilateral but operates as a kind of moral binary, sorting out the good from the bad on the basis of capacities to contribute."[36] The "financialization" of racial qualities we see at work in Cold War model minority discourse effectively differentiated Asian Americans from other "at-risk" or "unmanageable" minority groups and, at the same time, framed them as an internally coherent group of ethical, economically savvy model citizens.[37]

Despite their explicitly condemning the "flagrant" injustice of internment and the official explanation of "military necessity," we find social theorists like William Petersen echoing Warren and DeWitt, not least in approaching Japanese Americans as a group for which the "best theories" of modern sociology (as opposed to modern political economy) simply "do not apply."[38] For it was not simply that Japanese Americans deftly exploded the theories of social pathology that applied to so many other nonwhite minorities; they also failed to conform to the theories of assimilation that had long explained the transition of European immigrants. The latter's second, American-born generation had historically been afflicted with "unusually high" rates of juvenile delinquency, for which "sociologists ha[d] fashioned a plausible theory" to explain: namely, the challenge to patriarchal authority posed by the second generation's "contempt or shame" for their uneducated, non-native-speaker fathers. Yet delinquents among the American-born nisei—whom the legal restrictions on their immigrant parents' citizenship and property rights thrust into "adult roles early in life," such that we would have expected "not merely a high delinquency rate but among the highest"—were strikingly few and "anomalous."[39]

The model minority *was* that theory. But it was not so much a racial theory, as has been traditionally assumed, in the sense of an explanatory model for Asians' racial exceptionalism (the ingrained racial traits that explained their success, or, conversely, which accounted for African American failure). Indeed, it may come as a surprise to contemporary readers that the earliest accounts of the model minority bore little resemblance to those aspects with which we are now most familiar: a perception of Asians' exceptional intelligence, particularly in math and science, and equally exceptional meekness or obedience. Indeed, Petersen in 1966 came to the same conclusion Frank Wu and researchers on the link between race and academic success would twenty-five years later: beyond a few "outstanding individuals," Japanese Americans, on the basis of their academic records, were on the whole a remarkably unremarkable group, with little evidence of the innate "extraordinary academic worth" that is now inextricable from the stereotype. "The key to success in the United States, for Japanese or anyone else, is education," Petersen concluded.[40] Japanese American success was due not to deviating from, but rather doggedly cleaving to, the "American" conviction that higher education could serve as what Mills described as a "social elevator" for the children of the lower and less-privileged classes.

Critics have historically focused on the model minority as a "theory" in the sense that it explained why Asian Americans had succeeded where other minorities had failed. Yet, as Petersen's above comments already suggest, this is only half of the picture; model minority discourse was, further, an explanation of why Asian Americans had been able to succeed where even the majority of white Americans had not. Indeed, contrary to popular assumption, Petersen's article ultimately seemed less interested in holding up Japanese Americans as a punitive example for blacks. If anything, he considered the former a far more effective parable for white Americans. "By any criterion of good citizenship that we choose," Petersen observed, "the Japanese Americans are better than any group in our society, including native-born whites."[41] Asian Americans had, as the title of a 1971 *Newsweek* article proclaimed, "outwhited the whites."[42] These were not, in other words, merely model *minorities*, but model *Americans*.

What made Japanese Americans an ideal model for white middle-class Americans was not their exceptional qualities but, counterintuitively, the exemplary "everyman" status that Petersen had observed. In other words, Asian Americans were to the model minority as games were to game theory: the privileged vehicle for a conceptual model of social relations— and specifically economic ones. Indeed, the model minority was itself a game theory: a conceptual model of the world not as a game of strategy, as in von Neumann's and Morgenstern's theory, but rather as a game of chance. In Petersen's account, Japanese Americans' astonishing ability to be "Six Times Down, Seven Times Up" was the product of their gambling spirit.[43] Yet if racism were to blame for transforming what should have been a fair competition into a "crooked game" of overwhelming odds for

Japanese-American Cub Scouts in Gardena, Calif.: Wasps at heart?

Figure 3.1. This image appeared in *Newsweek* with the telling caption "Japanese-American Cub Scouts in Gardena, Calif.: Wasps at heart?" Charles Michener, "Success Story: Outwhiting the Whites," *Newsweek*, June 21, 1971. Photo by Lester Sloan.

racial minorities, this was at the same time a scale model of the broader "ridiculous game of chance" in which middle- and working-class white Americans had long felt themselves trapped.

In suggesting that Japanese Americans had become more American than Americans themselves, the explicit goal of model minority discourse—in the words of Petersen, to better understand "what manner of people" were these remarkably successful Japanese Americans—is thus itself better understood as an attempt to comprehend the essence or "spirit" of Americanness that was rapidly fading. Indeed, the combined admiration and awe with which Petersen and innumerable other writers contemplated Japanese Americans' "spectacular comeback" gains additional relevance once understood within the context of a broader mid-century quest for a bygone "success story" that had somehow been lost to American culture at large—and of which this plucky minority represented not a fringe anomaly, but one of the last remaining vestiges.

Model Models

The model minority's redemption of gambling from parasitic to productive ideal was itself modeled on the nineteenth-century domestication of gambling from vice to virtue that we saw in chapter 1. So, too, can the emergence of the Asian American family as a moral paragon be understood as an extension of the romanticized figure of the heroic frontier gambler, which had become a convention of Western fiction through none other than Bret Harte. Transforming the Western gamesman from a morally suspect figure conventionally associated with frontier humor into a virtuous exemplar, Harte's "major contribution to the frontier myth," Michael Oriard observes, was the figure of "the heroic gambler risking his life as readily as his fortune on the turn of a card."[44] Like the model minority willing to "risk their lives" even in a crooked game, the gambler in Harte's hands had become by the 1880s "a highly romanticized figure. If a gambler, he was a strikingly domesticated one . . . made to serve charity, high culture, and law . . . rendered unobjectionable by serving sentimental ends."[45]

This redemptive view of gamblers remained as compelling in 1960 as it had been in 1882. Such was also the conclusion of sociologist Erving Goffman, who in 1967 contemplated a unique brand of rugged American masculinity unique to frontiers, underworlds, and, most important for him, casinos. "In removing themselves further and further from the substance of our society," Goffman suggested, such "puddles of people" as cowboys, detectives, and gamblers counterintuitively "grasp more and more of certain aspects of [society's] spirit"; "their alienation from our reality frees them to be subtly induced into realizing our moral fantasies." In their aberrant, antisocial version of American habitus, gamblers in particular memorialized a vicarious national romance with what Goffman called "fatefulness": "the chancy deeds of an honorable life . . . all those activities that generate expression, requiring the individual to lay himself on the line and place himself in jeopardy during a passing moment."[46]

Reframing the American dream as an adventurous quest to discover "where the action is," Goffman's little-known ethnographic analysis of Las Vegas casinos offers a novel vantage point to explore the relationship between "margins and mainstreams," a phrase historian Gary Okihiro

FRONTIERSMAN — A Chinese-American boy adopts Western garb.

Figure 3.2. The original image caption reads "FRONTIERSMAN—A Chinese-American boy adopts Western garb." William McIntyre, "Chinatown Offers Us a Lesson," *New York Times Magazine*, October 6, 1957.

coined to argue that "the core values and ideals of [the United States] emanate not from the mainstream but from the margins—from among Asian and African Americans, Latinos and American Indians, women, and gays and lesbians."[47] Drawing on the insights of postcolonial theory, Okihiro's assertion that "the mainstream derives its identity, its integrity, from its representation of the Other" was premised on his belief that such a process reveals the "true significance of Asians in American history and culture." Their liminality within a black-white racial spectrum and repeated attempts to seek "inclusion within the promise of American democracy" have "helped to preserve and advance the very privileges that were denied to them, and thereby democratized the nation for the benefit of all Americans."[48] This potential "payoff," here conceptualized as a trickle-down reward for the entire nation, was, as we saw in the previous chapter, a central dynamic of the loyalty question-naire. Nisei men's' yes-yes answers were attestations not merely of their loyalty but their willingness to gamble on the American dream: that is, to risk—and frequently lose—their lives in the hopes of having their and their immigrant parents' Americanness legitimated.

This wartime gamble exemplified one of the major character traits Goff-man considered crucial to these marginal figures' ability to "manage . . . fateful events." "Gameness," as he labeled it, was "the capacity to stick to a line of activity and to continue to pour all effort into it regardless of set-backs, pain, or fatigue, and this not because of some brute in-sensitivity but because of inner will and determination."[49] In this light, Petersen's own admiration of Japanese American "perseverance" before, during, and after the war is as much an acknowledgment of the model minority's aleatory affinity as the many explicit gambling metaphors he uses. For, once again, it was not the materiality of gambling as a pastime but what gambling represented as an ethos that was being invoked. The "game" on which the Asian immigrant had staked his life was the Amer-ican dream—and the payoff of that gamble was not simply money, but social and cultural capital, embodied in the form of the Asian American family.[50] Thus it was that Cold War media would frame Asian American "family values" as both the modern-day alternative to the immigrant bachelor societies of the previous century and, at the same time, as a nostalgic harking back to those fateful days.[51] For while the model mi-nority was in part the face of a new world order with the United States at the helm, it was at the same time a deeply nostalgic, even antiquated figure, one intended, as David Palumbo-Liu pointed out, "to remind Americans of the traditional values [the nation] had cast aside in its rush to modernization."[52] It was, in short, not simply a wholesome image of 1950s Americana that Asian Americans had come to represent, as schol-ars have rightly noted, but also a 1950s that was itself looking back to its nineteenth-century manifest destiny heyday, and specifically toward the now-closed frontier.

Indeed, in the model minority rhetoric of mainstream media from the late 1950s onward, one finds Asian Americans cast not only as deeply traditionalist, but as a kind of living fossil from a simpler, happier age, one that modern Americans would do well to learn from. In a 1957 *New*

York Times Magazine article titled "Chinatown Offers Us a Lesson," William McIntyre wistfully described Chinese American family life as "so wholesome that it seems almost anachronistic in our epoch of anxieties." In this sentimental diorama, which found both textual and visual expression in publications ranging from the *New York Post* to *Look* magazine (a lifestyle publication similar to *Life*), Asian Americans remained uncontaminated by the "superficial, Hollywoodish goals" and rampant consumerism of modern life, as well as the "immorality" and "instability" engendered by liberalizing attitudes toward sex and gender, and the growing participation of mothers in the workforce.[53]

The domesticating function of this morally exemplary racial domesticity is emblematized by the cover image of McIntyre's article (fig. 3.3), which visually replaced the threatening foreignness of pai gow played in Chinatown gambling dens with the idyllic image of three generations of Chinese Americans assembled for an evening of wholesome family fun. While the trio of impeccably dressed and coiffed women chat and admire a well-behaved infant, the three men, undistracted by television or newspapers, focus their attention on what appears at first glance to be a game of Scrabble—but which, upon closer inspection, turns out to be a model airplane kit. As an illustration of the "lesson" aimed at "us," however, this choice of recreation is even more apropos than the familiar family pastime of the competitive board game. The introduction of injection-molded plastic model kits in the 1950s revitalized a hobby that had defined the Great Depression era but had subsequently fallen into obscurity. Newly redeemed and hailed as the "perfect man's hobby" in publications ranging from *Today's Health* to *Businessweek*, model building now offered "fathers and sons a psychological space of their own in the house where the father could relive his boyhood and the son could dream of his future."[54]

Elevated to the level of hobby or home craft rather than mere "toy," modeling, as it was often called, made headlines as the "way to men's hearts" in language strikingly similar to that which celebrated Asian Americans' model assimilative successes.[55] For if Asian Americans were framed as "role models" for American readers—one article concluded that "it wouldn't hurt us a bit to try keeping up with the Wongs, Lees and Engs"[56]—the clear-cut, reproducible image of success presented in figure 3.3 was itself like the one printed on the model kit box. Indeed, much

Figure 3.3. The original image caption reads "Chinatown family—'The child of Chinese-American parents is treated with affection, firmness, dignity and good humor.'" William McIntyre, "Chinatown Offers Us a Lesson," *New York Times Magazine*, October 6, 1957.

of the charm of Manhattan Chinatown, for McIntyre, was its resemblance to a scale model: a "city within our city" that was simultaneously "a miniature of China" and a *tableau vivant* of America's heyday.[57] It was just such a play at home, "do-it-yourself" model that politicians like Arthur Klein referenced when encouraging others to take a lesson from his exceptionally rule-abiding constituents in Chinatown, who "follow a way of life that deserves to be known, applauded, and emulated."[58]

Assembled in a carefully planned sequence for the newspaper photograph, on display for the admiration of American readers, the Chinese Americans in the image are in every way staged to give the impression of themselves as an all-American family. The obvious artificiality of that staging, however, simply draws attention to the fact that, like all models,

Asian Americans were not the same as the "real thing:" they were, as the caption in figure 3.1 suggests, WASPs only at heart.[59] Yet the very ludic means in which that asymptotic relationship to whiteness was established is instructive. Asianness is to whiteness, from this perspective, as model airplanes are to real ones: a "to-scale" representation neither inferior nor antithetical to the simulated "original," but an aesthetically pleasing image of it. Asian Americans become, as one news report put it, "a model of the way that white Americans like to think of themselves."[60]

Model Gamblers

Given that we have taken such pains to establish the link between race and gambling in terms of immaterial discourse rather than the more familiar material forms of gambling, it may seem strange to conclude with a look at "real" Asian American gamblers: that is, those who stake not life but simply wages on lotto tickets and Las Vegas casinos. There is certainly no paucity of material for such an analysis: indeed, gambling is mentioned in such a wide range of Asian American historical as well as literary narratives that the comparative lack of critical interest it has garnered is surprising, particularly since it is so often linked to the "articulate silence" that critic King-Kok Cheung has identified as a central trope of Asian American literature. Consider a classic example from Maxine Hong Kingston's *The Woman Warrior*, where gambling both instantiates and obviates a rare moment of classroom volubility by the normally taciturn young Chinese American narrator. Upon seeing her father's occupation incorrectly listed in her elementary school file, "I exclaimed, 'Hey, he wasn't a farmer, he was a . . .' He had been a gambler. My throat cut off the word—silence in front of the most understanding teacher. There were secrets never to be said in front of the ghosts, immigration secrets whose telling could get us sent back to China."[61] Such tantalizing glimpses into the details of an immigrant identity that remains, for the most part, as much a secret to the narrator as to the reader, are made especially precious in such second-generation narratives.

Gambling need not always be pathological; it is, after all, an important feature of social life in numerous Asian cultures, particularly as part of New Year festivities. Yet recent polls of San Francisco's Chinatown suggest that for many Asian Americans, gambling far exceeds such boundaries: nearly 37 percent of the almost two thousand respondents identified themselves as either problem or pathological gamblers.[62] In the most recent edition of the *Diagnostic and Statistical Manual of Mental Disorders (DSM-5)*, long the industry standard for mental health diagnoses, Asian Americans were, however, the only racial group not explicitly mentioned in the "Gambling Disorder" chapter, which lists a racial breakdown of "the lifetime prevalence of pathological gambling" as compared to the general population (~0.4–1.0%), and which "among African Americans is about 0.9%, among whites about 0.4%, and among Hispanics about 0.3%."[63] Like the scene in *The Woman Warrior*, such statistics reflect and reinforce the extremely low numbers of Asian Americans who seek treatment for gambling addiction, leading to a disturbing silence surrounding what many researchers have understood as Asian America's hidden epidemic.

These collective silences surrounding "real" Asian American gambling might seem little more than an effort to suppress that which does not align with the moral and economic virtues of the model minority image, a cover-up in which the community itself is understandably deeply invested. Yet it is only after juxtaposing gambling's silencing effects with its voluble celebration in model minority discourse that we can see the former not as a distraction from but a prerequisite for the latter. That is, for the model minority as heroic "gambler" to function effectively, "real" gambling—the demonized material[64]—must first be banished and redeemed as, instead, the idealized metaphorical. Recognizing the broader stakes of that representational transformation—attending, as we have been, to what gambling *means* for racial politics—allows us in turn to introduce a new critical focus to the issue of "real" gamblers in terms of the epistemological rather than material promises and perils they present to Asian America's self-conception.[65]

Much as their idealized counterparts did with American sociology, Asian American gamblers reveal the limits of current disciplinary paradigms in Asian American studies, and especially Asian American literary criticism. Viet Nguyen and Christopher Lee have noted that the heroic exemplars of Asian American studies tend to be those non-model minorities or "bad" subjects—whether living or fictional—who refuse to conform to racial expectations, and hence evolve into the field's "idealized critical subject."[66] As Nguyen points out, however, the construction of the "bad" subject (bad from the vantage point of the state, good from the vantage point of the Asian Americanist) poses a false binary between this idealized critical subject and its counterpart—the "good" model minority—when in fact the two are interdependent.[67] At the same time, that binary exacerbates an overly constraining and idealistic notion of "resistance" that presumes some demonstrable degree of intentionality and agency on the part of the subject (not to mention assuming the existence of some demonstrably distinguishable entity called a "subject"). This is a dangerous assumption. For as we saw in the previous chapter, for choices to matter, they must be seen *as* choices (i.e., intentional *and* voluntary), and this has been as true of the way we have historically interpreted Asian American political gestures as Asian American loyalty. Asian American gamblers, particularly of the pathological, silence-inducing variety, trouble the assumptions that underlie traditional approaches to theorizing the Asian American subject of resistance. Gambling, at first blush, would seem to be the antithesis of "good," model minority behavior. It might, indeed, be said to constitute an ideal form of social rebellion against American injustice, a means of what Erving Goffman described as decreasing one's social utility to a capitalist system—"the less uncertain his life, the more society can make use of him"[68]—and hence an exemplarily "bad" Asian American subject position. However, insofar as gambling effectively *eliminates* the agency of the player once she has made the decision to play the game—leaving her wholly at the mercy of the roulette wheel, the next card in the deck, and so forth—it frustrates both moral and political distinctions of good and bad, complicity and resistance, exception and model. How, then, do we evaluate these seemingly "bad" (i.e., "ideal") Asian American subjects who arrive at that position not by choice but by blind chance?

This question is at the heart of Hisaye Yamamoto's "Las Vegas Charley" and Wakako Yamauchi's "The Sensei," two mid-century short stories that utilize the figure of the Asian American gambler in the seemingly anachronistic setting of the frontier to capture the unique pathos facing Japanese Americans during the postwar years. Yamamoto and Yamauchi, both nisei authors born in the early 1920s, are best known for their short stories (and also, in the latter's case, a play), most of which depict pre- and post-internment Japanese Californian communities, with an especial focus on rural farmers in the Imperial Valley. While Yamamoto had enjoyed some success as a writer in the immediate postwar years, with a handful of short stories published in *Harper's Bazaar, Partisan Review*, and *Best American Short Stories* (1952), it was not until 1974, with the publication of *Aiiieeeee! An Anthology of Asian American Literature*, that both women were recognized as canonical postwar Asian American writers, joining the ranks of John Okada, Toshio Mori, and Louis Chu as "real" Asian American artists.[69]

Yamamoto's "Las Vegas Charley," published in *Arizona Quarterly* in 1961, traces the tragic life and death of a dissolute issei whom "everyone knew as Charley." Having moved to Las Vegas soon after the end of the internment, Charley, who is partially based on the author's father,[70] works as a dishwasher to support his voracious gambling habit; the story concludes with Charley dying of stomach cancer and leaving his sizable debt to be shouldered by his embittered son. Yamauchi's "The Sensei," the original version of which appears to date to within a few years of Yamamoto's "Charley,"[71] tells a strikingly similar story. Narrated from the perspective of a young nisei woman in Los Angeles, "The Sensei" recounts a series of encounters she and her husband have in late 1940s Las Vegas with an older issei man, once a powerful leader of the pro-Japanese movement in the internment camps, now a destitute and degenerate gambler.[72]

Although a few of Yamamoto's earlier short stories included representations of gambling,[73] the setting of Las Vegas constitutes a striking exception in both writers' oeuvres, nearly all of which take either the Imperial Valley, or in some cases Japan, as their primary setting. While Yamauchi, a painter before becoming a writer, is best known for incorporating landscapes into short stories, it is Yamamoto that makes most explicit the atmospheric connection between Las Vegas and internment camps like the one in Poston, Arizona, where we will eventually learn that Charley and his sons were imprisoned, buffeted for four long years by endless "heat and dust and mud storms."[74] "Charley" accordingly opens with a panorama of the Nevada desert outside of Las Vegas, "that arid land where, as far as the eye can see . . . there are only sand, bare mountains, sagebrush, and more sand."[75] Evoking, in other words, the barren and harsh desert landscape encountered by internees and which has remained a central image in internment literature, Las

Vegas functions from the very first sentence of the story as an ecological counterpart to the internment experience.

Like Las Vegas, the internment camps, built in isolated areas of the United States, have been historically associated with a curious "frontier" spirit. Not only were they initially framed, by certain officials, as a kind of untapped fertile land, but the lawless conditions that presided in the camps, where "gangs" of children roamed alongside adult "goon squads" led by men like the sensei, combine with the harsh climate and inadequate living conditions to evoke a kind of borderland atmosphere.[76] Certainly in the stories, Las Vegas itself becomes an extension of this same spirit: Charley spends most of his time (and all of his money) "in places called the Boulder Club, the California Club, the Pioneer Club, or some such name meant to evoke the derring-do of the Old West";[77] while in Yamauchi's story, the narrator and her husband begin their expedition at the Golden Nugget before also making their way to the Boulder Club, where they first meet the sensei. Such scenes effectively emphasize that these characters are not just gambling with money, but replaying the memory and logic of internment.

Those disturbing memories of the internment are stirred up by the presence of the sensei (an honorific term usually translated as "teacher") in Las Vegas. The sight stuns and horrifies the narrator, Utako, and her husband, Jim: not only, as she observes, because of the rarity of seeing a Japanese face, nor even because of the man's ignominious descent into poverty and gambling addiction, but because he acts in an utterly unexpected, "un-Japanese" manner: upon seeing the couple, he asks them for money. "I can't get over it," Jim keeps repeating afterward. "A Japanese begging."[78] Given the devastating economic losses suffered by the Japanese American community as a result of the internment order, the presence of an impoverished Japanese American, particularly in the immediate postwar years, when anti-Japanese sentiment remained high, would not seem a particularly unlikely event. Yet to Jim the sensei's behavior is utterly unthinkable, particularly in comparison to the man's previous life as a Buddhist priest at Tule Lake (the camp where no-no boys and other "problem" internees were sent). "He was a powerful man in camp—feared and respected," Jim confides to his wife. "He had a big following. Fanatics . . . they moved in bands and terrorized people."[79] For Jim, the trajectory from internment leader to begging gambler in

Las Vegas is inconceivable. Yet Yamauchi's short story, like Yamamoto's "Charley," seems to suggest that the connection is not illogical, but may in fact even be inevitable.

That both Charley and the sensei would, after the internment, find their way from one barren desert to another is thus framed as disturbing but not altogether surprising. Indeed, Charley recalls that once he became "accustomed" to the harsh conditions of the internment camp, it was "not too unbearable."[80] In fact, at the end of the war, when "the day of decision" arrived for internees, he muses that "he would be quite content to remain in this camp the rest of his life—free food, free housing, friends, flower cards; what more could life offer? . . . [He] was far from agreeing with one angry man who had one day, annoyed with a severe dust storm, shouted, 'America is going to pay for every bit of this suffering! Taking away my farm and sending me to hell! Japan will win the war and then we'll see who puts who where!'"[81] As startling and repugnant as Charley's sentiments first appear, the narrators take special pains to remind us that for all their pathos, Charley and the sensei are not quite as miserable as we might think. Just after we learn that Charley, despite working ten hour days as a dishwasher, inevitably gambles away everything he makes—"It never failed: at the end of the month he was quite penniless"—the unidentified narrator hastens to add, "Not that life was bleak for Charley, not at all. Each day was exciting, fraught with the promise of sudden wealth."[82] And Utako, even after recognizing the pitiable state of the sensei, whom she speculates may indeed be gainfully employed—"I could see the Sensei sweating all week at some miserable job, maybe washing dishes, only to lose his pay at the tables, and I knew the hopelessness he felt as the last of his money slipped away"—finds herself comforted when the sensei shows no resentment toward his adopted home. "Still I love Las Vegas," he tells her—and, she tells us, "that made me feel good."[83] Gambling, in short, begins to serve as the vehicle for a kind of national rehabilitation, emptying the sensei's politics as well as his purse. Through gambling he loses both his money and, from Jim's perspective, his Japaneseness: that is, both his "dignity" and his fanatical Japanese nationalism.

Charley's addiction has also effectively destroyed his relationship with his remaining family, an adult son with two children of his own. Yet what gambling does to guarantee Charley's divorce from blood family ties in the form of his son and grandchildren, it also does to construct an alternative kinship system and sense of belonging he finds quite satisfactory. Charley sees no contradiction in developing friendships with his Chinese immigrant co-workers despite their respective homelands' long-standing antipathy, nor with the white waitresses whose casual racism toward those Chinese he brushes off with equal apathy. Charley's world is, ironically, something of an all-inclusive, multicultural utopia; Las Vegas gambling comes to provide, as it did in Erving Goffman's own account of the city, "a freemasonry of individuals who would otherwise be strangers . . . a temporary coalition against the society of the respectable. . . . The traditional mechanisms of acquaintanceship and personal invitation are not needed to restrict participation; the risks of participation serve instead."[84]

The game-theoretical reading of the internment pursued in the previous chapter offers further insight into why the particular risks associated with Las Vegas might make the destination especially attractive to Japanese Americans like Charley and the sensei. While the thrill of gambling is obviously a global phenomenon, the unique circumstances of Japanese Americans, both before and after the internment, arguably created a matrix of particular appeal. The internment produced a widespread sense of the inherent contingency and suspended agency of the racialized experience of nonwhite Americans—above all, a sense of the capriciousness of that existence, in which one's entire life could be suddenly, radically, and permanently altered by a single unanticipated event over which one had little to no control. This sense of helplessness permeates both "Las Vegas Charley" and "The Sensei" as it did Okada's *No-No Boy*; yet here, we see the crucial question that animated Kiyo in *All I Asking for Is My Body* and in game theory more broadly—"What would you do?"—being transformed into the rhetorical shrug of "What can you do?" In "The Sensei," Utako's frustrated resignation at the initial experience of internment—"[I was] very resentful of my loyalty being questioned and my rights being violated, but at seventeen, what could I do?"—is echoed later as a response to Jim's horror over the sensei's degraded condition. "What could you do?" she asks Jim. "Who can be responsible for all the Japanese the world over?"[85]

Just as Asian American "industriousness" was used in model minority discourse to establish a consonance between Confucianism and the Protestant work ethic, Bret Harte's frontier gambler—whose material conditions resemble Charley's and the sensei's as its metaphorical ones do the model minority—was used in both mainstream media and by writers like Yamamoto and Yamauchi to yoke together "Asian" and American value systems, although to markedly different effect. As Michael Oriard notes, the heroic gambler of Harte's fiction "emerges as a gamesman by trade but a transcendent sportsman by instinct and action. He is a fatalist in a world dominated by chance, but his absolute commitment to honor and fair play lead to an ambiguous sentimental salvation."[86] Model minority narratives rehearsed this same combination. In a 1971 *Newsweek* article, Charles Michener argued that, alongside the "Japanese" values of "*Enryo* (reserve, restraint) and *gaman* (patience, perseverance)," Japanese Americans during the internment demonstrated "an enormous fatalism and respect for authority [which] shaped their acquiescence to the evacuation order and enabled them eventually to overcome."[87]

In "Las Vegas Charley," this fatalism reaches near-Bartlebyian proportions. While interned, the experience that puts Charley "on the road that would lead, inexorably, to Las Vegas" is a failed attempt to get remarried: "After this rejection he had returned to his passion for flower cards. What else was there to do?"[88] When confronted years later in Las Vegas by a drunk soldier who "apologized for the heinous thing he had done to Charley's people"—dropping the atomic bomb—Charley remains silent; not out of anger, but because "what was there to say?"[89] When Charley falls ill and imposes on his son's hospitality, he feels "unwelcome" but reasons that "there was no help for it."[90] Taken together, these scenes of suspended or disavowed agency not only dramatize the sense of helplessness and frustrated impotence produced and reinforced by the internment, but reveal the disturbing postwar afterlife of the mind-set as the characters begin to internalize that state of evacuated agency as the status quo. Indeed, a significant but little discussed part of what draws Charley and the sensei to Las Vegas is precisely the city's astonishing ability to transform that sense of helplessness into its own source of excitement and anticipation.

In yellow peril discourse, attraction to games of chance was seen as responsible for destroying the dreams of would-be Chinese sojourners in a single instant, leaving them penniless and forced to stay in the

United States—to become, in other words, Asian Americans. In these short stories, however, it is precisely gambling's ability to "negate . . . work, patience, experience, and qualifications" that accounts for the irresistible attraction of such games to Charley and the sensei.[91] For in games of chance, as Roger Caillois has observed, "not only does one refrain from trying to eliminate the injustice of chance, but rather it is the very capriciousness of chance that constitutes the unique appeal of the game."[92] By accepting and even embracing rather than attempting to resist such "injustice," gamblers thus counterintuitively enjoy a rather different sort of egalitarianism, of the "anybody can become anything," roulette-wheel variety earlier described by Amy Tan and Pierre Bourdieu.

While "Las Vegas Charley" and "The Sensei" have produced numerous critical interpretations that hinge on the lamentable pathos of figures like Charley and the sensei, the tendency to treat these stories as alternatives to, or even subversive of, the model minority myth limits our ability to recognize the extent to which the Asian American gambler serves as a crucially legitimating "negative analogue" for the model minority. That is, reading the gamblers in "The Sensei" and "Las Vegas Charley"—as the majority of critics have—as tragic allegories for "the damaged sectors of the Japanese American community that could not make a comeback after the war" or as "a metonym of failure that represents the emasculation of *Issei* male culture" rightly accounts for the authors' efforts to explode model minority stereotypes.[93] Yet seeing Charley and the sensei as representative of particular nonnormative "sectors"—and hence as "idealized critical subjects"—obscures the fact that they shed light on a broader phenomenon that afflicts Asian America as a whole. Insofar as these stories function as allegories, what they dramatize is not so much the failure of a few tragic individuals to "live up to" the model minority image, but the lure and redemptive potential of gambling as a means of reconciling one's failure and providing alternative, equally seductive forms of pseudo-national inclusion.

When, following Charley's death from liver cancer, the nisei doctor tries to comfort Charley's son Noriyuki (and, it would seem, himself) by pointing out that "at least your father had a good time—he drank, he gambled, he smoked. I don't do any of those things; all I do is work, work, work," Noriyuki recognizes—as the reader herself is meant to— that Charley was no freewheeling exception, but "one man among so many who lived from day to day as best as they could, limited, restricted, by the meager gifts Fate or God had doled out to them."[94] In finding that he "could not quite agree" with the doctor's assessment, Noriyuki's silence is a reminder that he as well as the doctor, both "success stories" and model minorities by the reigning standard, are yet themselves part of that same, tragic struggle. Charley was in fact not their opposite but another exemplary model; he, like the sensei, reinforces and even celebrates the extent to which success had become the "accidental and irrational event" Lowenthal described.

Recognizing the dialectical relationship between the Asian American gambler and the model minority allows us to attend, once again, to how the two figures collectively anticipate a fuller picture of the workings of racial capitalism in the neoliberal moment. What made Asian Americans models was not only the embrace of financial risk understood to be the basis of their post-internment economic recovery, but also the state of debt and financial precarity that characterizes the existence of Charley and the sensei. Critics like Annie McClanahan, Miranda Joseph, and Maurizio Lazzarato have emphasized the extent to which debt, as the "defining feature of economic life today," has produced a vexed subject position Lazzarato dubs the "indebted man," caught at the intersection of "a particular regime of capital accumulation and a regime of biopolitical governmentality," of "ethics and economics," "rationality and responsibility."[95] While, in these accounts, modern "credit-crisis culture" is exemplified by the 2007–10 nationwide banking emergency known as the subprime mortgage crisis, it is interesting to note the extent to which internees model the indebted relationship resulting from an analogous economic "crash," in which property loss and asset seizures of all kinds effectively nullified, in a single moment, decades and even whole generations of time and money invested into creating successful Japanese American business ventures. Such parallels importantly underscore Andrew Hoberek's directive to attend more closely to the economic disparities and class dynamics of the postwar period in order to remedy what he notes as the tendency for scholars of postwar culture to downplay economic issues in favor of psychological ones, in part due to the assumption of the era's relative prosperity, economic calm, and "classlessness."[96] Indeed, part of what made Japanese Americans model minorities was that while they, too, were enjoying such comfort and prosperity as found among many of their white counterparts, their achievement of such success was understood to be the result of personal effort rather than national boon. Randy Martin's observations helped us to recognize risk's role in producing moralized racial dichotomies on the model of William Petersen's "success story." McClanahan's and Lazzarato's insights further underscore the effect of chronic debt relations plaguing "losers" like Charley and the Sensei. As Lazzarato points out, "Debt represents an economic relationship inseparable from the production of the debtor subject and his 'morality,'" one which, McClanahan reminds us, profoundly shapes "our ideas of personhood and moral character."[97]

At stake in model minority discourses and counter-discourses is thus not simply a rehabilitation of Asian Americans from yellow peril to all-American exemplar, but a rehabilitation of a particular set of attitudes about chance and competition, ability and luck—and alongside them, the oncoming tide of a ruthless neoliberal "financialization" of everyday life. While the American dream appears to be about the elimination of risk and the guarantee of success through hard work, in reality social mobility is as much the result of random events beyond one's control, and as such is far more akin to winning the lottery. Stories like the ones discussed in this chapter turn away from the familiar American exceptionalist rhetoric of equality, liberty, or justice, reminding us that immigration and assimilation are fundamentally agonistic processes, opportunities to *compete* equally in a perverse contest to prove one's racial equality.

Gambling plays a powerful material and rhetorical role in naturalizing and perpetuating these contests. For gambling is at once a way to make money and a way to explain why some people "make it" and others do not; a way to buy and to buy into a seductive fantasy of self-determination—"What would *you* do if you won the lottery?" These are the sorts of dangerous fantasies through which systemic failures can be transformed into personal ones. To take them seriously is thus to account for both the fictional *and* the material means through which racial inequality has been rationalized and economic inequality racialized. "The primary function of racialization," Jodi Melamed reminds us, "has been to make structural inequality appear fair."[98] Games of chance constitute one of the seemingly "free" or "innocent" mechanisms through which that illusion of fairness is achieved, revealing the logic of racialization as well as its effect.

Marco Polo in the Virtual World

PART II

Marco Polo in the Virtual World

The Pitch

Freeplay

4

West of the Magic Circle

The Orientalist Origins of Game Studies

The "founding fathers" of modern game studies, Dutch historian Johan Huizinga (1872–1945) and French sociologist Roger Caillois (1913–1978), were the first to undertake a systematic analysis of the seemingly limitless range of human activities described as play. Where earlier discussions of play—like Freud's theory of humor, or Baudelaire's "The Philosophy of Toys"—had tended to narrow their focus to specific ludic genres, Huizinga and Caillois strove to discover the characteristics common to parlor games as well as poetry, to stagecraft as well as soccer.[1] The fruits of this labor were first captured in Huizinga's *Homo Ludens* (1938), wherein play is characterized as "a free activity standing quite consciously outside 'ordinary' life as being 'not serious,' but at the same time absorbing the player intensely and utterly. It is an activity connected with no material interest, and no profit can be gained by it. It proceeds within its own proper boundaries of time and space according to fixed rules and in an orderly manner. It promotes the formation of social groupings which tend to surround themselves with secrecy and to stress their difference from the common world by disguise or other means."[2] This definition of play as a "magic circle" set apart from everyday life has been enormously influential, serving as the de facto starting point for innumerable works of contemporary scholarship on games, sport, and role-playing. It has provided both a critical vocabulary and a conceptual framework for analyzing games and play in terms of their spatial and temporal delineation of "second worlds," their engaging "immersiveness" and realism, and the enduring player communities that have sprung up around online multiplayer games like *World of Warcraft*.[3]

Roger Caillois's *Les jeux et les hommes* (*Man, Play, and Games*, 1958) extended Huizinga's insights to produce its own conceptual schema in the form of a ludic taxonomy. Caillois subdivided games into four categories—competition, chance, mimicry, and vertigo (sensorial disorientation)—and offered an in-depth analysis of the unique structure, function, and pleasure provided by each type of game. This typology has fundamentally shaped the course of contemporary discussions of gaming across a wide range of media, from console and handheld games to roulette and poker. Indeed, as we have already seen in part I of this book, Caillois's in-depth structural analysis of games of chance is especially instrumental to understanding the racial typologies that arise from games: allowing us to recognize, for example, the appeal of gambling as both matter and metaphor to yellow peril and model minority discourses, or the rhetoric of contingency and risk to Japanese American internment narratives.

While Huizinga's and Caillois's pioneering efforts have allowed us to rescue games from their vernacular triviality as "child's play" and place them instead under the microscope of scholarly inquiry, the lenses they have provided for examining the intricate internal machinery of ludic activity have also resulted in a bit of tunnel vision that has discouraged our turning a similarly inquiring eye to the theories themselves. In the most literal sense, this has involved limiting our focus to the first one or two chapters of each book—in which Huizinga's definition and Caillois's taxonomy appear—rather than the sizeable remainders that follow. This tendency is apparent in the consistently narrow citational scope of scholarship that references these theorists, and in the selection of front-loaded excerpted content found in game studies anthologies intended for classroom use. Yet the definitions and taxonomies for which these theorists are now remembered were in fact, for them, only starting points for much broader ethnographic projects that have since been largely forgotten.

Whereas their predecessors had viewed play as a physiological reflex or release of pent-up energy, or as a didactic tool in adolescent development, Huizinga and Caillois considered the true value and novelty of their work to lie in their assertion that play served a "cultural" function. Indeed, Huizinga's assertion was that play gave rise *to* culture, setting in motion the "civilizing" process whereby humans imaginatively represented the world, imposed order on a chaotic universe, and gave meaningful form to social interaction. In the foreword to *Homo Ludens*, he thus recounts his frustration with the many well-intentioned editors and organizers who had altered the title of his early lectures on the subject—then called "The Play Element of Culture"—to "The Play Element in Culture." For, Huizinga emphatically reminds us, "it was not my object to define the place of play among all the other manifestations of culture, but rather to ascertain how far culture itself bears the character of play."[4] In other words, the discrete ludic artifacts—video games, sporting contests, et cetera—that game studies scholars have subsequently used Huizinga's theory to analyze were for him, and for Caillois, only the residual traces of a far more important and diffuse historical phenomenon: the institutionalization of play and its absorption into the social infrastructure, which paved the way for the progression of human civilization (a term both theorists used interchangeably with "culture").[5]

As literary critic and fellow ludologist Jacques Ehrmann has noted, "culture" in Huizinga's theory, and later in Caillois's, functions as a fixed, stable, a priori referent on which their definitions of play are built, leading them to evaluate both culture *and* play from what seems to be a universalist definition of those terms but which is, in fact, "only valid in relation . . . to the observer": in this case, an early to mid-twentieth-century white, Western European academic.[6] Ehrmann describes the "simplistic and ethnocentric metaphysics of consciousness" that led the theorists to, quite unconsciously, take a particular tableau of Western modernity as the basis for a universal and timeless definition of "culture" and "reality" as such. One example among many of this tendency is the economic opposition they set up between play and productive labor, with Huizinga's assertion that play is associated with "no material interest" being echoed by Caillois's characterization of play and work, respectively, as "time lost [as] opposed to time well spent."[7] However, the validity of the work-play, labor-leisure opposition is, as Ehrmann reminds us, wholly contingent on the specific cultural milieu of early twentieth-century industrial capitalism (and even there, the binary is hardly so clear-cut as they suggest). It is in such moments, where the relativity and reductivism of these theorists' foundational concepts go unquestioned by their users, that Ehrmann compellingly demonstrates how Huizinga and Caillois "reveal unwittingly their implicit values and undermine their own analyses."[8]

This Eurocentric viewpoint, in which "culture" implicitly means Western European culture of the sort that had produced both Huizinga and Caillois, is further evident in their tendency to use the term "culture" (and "civilization") as if it were merely a neutral description of the attitudes and behaviors of a society. Yet "culture," as numerous scholars have amply demonstrated, has historically been invoked as a more palatable euphemism to obfuscate or naturalize thornier issues of structural inequality, particularly with regard to race and ethnicity.[9] Thus Huizinga's assertion of play *as* culture—as that which gives rise to culture—was, as Ehrmann suggests, itself reflective of an ethnocentric understanding of human history as a trajectory that, "starting with primitive man would lead necessarily, in its 'superior' stage, to civilized (cultured) western-man."[10]

If to use the term "civilized" in the early twentieth century was to borrow from an established discourse of primitivism a racialized dichotomy inextricably linked to "the dark continent" of "savage" Africa and "enlightened," "civilized" Europe, to speak of "culture" in this moment was to inevitably invoke the equally insurmountable (and still racially subtended) "cultural" differences between the "Orient" and the "Occident" that had shaped the European worldview for centuries.[11] Edward Said's monumental and controversial work *Orientalism* offers innumerable examples of how the "Orient," as a region roughly corresponding to the Middle East and East Asia, "has helped to define Europe (or the West) as its contrasting image, idea, personality, experience." Indeed, the very possibility of something called the "Occident" (i.e. the "West") depends on the presence of something which is the "Orient" (i.e., the "East")— and vice versa. After all, the terms "Occident" and "Orient" do not refer, etymologically, to specific locations, but rather to a spatial relation: the Orient is simply "a region situated to the east of a given point" and the Occident, its directional counterpart.[12] To be the "West," then, means to be West *of somewhere else*: without the East there can be no West. Just as that elsewhere is rendered meaningful only in reference to oneself—as East of (i.e., Oriental to) Europe—the absence of that Oriental Other would evacuate the very concept of Western Self, of Self *as* Westerner. To define play as a cornerstone of "Western civilization," as Huizinga and Caillois both sought to do, thus inevitably meant being drawn into a diametrically opposed conception of West and East: of the world divided into antithetical yet complementary halves.

If Orientalism has been discussed in game studies at all, it has nearly always been in relation to certain video games' exotifying, functionalized representations of East Asia and the Middle East (particularly as they reflect the military entertainment complex's vision of a post-9/11 world order), or, to a lesser extent, in reference to the Asian origins of the video game industry.[13] These concerns are not irrelevant—indeed, the latter is the focus of the next chapter—but they often reflect too narrow a definition of Orientalism as a feature of game content or a factor in game reception rather than a methodological and metaphysical tradition in which the field's foundational theorists were in fact already steeped, and hence a fundamental part of their theories of games.

While Orientalism was arguably endemic to nineteenth- and twentieth-century Western history and philosophy as a whole, Huizinga and Caillois were particularly intimate with Orientalist beliefs and practices, for it was a scholarly project in which they actively participated throughout their academic careers. Huizinga was trained as an Orientalist at the University of Leipzig in 1897, pursuing advanced studies in Sanskrit and completing his doctoral dissertation under the prominent Orientalist Hendrik Kern on the subject of the *vidushaka* (court jester) in classical Sanskrit drama. In 1903, he joined the University of Amsterdam faculty as a lecturer of ancient Indian culture and literature, eventually becoming a professor of history at the University of Leiden, home of the most renowned Oriental studies department in the Netherlands. Caillois's Orientalist interests were less formal but no less ambitious, evidenced by a wealth of editorial work spanning anthologies like *The Dream Adventure* (1963), a selection of dream-related excerpts and stories drawn in the main from classical Chinese texts; the complete works of French Orientalist author Montesquieu; and the interdisciplinary journal Caillois co-founded and edited, *Diogenes*, which featured special issues dedicated to such subjects as "Man and the Concept of History in the Orient."

Given these scholarly credentials and research agendas—and the numerous references in both *Homo Ludens* and *Man, Play, and Games* to the "Orient," as well as to Orientalist accounts of Asian play and games—it seems inevitable that Huizinga's and Caillois's theories of play, too, would carry the mark of a binaristic perception of the East as mystical, timeless, childlike, "different"; and the West, in contrast, as rational, chivalrous, mature—in a word, "normal." The question I am interested in, however, is not so much, What was Orientalist about their ludic theories?—for essentially *all* European history and philosophy produced during this time period can be described as Orientalist in one way or another—but rather, What was ludic about their Orientalism? That is, given their view of culture as play, how did Huizinga and Caillois use the tenets of Orientalism to produce, beyond the usual conclusions about "Oriental" culture, conclusions about *games*—about play's "essential traits," its marginality to a (Western-defined) reality, its civilizational origins and destinies?

This chapter's focus, then, is not only on the moments in which Huizinga and Caillois deliberately invoke Asia, but those moments where, as Ehrmann put it, they "unwittingly" reveal the implicit role of the Orientalist imaginary as the formal logic guiding their ludic theories. This is a dynamic and a method with which we are already familiar from the previous chapter, where the gambling metaphors used in model minority discourse were shown to be only the most obvious signs pointing to gambling's more fundamental allegorical role as a racial ethos. This chapter, likewise, uses the manifest Orientalist content of *Homo Ludens* and *Man, Play, and Games* as a way to get at its subterranean, "metaphysical" significance. In short, I understand these explicit Orientalist references the way Huizinga and Caillois themselves understood games: as residual traces of a far deeper, culturally formative enterprise.

"The point," here as it was for Said, is that "even if it does not survive as it once did, Orientalism lives on academically through its doctrines and theses about the Orient and the Oriental."[14] In other words, we overlook these ludo-Orientalist resonances at our own peril, for doing so produces a series of blind spots in our own analyses that unwittingly reproduce some of the original theories' most problematic ethnocentric assumptions. When we fail to acknowledge the East/West distinction as both the foundation for and a stumbling block in Huizinga's and Caillois's own binaristic conceptions of play and seriousness, magic circle and ordinary life, competition and chance, and so on, the limitations of their theories become our own.

East of Agon

East Asia plays an integral yet equivocal role in Huizinga's *Homo Ludens*. At times, it functions as an intermediate culture sandwiched between the civilized and the primitive; at others, as a sort of global model minority untainted by the "corruption" of Western play by industrial modernity.

The "East" often exemplifies for Huizinga play's "inherent" universality, the fact that "all peoples" play: hence his endless descriptions of everything from Tibetan shamanism to Chinese martial etiquette to the Japanese lexicon for play, all drawn from the "authoritative" accounts of a well-established canon of Orientalist scholars. Huizinga's claim that the "play-element" was universal among human societies—associated neither with any particular culture, nor "any particular stage of civilization or view of the universe"—was, however, quite radical for its time. It was, in fact, in direct opposition to the then-reigning perception among European historians and sociologists, exemplified by Swiss cultural historian Jacob Burckhardt's *The Greeks and Greek Civilization* (*Griechische Kulturgeschichte*), that culturally significant contests were essentially and uniquely Hellenic—and, even then, of relatively minor historical interest to those studying modern Europe.[15]

Coining the term "agonal" to describe the political and religious function of athletic contests in the sixth century BCE—the moment of Hellenic expansion and the national Olympic games—Burckhardt argued that in the institutionalization of agonism as at once event and ethos, "the Greeks stood alone . . . the *agon* was a motive power known to no other people."[16] *Agon*'s ostensible uniqueness as a Greek institution was used, in traditional Orientalist fashion, to claim it as a distinctly "Western" legacy. Thus, Burckhardt argued, "in the Asiatic cultures, despotism and the caste system were almost completely opposed to such [agonal] activities," while "even now the eastern custom is not to compete among equals but rather to have mock fights performed as a spectacle by slaves or paid entertainers."[17] Historian and fellow Orientalist Victor Ehrenberg, one of Huizinga's contemporaries, put an even blunter point on it: "to the Orient," he remarked, agonism has "remained alien and antipathetic."[18] In order to refute these perceptions, then, Huizinga had to demonstrate that play was both universally significant—that is, not just Greek—*and* historically autonomous—that is, not a derivative residue but a deterministic driver of Western civilization.

Although it would seem that the ethnocentrism of these accounts of *agon* was itself the greatest hindrance to Huizinga's desire to develop a "general sociology" of play, his solution to this dilemma, somewhat counterintuitively, was to reinvoke—and reproduce—their Orientalism in a slightly different form. Thus we find him drawing extensively on the work of French sociologist and sinologist Marcel Granet, whose account of premodern Chinese contests and rituals—"as simple as it is convincing and scientifically accurate"—Huizinga used to refute both the sociological triviality and the essential Greekness of play.[19] Granet's characterization of Chinese social organization, like Huizinga's of culture writ large, relies fundamentally on the "civilizing"—that is, culturally productive—potential of play, which Granet argued was the result of an evolution from "rustic games" played between individuals or small groups to "rivalries between societies" for prestige. While even Huizinga is forced to acknowledge that such a grand ludic genealogy may be slightly overstating things—"even if we hesitate to go all the way with Granet, who derives the whole hierarchy of the later Chinese state from these primitive customs"—he nonetheless maintains that Granet "has demonstrated in an altogether masterly fashion how the agonistic principle plays a part in the development of Chinese civilization far more significant even than the agon in the Hellenic world, and in which the essentially *ludic* character shows up much more clearly there than in Greece. For in ancient China almost every activity took the form of a ceremonial contest; the crossing of a river, the climbing of a mountain, cutting wood or picking flowers."[20] Here, "Chinese civilization"—the singularity of which is even more a fantasy than that of the "Hellenic"—is not simply one particular example among many of play's universal reach beyond ancient Greece, but the crucial embodiment of culture's "essentially ludic character" on which a general theory of play and culture can be derived.

A hallmark of Orientalism is the way in which it takes the "West" as a universal point of reference against which Asia has been defined as an often inferior particularity.[21] While Huizinga's invocation of China may seem to—and was perhaps even intended to—refute not only the anti-ludic prejudice but the Orientalist ethnocentrism of his forebears, his various discussions of "Oriental" agonism, which continue elsewhere in lengthy speculations on the Japanese word for "play" and the ludic rituals of "the India of the Mahabharata," ultimately presented little challenge to their fundamentally Orientalist perspective of the "Far East" as an irreducible and conspicuously particularized Other. What might appear, in Huizinga's initial invocation of Granet in the long passage quoted above, to be a "progressive" elevation of China to equal footing with the Hellenic on the basis of the play-element is subsequently used to reinforce the Orientalist divide.[22] For the very hypervisibility of *agon* (competitive games of skill) in the Chinese context—where, Huizinga suggests, it can be seen more nakedly even than in the agonic Greek age—becomes, a few pages later, evidence of a sort of pedantic primitivity he will later explicitly call "puerilism": an instance where *agon* has been extended far beyond its Sophist ideal into a near parody of itself. As his discussion shifts to the "courtesy-match"—the types of social games in which competitors attempt to one-up each other through displays of excessive civility or generosity, as in paying a restaurant bill—we see Huizinga falling prey to what Edward Said refers to as the "imaginative mode" of Orientalism: the host of fantastic and often contradictory stereotypes and narratives historically associated with the Orient (e.g., as refined but also savage, meek but also quick to anger).[23] Here, it is the stereotype of the "Oriental" as hyper-polite, obsessively concerned with courtesy, protocol, and mannered language, that Huizinga finds an invaluable portrait through which to shore up his argument about the civilizing properties of agonism. Thus he concludes that although "the courtesy match is to be met with all over the world . . . [it] is nowhere as formalized, perhaps, as in China," where a supposedly unrelenting setting of hyper-formality gives every conversation, or even a single word, an overinflated "technical significance as marks of shame or honor."[24] By taking as fact such Orientalizing portraits of "Asiatic culture," Huizinga thus perpetuates established fictions about the radical particularity of the Orient even as he seems to refute them.

What makes this discussion of China not merely Orientalist but exemplary of the mutually constitutive mechanism of race and play that I have been calling ludo-Orientalism is the ludic use to which Huizinga puts these Orientalist discourses. That is, Orientalist stereotypes are here first used not, in typical Orientalist fashion, to make claims about China's radical particularity and difference from the implicitly universalized West, but as evidence of *play*'s universality. This seemingly objective ludic claim is then used, in the style of a feedback loop, to "discover" evidence of China's particular hyper-formality.

The Occidental Dream

China's value to Huizinga extends beyond its historical status as the (culturally inferior) counterpart to ancient Greece; his interest in the

formal games played in China simply makes explicit the more foundational role China plays as an exemplary model of play. The puerilism
that Huizinga attributes to the Chinese can be understood as a criticism, evidence of their lack of "true" playfulness, in the sense that they
take play so "seriously" that it can never be just a game. But it can also
be understood, from the other direction, as asserting Huizinga's sense
of China as the *purest* embodiment of play, the very essence of culture's "play-element" as such, in the sense that everything, even the
most ordinary of activities, becomes infused with ludic potential. The
ludo-Orientalism of *Homo Ludens* might then be said to lie not simply in its explicit reproduction of the *content* of Orientalist stereotypes
about Chinese culture, but rather in its implicit, *formal* reproduction
of the East/West relation. The explicitly spatial and temporal terms in
which that East/West distinction signified became the foundational
model for how Huizinga understood the relationship between play
and "seriousness" as oppositional. Indeed, in Huizinga's theory, games
become to "real life" what the Orient—or rather, what V. G. Kiernan
aptly described as "Europe's collective day-dream of the Orient"—had
historically been to the Occident.[25]

Here we come to a meaning of ludo-Orientalism slightly different
from what we saw in part I. There, the term captured the rhetorical
force and material consequences of describing a racialized body or relation as a game—for example, Bret Harte's allegorizing of Chinese labor
disputes as a euchre game. We have already noted similarities between
this descriptive ludo-Orientalism and the sort we find in Huizinga's and
Caillois's efforts to define games or play in terms of racial (or "cultural")
differences. But if in part I we described the ludo-Orientalist process as
one of "gamifying" race—of defining race in ludic terms—then we might
provisionally call what we are already seeing in *Homo Ludens* a process
of "Orientalizing" play. By this I do not mean simply using Orientalist references, but seeing play as the Orientalist had long been accustomed to seeing the Oriental: as occupying "a different but thoroughly
organized world of his own, a world with its own national, cultural, and
epistemological boundaries and principles of internal coherence."[26] Describing Orientalism as an act of "imaginative geography," Said draws
our attention to the cartographic fictions whereby collectively authored
acts of make-believe about who or what the "Oriental" is have acquired

the authority of commonplace truth—and where the "magic circle," in Huizinga's theory, also acquired its ironclad authority. For there exists a striking formal parallelism between Orientalism's imaginative geography of an absolute divide between East and West, and Huizinga's conviction in an absolute, zero-sum divide between imaginative play and reality, with the former's spatial limitations becoming one of its most defining characteristics. Consider, for example, how Huizinga first defines the "magic circle" of play: "All play moves and has its being within a playground marked off beforehand either materially or ideally, deliberately or as a matter of course. . . . The arena, the card-table, the magic circle, the temple, the stage, the screen, the tennis court, the court of justice, etc., are all in form and function play-grounds, i.e. *forbidden spots, isolated, hedged round, hallowed, within which special rules obtain. All are temporary worlds within the ordinary world*, dedicated to the performance of an act apart."[27]

The magic of the magic circle—the illusion that is play[28]—is framed in both cartographic and administrative terms. On the one hand, it is a boundary-drawing exercise, the mental or material cleavage of life into two parts: "ordinary" reality and "extraordinary" play, an "in" and "out" of bounds. But it is also a rule-making exercise: what makes the magic circle hold its shape is its irrational but internally coherent set of rules, its self-governing tyranny, and all manner of other complementary contradictions. For although it does not follow the "rational" rules of reality, "inside the play-ground an absolute and peculiar order reigns."[29] In these few sentences we see all the well-worn stereotypes of the Orientalist imaginary, seemingly emptied of both racial content and national context, being redeployed instead as formal qualities of the imaginative process called play: the "forbidden" and "isolated" place, transient and ethereal, with its irrational customs and "peculiar" laws. The magic circle of the Orient is, in this passage, framed in opposition to the "serious" reality of the Occident. Play is enclosed, but it is not truly sovereign: it is defined first and foremost by what it is not, which is reality (or its synonyms, "life" and the "ordinary world"). Hence we say, "It's just a game" (It's not real life), or "I was only playing" (I wasn't being serious). Yet the dynamic of antithetical complementarity with which we are now becoming familiar is also reasserted in *Homo Ludens'* ludo-Orientalist framing of play as reality's foil. Play is "an accompaniment, a complement" to "real" life and "in this respect is indispensable"—yet at the same time, "gratuitous" and thus ultimately "secondary" in status.[30]

Huizinga's theory of play reproduces, as method, the same self-affirming fantasies through which Orientalism, by spatializing the Other, became "a political vision of reality."[31] In doing so, it also amplifies the precariousness that accompanies such binaristic fictions. For in Huizinga's theory, "reality" comes to serve an analogously problematic role to that of "culture," in the sense of being an a priori referent against which play is privatively defined. Ehrmann nicely sums up this circular problematic: "Just as in our first section we reproached them [Huizinga and Caillois] for evaluating play in opposition to and on the basis of a 'reality' which was never questioned even though it was only valid in relation to a given culture, itself relative to the observer, we can now reproach them for evaluating play in opposition to and on the basis of a conception of culture which is never questioned even though it is only valid in relation to a given 'reality,' which is relative to the observer."[32] Taken together with our discussion of Orientalism, Ehrmann's insights help explain why game studies has had an especially difficult time accounting for the increasingly blurred boundaries in contemporary life between play and reality, specifically in relation to the emergence of "augmented reality" or "pervasive" games like *Ingress* and *Pokémon GO*. Take Ian Bogost's and other game scholars' efforts to contest the explosive popularity of "gamified" apps and programs like Fitbit, *Class Craft*, and HabitRPG, which have profitably utilized mechanics like scoreboards, leveling systems, and contests to motivate user behavior in the realms of exercise, education, and even housekeeping.[33] The vague definition of gamification remains that of "the application of game-design elements and game principles in non-game contexts."[34] But what, exactly, defines a "non-game context"? If the application of game "elements" and "principles" does not by itself make something into a game, then wherein does its true "gameness"—and hence its distinction from "non-game contexts"—lie? The tautologies implicit in the original theories are made problematically hypervisible.

There has been a temptation to think that the problem lies with the "antiquated," analog context of Huizinga's and Caillois's theories and hence evidence of their unsuitability for contemporary digital games and life. Yet the recent proliferation of new theories derived from video games, for all their medium specificity, have not only failed to supplant the originals but, in some sense, heightened the contradictions at their center. Mark Seltzer critiques two of these recent works—Jesper Juul's *Half-Real: Video Games Between Real Rules and Fictional Worlds* (2011) and McKenzie Wark's *Gamer Theory* (2009)—for what he sees as their undertheorization of the relation between game and nongame:

> We might say too then that this game outlook on life amounts to "expanding the game to the whole world," or that a world that's like a game is thus part rules and part fiction—or "half-real"—as two recent, and influential, accounts of gamer theory have it. But both notions—the notion of the expansion of the game to the whole world, the division of real life by halves—are too crude to do much work with. For one thing, in both, the unity of the difference between game and world is left uninterpreted. For another, so are the social conditions that make for the form of the distinction in the first place.[35]

This is, as we have seen, not a new problem. What for Seltzer marks a "blind spot" in contemporary game studies was the very same ethnocentric fallacy, in Ehrmann's Derridean critique, on which Huizinga's and Caillois's theories rested. This "unwitting" ethnocentrism is what we see being unconsciously reproduced in, for example, Juul's theory of games as "half-real." Indeed, one is hard-pressed to find a pithier description of ludo-Orientalism's legacy than what Seltzer refers to as "the division of real life by halves": that is, the complete and unconscious lamination of the East/West binary onto the game/reality binary.[36]

Alongside the "reality" problem, we have that of analyzing "realism" in games. Ehrmann long ago cautioned that the critic's job is not to evaluate a text as realistic or unrealistic.[37] The pressure to do so, however, has been amplified by the increasing sophistication of video game visuals and "real-time" games, as well as the emergence of a whole genre of self-described "reality games" that directly reference contemporary events. This has given rise to the belief that the *real* problem is the undertheorization of realism in video games, and hence we need a medium-specific definition for it. Thus Alexander Galloway, for example, has called for games to demonstrate "some kind of congruence, some type of fidelity of context that transliterates itself from the social reality of the gamer, through one's thumbs, into the game environment and back again. This is what I call 'the congruence requirement,' and it is necessary for achieving realism in gaming. Without it there is no true realism."[38]

Such a theory is hindered not only by its vagueness—What, precisely, is the "social reality of the gamer"? And what makes this reality social?—but its tendency to treat realism as an intrinsic quality of the product and hence implicitly place the responsibility on the game designer to create "realistic" games. At the same time, however, Galloway's critique usefully emphasizes the perspectival nature of reality that Ehrmann also pointed to and which has long been the conclusion of ethnic studies scholars in relation to the indefinable criteria of "authenticity" (and, for that matter, the conclusion of literary scholars in relation to the criteria of "realism"). Evaluations of ludic realism (and the very question of what "realism" means in the context of games) in this sense resemble the imaginative geography of Orientalism, ultimately revealing as much about the evaluator and their context as about the games: perhaps more, in fact, since the very same game could conceivably be described as "realistic" by one player and "unrealistic" by another. Classifications of a game as "realistic" might thus be thought of as not only aesthetic but ethnocentric evaluations, in the sense that such a judgment tends to be contingent on the critic's familiarity with the representation or experience being evaluated.

Homo Sapiens, Sub Specie Ludi

Now that we have a better grasp of the stakes of Huizinga's ludo-Orientalist legacy, let us turn to the other half of our inheritance: Roger Caillois's *Man, Play, and Games*. For it is through this later text that we can see more clearly how the theories themselves have become artificial yet absolute self-legitimating fictions of their own. That is, scholars have tended to accept as equally axiomatic Huizinga's and Caillois's definitions of play, on the one hand, as a "free," self-enclosed enterprise with no connection to "material interest"; and the two men's characterization of their own work, on the other hand, as a "free"—that is, disinterested—scholarly endeavor. Take, for example, the editorial introduction to an excerpt of *Man, Play, and Games* in one of the most widely taught contemporary game studies anthologies, which informs students that Caillois's work was motivated "by a desire to study play in and of itself" and glosses the non-excerpted remainder thus: "In the rest of the book, Caillois applies this taxonomy to play activities from a range of world cultures."[39] This latter chronology, which is also described in the translator's introduction to *Man, Play, and Games*, recapitulates Caillois' own assertion—made implicitly through the sequential order of the book, and explicitly halfway through it—that his taxonomy of games precedes his taxonomy of cultures. In his own narrative of the book's genealogy, he claims that it was only *after* establishing his "sociology of games"—a series of rubrics that will be discussed in detail shortly—that he hit on the idea of a "sociology derived from games": that is, a classification of human cultures (i.e., civilizations) according to their ludic preferences.

Yet there is reason to doubt the veracity of this origin story: indeed, as we will see, it seems more accurate to say that the taxonomy for which Caillois is best known was not applied to but derived from "world cultures," and specifically from the relation between East and West. The equivocal status of cultural origins, as such, is in fact one we see at work in his wonderfully bombastic claim that "it is not absurd to try diagnosing a civilization in terms of the games that are especially popular there. . . . They necessarily reflect its culture pattern and provide useful indications as to the preferences, weakness, and strength of a given society at a particular stage of its evolution. The contrast with games preferred by neighboring peoples does not provide the surest method of determining the origins of psychological incompatibility, but it can provide impressive illustrations, after the fact."[40] Caillois is clearly no less credulous than Huizinga of the "fact" of cultural "incompatibilities" or the trajectory of civilizational "evolution" leading, as we saw before, from "primitive" to "Western" man. Yet he exceeds even Huizinga's ambitions in his promise to not merely find further evidence of such differences but to "determine their origins"—which is to say, to demonstrate how a given society's ludic preferences have *causally* determined its present state as well as its long-term "chance to flourish or stagnate."[41]

The explicitly Darwinist tones of this claim make it at once more retrograde and more radically progressive than those offered by the eighteenth- and nineteenth-century enterprise that has come to be known as "scientific racism," which tended to limit itself to identifying the physiological and psychological symptoms of ostensibly biological racial differences: more progressive in the sense that it framed civilizational (and thus, implicitly, racial) differences as potentially advantageous evolutionary adaptations rather than pre-given and immutable curses or boons; more retrograde in the sense that it understood the relation between cultures to be arranged not along a hierarchy of comparative superiority/inferiority, but rather as incompatible evolutionary tracks.[42] Caillois will in fact go on to explicitly frame civilizational "strength" as the cultural equivalent to developing a spinal cord—and "primitivity" to the lack of such a backbone. In his view, the two form "a dichotomy as radical . . . as that which separates cryptogamous from phanerogamous plants and vertebrate from invertebrate animals"—or, to use his own example, the Occident's golf ("the Anglo-Saxon sport, par excellence") from the Orient's chess and checkers (which "the Chinese place . . . among the five arts that a scholar must practice").[43]

For all his Darwinian flourishes, however, Caillois was ultimately less interested in discovering the environmental factors that might have resulted in this phylogenetic divergence than in emphasizing the absolute, zero-sum nature of the divergence itself, appropriating "survival of the fittest" logic to naturalize the strength of Western civilization as evidenced through its national (and racial, as his "Anglo-Saxon" golf example makes clear) games. Like Huizinga, Caillois's ludo-Orientalism manifests as a feedback loop; but where Huizinga used Asian particularity to demonstrate ludic universality and vice versa, in *Man, Play, and Games* it is the presumed universality of ludic and hence cultural divergence—the particularity of both East *and* West, of chess *and* golf— that is established by way of the Orientalist imaginary.

This dynamic is made clear early in the book as Caillois proposes that games can be classified according to the degree of regulation or constraint they impose on player action (table 4.1). Thus at one end of the continuum, which he dubs *paidia* (the Greek word for "child"), we find "unregulated" or spontaneous play forms such as impromptu wrestling matches and make-believe games; at the other pole, which he calls *ludus*, the highly disciplined, rule-governed activities of professional athletic competitions and crossword puzzles. As polarities, *paidia* and *ludus* are initially framed through a relation of "continuous opposition," characteristic of the competing human impulses for disorder and paroxysm, on the one hand, and disciplined order, on the other. At the same time, however, the continuum that stretches between them is meant to capture an evolutionary narrative of the sort we have been discussing. It is no coincidence that most of the games that fall on the *paidia* extreme of the spectrum are those popularly associated with childhood (make-believe, staring contests, tumbling), and those on the *ludus* end with adulthood (crossword puzzles, chess, solitaire): the relation explicitly functions as a metonym for a broader historical shift from "premodern" to "civilized" man.

But the path to "civilization," although it may always begin with the "free energy" of *paidia*, does not everywhere result in *ludus*. Indeed, Caillois sees *ludus* as a uniquely Western mode of disciplining *paidia*, of putting playful impulses to work in the service of culture building. The particularity of this ludic narrative of manifest destiny—of the West's civilizational pubescence into a state of "purposive innovation"—is established by way of contrast to (what else?) the East's, and specifically China's. "Wisely and circumspectly, Chinese culture . . . worked out a different destiny for itself," channeling *paidia* in a direction "better suited to its supreme values." The origins of the "psychological incompatibility" between Occident and Orient, then, lie in the moment at which the Occident "oriented [itself] towards process, calculation, [and the] spirit of enterprise" and the Orient, instead, in the direction of "calm, patience, and idle speculation."[44]

In short, Caillois is suggesting that the Orient *became* the Orient— its civilizational fate and its divergence from the West sealed in the same moment—by way of an "implicit but fundamental and significant choice" toward *wan* (玩, glossed in English as "play" or "game"). Caillois's choice of that term, along with the various alternatives he considered and ultimately discarded, is discussed at length and with relish in subsequent pages, aided by the source text he used: British consul Herbert Giles's *Chinese-English Dictionary*. The Orientalism of Giles's dictionary lies less in its form than its intended function: it was written with the sole purpose of facilitating British colonial administration over Hong Kong. That this dictionary of the empire would then serve as a privileged hypotext for Caillois's own ludo-Orientalist endeavors is especially fitting given the latter's own appetite for bureaucratic standardization and the taxonomic classification of foreign entities. Unfortunately, such passion is in short supply in the actual content of Giles's dictionary, which is, even by dictionary standards, dry and interminable. But perhaps that is, in part, why Caillois selected it over other Chinese-English reference works: his concern is neither with passion—nor, for that matter, with accuracy; Giles's dictionary was widely criticized as a "ghastly failure" and "in no sense a dictionary at all"[45]—but with the weight of Orientalist authority. And what could be weightier than that conferred by a 1,700-page dictionary—except, that is, the verbatim rendering of no less than eleven separate entries from said dictionary into prose? For that is, essentially, what Caillois's discussion of the various expressions for play in Chinese boils down to: an exhaustive and droning series of definitions—often incorrectly spelled and cited, in unintentional homage to the source material's own flaunted inaccuracy—for every word in the dictionary even vaguely related to the concept of play.[46] *Wan* becomes Caillois's ultimate choice less because of its more encompassing denotative range in Chinese than its implicitly Orientalist connotations. The term, "according to some"—here Caillois, thankfully, releases his grip on Giles to cite Dutch Japanologist J. J. L. Duyvendak and French sinologist Andre D'Hormon—"would etymologically designate the act of indefinitely caressing a piece of jade while polishing it, in order to savor its smoothness or as an accompaniment to reverie."[47]

Caillois's conclusion—that "the example of the word *wan* shows that the destinies of cultures can be read in their games"—makes it clear that *ludus* and *wan* are not simply two different names for the human play impulse, but mutually exclusive evolutionary tracks, the source of the phylogenetic divergence Caillois set out to explain.[48] Such is what makes the argument not an Orientalist but a ludo-Orientalist one. That is, Caillois's discussion of *paidia/wan* initially appeared to be simply the usual path taken by innumerable Orientalists who, in Edward Said's account, "have accepted the basic distinction between East and West as the starting point for elaborate theories, epics, novels, social descriptions, and political accounts concerning the Orient, its people, customs, 'mind,' destiny, and so on."[49] Yet the common starting point of the East/West division—the *paidia* of academic inquiry—is channeled, in *Man, Play, and Games*, not into familiar Orientalist conclusions "about" the Orient, but into ludo-Orientalist conclusions about *games*, which are in turn used to "explain" the Orient's divergent destiny. Ludo-Orientalism, seen in this light, names a disciplinary choice that is analogous to, and no less fundamental and significant than, that of *ludus* over *wan*.

Homo Ludens, Asiaticus Aleis

The *paidia*/*wan* discussion finds Caillois rehearsing the now-familiar ludo-Orientalist tautology wherein what is "discovered" by way of ludic inquiry—the "fact" of East/West divergence—is the same Orientalist assumption on which the inquiry was initially predicated. This recursive dynamic is clearly of a piece with the other logical inconsistencies resulting from the ethnocentric metaphysics of consciousness Ehrmann critiqued. And here, as with Huizinga, these "blind spots" have been as much a part of the legacy of *Man, Play, and Games* as the insights it contains, shaping the way that we as readers see—and fail to see—games and game theories.

Thus we have good reason to ask whether the direction of influence between Caillois's "sociology of games" and his "sociology derived from games" is as linear or unidirectional as he claims—and as we have believed. The *paidia*/*ludus* division makes up one half of this "sociology of games"; the other is the four-part taxonomy illustrated in table 4.1, which reflects Caillois's creation of four subcategories within which to classify games according to whether the role of competition (*agon*), chance (*alea*), simulation (*mimicry*), or vertigo (*ilinx*) is dominant. Skill-based games in which the strongest or most intelligent competitor wins are thus named *agon*, and those in which chance alone determines the outcome, *alea*; games of make-believe and role playing fall under *mimicry*; and *ilinx*, finally, refers to games played for the pleasure of sensorial disorientation, as in the children's game of using a bat or stick as a fulcrum for rapidly spinning oneself around until "voluptuously" dizzy.[50]

Despite Caillois's initial claims about the universalism of this schema, the taxonomy's all-Greek naming system, and the fact that it is entirely composed of "Western" games, suggests otherwise. Together, they hint at the extent to which Caillois's taxonomy is from the beginning derived from world cultures—in this case, the ludic tradition of the Hellenic world discussed above—long before it is applied to them. To this we might add the influence of a long tradition of Eurocentric taxonomy established by Swedish naturalist Carl Linnaeus, for Caillois has here

Table 4.1. Caillois's classification of games, from Man, Play, and Games (1958; repr., Urbana: University of Illinois Press, 2001).

AGÔN (Competition)	ALEA (Chance)	MIMICRY (Simulation)	ILINX (Vertigo)
paidia Tumult Agitation Immoderate Laughter			
Racing Wrestling Etc. (not regulated) Athletics Boxing, Billiards Fencing, Checkers Football, Chess Contests, Sports in general	Counting-out rhymes Heads or Tails Betting Roulette Simple, complex, and continuing lotteries	Children's initiations Games of illusion Tag, Arms Masks, Disguises Theater Spectacles in general	Children "whirling" Horseback riding Swinging Waltzing Volador Traveling carnivals Skiing Mountain climbing Tightrope walking
Kite-flying Solitaire Patience Crossword puzzles *ludus*			

N.B. In each vertical column games are classified in such an order that the *paidia* element is constantly decreasing while the *ludus* element is ever increasing.

applied to games the same logic of essentialism that the "father of taxonomy" had used to classify the whole of biological life. That is, Caillois's "radical dichotomy" of a game-based civilizational typology proceeded in methodological lockstep with Linnaeus's massively influential *Systema Naturae* (first published in 1735), which hierarchically organized *Homo sapiens* according to its four racial "subspecies": *Homo sapiens Eoropeus albescens* ("white" people from Europe), *Homo sapiens Africanus negreus* ("black" people from Africa), *Homo sapiens Asiaticus fucus* ("dark" people from Asia), and *Homo sapiens Americanus rubescens* ("red" people from the Americas).[51] On this four-part geographical and chromatic rubric Linnaeus attached further binomial descriptors to capture each subspecies's essential "humors" and character traits: the "sanguine" European was *regitur ritibus* (ruled by custom); the "phlegmatic" African, *regitur arbitrio* (ruled by caprice); the "melancholic"

Asian, *regitur opinionibus* (ruled by belief); and the "choleric" Native American, *regitur consuetudine* (ruled by habit).[52]

The point here is not that Caillois's own four-part taxonomy of games corresponds exactly to the *content* of Linnaeus's racial taxonomy (although as we will see, it does in more ways than one), but rather to its *formal logic*: not just its quadrisectional division, but the concept that what made each quadrant internally homogeneous and different from the others was the way it viewed the game of life, the sorts of *rules* it played by (and was, at the same time, "ruled by"). Understood in terms of its Linnaean legacy, Caillois's "sociology of games" begins to look fairly indistinguishable from his "sociology derived from games," the former already being based on a schema that was from the very beginning made for classifying human beings.

This is not to say that Orientalism had no place in these taxonomies; indeed, the taxonomy depicted in table 4.1 may reflect the form of Linnaean taxonomy, but the way Caillois conceived of the relationships *among* the four categories reveals a far more "bicultural" lineage. Whereas Linnaeus had understood the four racial subtypes to exist within a hierarchy (with *Eoropeus albescens*, obviously, at the top), Caillois posited, in his own theory, a dualistic relationship between *agon* and *alea*, on the one hand, and *mimicry* and *ilinx*, on the other, closely resembling Orientalism's antithetical complementarity: "Nothing is more noteworthy in this regard than the exact symmetry between the natures of *agon* and *alea*: parallel and complementary. Both require absolute equity, an equality of mathematical chances of almost absolute precision. Admirably precise rules, meticulous measures, and scientific calculations are evident. However, the two kinds of games have opposite ways of designating the winner."[53] And later: "*Alea* and *agon* are therefore contradictory but complementary. They are opposed in permanent conflict, but united in a basic alliance."[54] Although *alea*, in its very name, initially appears to be as much a Hellenic cornerstone as *agon*, Caillois's subsequent discussions of games of chance suggests *alea*'s especial intimacy with the "East." In *Man, Play, and Games*, Caillois heaped scorn on the aleatory games that he saw "corrupting" modern life in the form of popular published horoscopes, ostensibly an offshoot of the "Chinese Zodiac," which according to him use one's birth date to "transform . . . each day and each week into a kind of promise or menace for their readers."[55] The situation was even more repugnant in "mixed societies" (by which he meant partially civilized ones) like those of Cuba, Puerto Rico, and Brazil. There the *charada china* or "Chinese charade"—a lottery game originating in China—had become a national obsession and crisis, an "incurable cancer on the economy" so severe as to warrant an explicit clause in the penal code outlawing it.[56]

Although Caillois considered *alea*, in the form of the Chinese charade, a material threat to the gullible masses, the charada china's metaphysical form—what he called "circular time"—was no less dangerous to the well-educated Western historian. His tentative musings on this "Oriental" temporality are given fullest expression in the 1963 special issue of the journal he edited, *Diogenes*, titled "Man and the Concept of History in the Orient," which opens with his own essay, "Circular Time, Rectilinear Time." Caillois's conclusion, in *Man, Play, and Games*, that "the destinies of cultures can be read in their games," takes on a double meaning in the *Diogenes* piece: destiny now means a culture's eventual trajectory according to its choice of games but also, equally important, the way it views the role played by fate as opposed to personal agency in shaping outcomes in the game of life. This is, of course, the most fundamental difference between *agon* and *alea* in Caillois's theory: in the former, one "makes one's own fate"; in the latter, fate is the maker. Now, however, *agon* and *alea* shift from a spatial symmetry, as initially depicted in the ludic taxonomy, to a temporal spectrum akin to the *paidia-ludus* continuum. Civilization becomes a process of transitioning from *alea* to *agon*, and in doing so "escap[ing] from the kind of time that lacks a usable past or a sense of the future—a time in which [the group] can only wait for the cyclical return of the masked gods, imitated at fixed intervals in complete unconsciousness of self."[57]

Caillois thus opens the *Diogenes* article by proposing that the "fundamental contrast" between East and West lies in their divergent conceptions of historical temporality: what he refers to respectively as "circular time"—the cyclical cosmology just mentioned—and "rectilinear time"—a developmental telos stretching from "unfathomable past" to "undefined future."[58] He takes China as representative of this Eastern, circular conception of time, extending Marcel Granet's description of seasonal rituals to consider Chinese civilization in terms of its calendar system. Although he does not explicitly say so, the "proof" he furnishes for Chinese conceptions of time seems to derive less from scholarly sources (of which there are virtually none cited) than what we might call a "commonsense" Orientalism: the sort of "knowledge" about China one might glean from, say, reading the horoscope placemats at a Chinese restaurant. Thus Caillois's analysis of the "Chinese cycle"—"or at least its popular version," which from his perspective is essentially the same thing—is predicated on a rambling yet reductive description of the "five-phase" or "five-element" conceptual schema (五种流行之气) and the twelve-year astrological calendar glossed in English as the Zodiac and commonly symbolized by animals (rat, tiger, ox, etc.). These temporal schemas, according to Caillois, produce in the societies that ascribe to them a resigned view of the world as an immutable, endlessly recurring, predetermined series of events that define an individual from the very moment of conception. In contrast to this "enclosed and catastrophic vision of history," the rectilinear model of the West views events "rationally," not as the result of cosmic laws but "simply the series of purely internal causes and effects which translates and constitutes the historical movement itself."[59]

This latter perspective, Caillois makes clear, is a fundamental precondition of the free will and "purposive innovation" he celebrated in *Man, Play, and Games* through the dichotomy of Western *ludus* as opposed to Chinese *wan*, and *agon* as opposed to *alea*. Thus, in rectilinear/Western time, "the responsibility for all that occurs, be it success or catastrophe, lies with the actors, who knew or ignored how to respond satisfactorily to the challenge of their milieu and their time."[60] The temporal division Caillois establishes here precisely replicates the *agon/alea* distinction he outlines in *Man, Play, and Games. Alea*, he observed there, "supposes on the player's part an attitude exactly opposite to that reflected in *agon*. In the latter, his only reliance is upon himself; in the former . . . winning is the result of fate," the outcome explained, as in the "Chinese" worldview, in terms of an event's "fortuity" or auspiciousness.[61]

Early in his *Dioegenes* essay, Caillois likens circular time to a foreign disease or invasion, a barbaric "aberration" that had occasionally interrupted the evolution of the West's rectilinear rationality: for example, in Etruscan texts that described temporality in terms of a twelve-millennia duration, each corresponding to a Zodiac sign.[62] Later in the essay, however, Caillois suggests that Asian cyclical time is less like a common cold than a lifelong addiction, a base impulse toward the opiate of aleatory fantasy from which the West was in perpetual recovery. In the conclusion of his piece, Caillois rues the fact that "the Western mentality [has] never disengaged itself completely" from the "insidious, unconscious passage from historical research to the philosophy of history," wherein the historian, "despite himself," gives into the "tenacious temptation" to view the past as an endless series of civilizations rising and falling through an inevitable cycle of "origin-maturity-decrepitude."[63] The West, in short, constantly threatens to "slip once more into the closed form of the circuits familiar to the East"—and, in doing so, to lose both its agonic and geographic identity as the West.

If the preceding has satisfactorily sketched out some answers to the query this chapter initially posed—what is ludic about Huizinga's and Caillois's Orientalism?—it has also raised an even more important question: what are we to do about it? If what appeared to be an "undertheorization" in contemporary game studies is in fact a manifestation of the spatial and racial dichotomies on which the original theories were based, this would imply that ludic theory in the post-racial moment has unwittingly taken on the role once served by explicitly racist theories. Whereas race was openly named in the Linnaean taxonomy, it has now been gamed, snugly embedding itself in seemingly colorblind, apolitical sites of play.

The dilemma we face, then, is precisely the nature of the structuralist paradox Jacques Derrida famously articulated in "Structure, Sign, and Play" by examining anthropologist Claude Lévi-Strauss's *The Raw and the Cooked*. "Whether he wants to or not," Derrida observed, "the ethnologist accepts into his discourse the premises of ethnocentrism at the very moment when he is employed in denouncing them."[64] There is no way out of this game; yet this does not imply "that all the ways of giving in to it"—or, we might say, playing it—"are of an equal pertinence": "The quality and the fecundity of a discourse are perhaps measured by the critical rigor with which this relationship to the history of metaphysics and to inherited concepts is thought. Here it is a question of a . . . critical responsibility of the discourse. It is a question of putting expressly and systematically the problem of the status of a discourse which borrows from a heritage the resources necessary for the deconstruction of that heritage itself."[65]

This chapter has sought to envision and to enact a critically responsible (and responsive) game studies. It has done so, in part, by analyzing game theories *as* games, by examining them alongside the particularity of the reality that shapes them. It has attended to Orientalism as something that goes much deeper than a game's representational content—exotic characters or settings—to a kind of worldview being created at the invisible level of game mechanics, one that is "ergodic" in the sense that Espen Aarseth used the term: a narrative that is not passively consumed but actively given meaning by the player.[66] It has, in short, proposed one of what will hopefully in the future become many ways that we might retain these indisputably valuable theories without falling prey to what Jacques Ehrmann identified, in the final analysis, as their greatest oversight: "Huizinga and Caillois erred principally in never doubting . . . that the player (themselves!) is the subject of play; in believing that, present in the game, at the center of play, they dominated it. They forgot that players may be played; that, as an object in the game, the player can be its stakes and its toy."[67] The path forward, then, may lie not in abandoning but in playfully maintaining our skepticism.

5

Mobile Frontiers

Pokémon *after Pearl Harbor*

Playing and mapping go hand in hand. To play is to make space—in the day, in the mind, in the earth—for playing; to mark space—as "playtime," as "make-believe," as a "playground"; and to map on these spaces a different set of rules, a different way of seeing, navigating, and measuring. To play is thus to reorient oneself within a new world; but it is also, as we discussed in the last chapter, to Orientalize that new space, to understand it as spatially, temporally, and metaphysically antithetical yet complementary to reality as we know it. Play is "not real," and reality is "not a game": the map, in short, is not the territory.

Or is it? It is no coincidence that the games that have most troubled our existing ludic definitions—namely, those "gamified" or "augmented reality" apps that starkly expose the precariousness of the play/real life binary—tend to be those that make the greatest use of modern mapping and location-based technologies. Obviously, without a GPS-enabled device and adequate cell phone reception or Wi-Fi, one cannot "check in" at a restaurant on Yelp, nor "capture" a wild Pikachu in *Pokémon GO*. But more important, there *is* no restaurant to "check in" at, no Pikachu to capture, if there is no map on which these entities appear. The restaurant itself may still exist as a physical eating establishment, but if there is no listing for it on Yelp—if it cannot be located through the app's interface—then from the perspective of the player (as opposed to the diner) it effectively does not exist. There is no game, no badges or bragging rights to be earned. Conversely, there may be no physical Pokémon to capture "out there" in the world, but because they appear on the game's map the creatures acquire a cartographically—and hence metaphysically—"real" existence.

This conceit, in fact, drove the global phenomenon of *Pokémon GO*, which began life as nothing but a Google Maps "hoax." It started in 2014 as just one among many April Fools' Day jokes the Silicon Valley giant had begun annually embedding in its products, a tradition inaugurated in 2000 with the release of "MentalPlex," a service that ostensibly allowed users to search the web telepathically.[1] The 2014 Google Maps "Pokémon Challenge" was a complex affair, comprising three distinct but carefully synchronized conceits. On the developer side, a team led by software engineer Tatsuo Nomura had secretly scattered throughout Google Maps a number of cute, cartoonish "pocket monsters" from the Japanese Gameboy games and *Pokémon* animated television show so popular among American adolescents in the late 1990s and early 2000s. Concurrent with the rollout of this developer "update," a promotional video appeared on the Google Maps blog and YouTube channel in the early evening hours of March 31, ostensibly prompted by the discovery that "dozens of wild Pokémon have taken up residence on streets, amidst forests and atop mountains throughout Google Maps."[2]

The slickly produced two-minute video opens on a scene of a young man clad in hiking gear, smartphone in hand, bushwhacking his way through a dense forest. As a voice-over extolls the adventurous spirit of "Pokémon masters"—a title the millennials in the audience would immediately recognize as the coveted objective of the original Gameboy games and TV show—we see the man come face-to-face (or rather face-to-screen) with a ferocious, dragon-like Pokémon: a Charizard in its cave. Crouched behind a rock, the man hurls a small red and white "Poké Ball" (the device used to capture the creatures in the original games). The fire-breathing monster vanishes mid-roar as an on-screen message appears over the darkened mouth of the now-empty cave: "GOTCHA! Charizard is caught!"

The scene is replayed several more times with different combinations of players and outdoor settings, intercut with shots of Brian McClendon, then vice president of the Google Maps team, announcing the search for the "world's best Pokémon master"—and Google Maps' newest team member. Interested parties were then directed, for further details, to the third and final piece of the April Fools' fiction: a job listing posted on Google's official blog.[3] The skills associated with the "profession" of Pokémon master are, it turns out, the very same qualities Google looks for in its employees—"risk-taking," "detail-oriented," "deep technical knowledge," and the ability to "navigate through tall grass to capture wild creatures." The ad jocularly invited prospective candidates to submit their qualifications via a newly developed "training tool," which turned out to be simply the most recent version of the Google Maps smartphone app. The objective, as job seekers were informed upon downloading and opening the updated app, was to search the Google Maps interface for Pokémon, leaving "no city unzoomed," and to "capture" the creatures they encountered by taking a screenshot.

A handful of static images might seem a rather anticlimactic payoff for what was, from the perspective of all parties involved, an extremely time- and labor-intensive undertaking. Such a dismal calculus is, perhaps, part of the very nature of hoaxes: the fun is only meant to last as long as the illusion does. But if the pleasure of April Fools' Day jokes lies in perpetuating the deception only in order to eventually expose it—and the victim—*as* an April Fool, then the Pokémon Challenge was both a terrible prank and a brilliant one. Terrible in the sense that it was not intended to deceive but to titillate: the video included an express disclaimer to that effect, while the job posting's facetious tone and the lack of functionality associated with the updated app accomplished the same. But brilliant in the sense that it had fooled people into thinking that they were the masters, the ones playing rather than being played. The ultimate "GOTCHA!" was not that there were no "real" Pokémon to catch, but that *because* there was no "real" job being offered at Google no labor was being performed on the part of the would-be candidates. Indeed, as the April Fools' Day jokes became ever more elaborate and expensive with each passing year, Google users increasingly came to see themselves as the beneficiaries of a spectacularly gratuitous labor expenditure that the company had undertaken purely for its audience's annual enjoyment.[4]

But such self-deceiving egotists were the true April Fools. For they cleaved to the illusion that the jokes were transitory ends in themselves, and in doing so failed to see the "hoaxes" as the means to larger and less innocent ends: that is, the perpetuation of the perception of Google itself as a fun-loving, creative-thinking maverick of just the sort ostensibly being sought in the Challenge. If the video tool was, in that sense, a genuine corporate recruitment tool disguised as a fake one—one aimed at securing not new employees but the image of the employer—the job posting on the blog was somewhat less subtle, although no less effective, in its efforts to maintain and expand the Google consumer base. The company had long ago learned to appreciate the value of the carrot over the stick when it came to influencing user behavior, whether through the appeal of an exclusive, "invite-only" email service like Gmail or the perceived scarcity of a "one-day only" April Fools' Day event. The latter, when combined with millennial nostalgia for a childhood game, was so strong as to make thousands of users leap to update to the latest version of the Google Maps app, making the hoax a far more effective tactic than those pesky "update available" app notifications. Equally effective was the job posting and video's seemingly offhand mention that the latest Challenge "hints and tips" would be made available to Google Maps' social media followers on Google+, Facebook, and Twitter.[5]

The Challenge, such as it was, ran for less than forty-eight hours. Yet the Pokémon's abrupt departure on April 2, 2014, turned out to be only a temporary hiatus. Two years later, they returned to Earth—or, rather, to Google Earth—in the form of a stand-alone mobile game that was essentially the Pokémon Challenge made playable. *Pokémon GO* was a collaboration between the Tokyo-based Pokémon/Nintendo company and the San Francisco–based Niantic Labs—whose CEO, John Hanke, had been a Google Maps employee at the time of the April Fools' joke. The game seemed to be the Google hoax realized: now players could, like the "digital explorers" featured in the original promotional video, travel to real (i.e., public, outdoor) places to capture Pokémon instead of just passively scrolling through the Google Maps interface. While users might be required to leave their living rooms and pound the pavement in search of Pokémon, however, it was not quite the experience portrayed in the Challenge: after all, the gameplay still took place entirely on the screen. There was no physical Poké Ball to hurl, no real risk of being singed by a Charizard's fiery breath.

In fact, what seemed like a hoax made real might ultimately be understood merely as the expansion of the hoax—and, in that sense, the marketing campaign underlying it. Indeed, *Pokémon GO* was an even more impressive showcase of Google Maps than the original Challenge had been, for the game demonstrated how GPS navigation technology could be used not just for the mundane purposes of obtaining driving directions or checking real-time traffic conditions—for the "work" of daily life in the age of smartphones—but also for the purpose of play. It was, after all, the very same smartphone and satellite technology being used to locate the nearest gas station in Google Maps, on the one hand, and the nearest cartoon quarry in *Pokémon GO*, on the other. The difference was simply that what had been laminated within a single interface in the Pokémon Challenge had now been divided into two (apparently) distinct applications.

The functionality of Google Maps thus authorized the location-based fictions that made *Pokémon GO* so fun. Yet the implications of this authority—what we might call the punch line of the real April Fools' joke—were not apparent until several weeks into the game's release, when concerns about privacy and data mining began to surface. In order to play the game, users were required to create a Pokemon.com account—or to sign in with their existing Google account. The convenience of not having to remember yet another password—and the fact that the Pokemon.com site was quickly overwhelmed and for a time no longer accepting new users—led numerous players to opt for the third-party, Google sign-in method. While entering one's Google credentials would have normally prompted a second screen in which users were asked to confirm the permissions they were providing—in this case, the granting of "full access" privileges to one's Google account by Niantic, and vice versa—a bug in the initial game skipped over this authorization screen, leading directly into gameplay. The "glitch" was quickly patched, but this simply meant that anyone wishing to play was now required to manually agree to their geospatial data—that is, information about where they were and had been, for how long, what speed they were traveling at, and so forth—being collected and shared between Google and Niantic, not that such data was no longer being harvested.[6]

Pokémon GO was certainly not the first app to use geospatial data to monitor its users' movements, nor to monetize that information—for example, by creating in-game incentives that directed players toward particular local businesses, as was the case with the three thousand McDonald's restaurants in Japan that were converted to Pokémon "gyms" (important landmarks where players congregated in order to compete with other trainers) following the fast-food chain's national sponsorship of the game.[7] But the game was doing more than simply jumping on the lucrative data mining bandwagon alongside innumerable location-based mobile apps like Fitbit and Foursquare as well as navigation apps like

Waze and Uber. For Google Maps did not simply make *Pokémon GO*'s conceit possible or plausible: rather, its location-based functionality constituted the game's core dynamic. That is, game developers were using the very same GPS technology to track and collect data about players even as the players themselves used it to track and collect nearby Pokémon. If the prospect of Google Maps employment—of putting one's gaming skills to work—was no longer an explicit framing narrative in *Pokémon GO* as it had been in the original April Fools' Day joke, this was simply because it was no longer needed to incentivize users. Indeed, disguising that work-play connection proved a more effective approach: far more valuable than a single employee was the uncompensated, voluntary microlabor performed by hundreds of thousands of aspiring Pokémon masters willing to trade their personal data in exchange for a "free" dose of nostalgic fun. The April Fools' Day prank had paid off in spades.

The foregoing is both an example of, and evidence of the pressing need for, the type of critically responsible and responsive approach to game studies discussed in the previous chapter. There, we began with the striking parallelism between the way Huizinga's and Caillois's theories have been applied by contemporary game studies scholars to analyze games, and the way the theories have themselves been read *as* games in the sense of being analogously "free": that is, apolitical, universal, and empirically objective. Upon comparing the seemingly "free" content of the theories with the historically bound context of their creation, however, we discovered that the illusion of ludic freedom, which both theorists so emphatically insisted was an inherent quality of play, was itself a scholarly fiction.[8] By turning to the academic and institutional sources of Orientalist authority from which Huizinga's theory of the magic circle and Caillois's taxonomy of games were derived, we found that these models not only reproduced, but fundamentally relied for their coherence and legitimacy on, the "natural"—that is, intrinsic and unbridgeable—differences between East and West. As the inheritors of this Orientalist legacy, game studies scholars face a dilemma: how might we continue to draw on and extend Huizinga's and Caillois's valuable ludic insights without at the same time unwittingly reproducing their ethnocentric biases?[9]

Let me briefly reiterate the historicist method proposed in response at the end of the last chapter, one which this chapter will demonstrate has equally productive possibilities for the analysis of games as of game theories. It was suggested that the first step in addressing this blind spot—which afflicts not only academic but "commonsense" understandings of games—is simply to acknowledge its existence. (This is harder than it sounds, not least because, as we just saw with the April Fools' jokes, the shards of our illusions may leave behind a disturbing impression of our own victimization, or worse, our unwitting complicity.) The second is to historicize the aporia: to contextualize the game theories—or, as in this chapter, the games themselves—within the particular national and cultural milieu, the political agendas and economic relations, the philosophical and methodological traditions within which they are both initially conceived and later consumed. This means acknowledging the porousness of the magic circle, the relationship between the game and the world from which it is supposedly isolated—or which it is seen to "realistically" reproduce. For then we can begin to consider the stakes of the a priori assumptions from which our games as well as our game theories obtain their veracity.

Historicizing *Pokémon GO* within its April Fools' Day context is just one way of applying this method. From this brief assay we have already gleaned two valuable historicist insights: first, the inextricability of the game's fictions from its material origins as a corporate PR campaign and Google Maps expansion; and second, how the explicit original fiction of a job opportunity became a disguised material reality through the labor of data creation and mining. The success of the deception was due in part to the widely held assumption that the "freemium" game, like the April Fools' Day joke, was an innocent, pleasurable pastime—and thus, like the game theories of the previous chapter, an "end in itself."

This chapter, like the last, seeks to explode that myth by expanding the scope of our scholarly map to include both sides of the Pacific, and both sides of the game/world binary. It attends to the postwar Japanese moment in which the original *Pokémon* franchise was produced as well as the late twentieth- / early twenty-first century moment in which *Pokémon GO* was consumed by global audiences. Doing so reveals a striking prehistory to the Google marketing campaign as an extension of a national rebranding effort that began in 1980s Japan, and which saw Pikachu and his "trainer" Ash Ketchum conscripted into service alongside characters like Hello Kitty and Mario. This approach also allows us to recognize in the later game's use of GPS technology and the Google Maps framework the legacy of a broader cartographic tradition of ideologically charged map making—one which imperial Japan had already put to sophisticated use to disseminate and rationalize its expansionist agenda during the early decades of the twentieth century.

In demonstrating how the mid-century contestation for physical spaces in East Asia has its counterpart in the contemporary contestation over the way those spaces are represented in and through Japanese video games, this chapter augments existing discussions of the ludic's role in Japan's strategic postwar shift from "hard" to "soft" power—that is, from violently enforced national ideologies to voluntarily adopted "cultural" values. *Pokémon GO* is a ludo-Orientalist artifact not because the original franchise (and, in fact, the idea for the later mobile game) comes *from* Japan, but because it is at every level informed by the way Japan is *perceived* by, and how it wishes to be perceived by, the "West"— and the way the latter, in turn, has been used by Japanese companies like Nintendo as a seemingly neutral, universalist model for developing "global" consumer products. As Nintendo of America's Pokémon brand manager Gail Tilden put it, "We try hard to keep American children from thinking of Pokémon as being from Japan. This requires localization, not to hide the fact that Pokémon is made in Japan, but to convey the impression that these are global characters. Therefore, we do not want to make Pokémon American, either. We want Pokémon to become global characters that children all over the world will find familiar."[10] Perhaps because they were already well versed in such ethnocentric perspectives, Americans have been especially receptive to such "performances of commodity white face," as anthropologist Christine Yano has called the Japanese marketing of Hello Kitty and other characters. The perceived non-Japaneseness of the cute and fanciful Pokémon may have facilitated their misrecognition as "American," in the sense that Yano means in suggesting that "what is interpreted as 'without nationality' is actually very much imbued with Euro-American culture or race—or at least one interpretation of it. To 'have nationality' is to exhibit traits that are distinct from Euro-America."[11]

As a ludo-Orientalist artifact, *Pokémon GO* further offers a useful foil to *Homo Ludens* and *Man, Play, and Games* because the critical and popular receptions of both have tended to privilege issues of content over those of context; hence questions of historical and national origins, racial politics, labor economies, and so forth have been seen as largely tangential or, as with the issue of data mining in *Pokémon GO*, an unfortunate contamination of the game as what should be, at least in theory, an end in itself. Beyond this, however, there is the strikingly similar role which Asia plays—or rather, seems *not* to play—in the cultural objects examined in this and the previous chapter. That *Pokémon GO* was a U.S.-Asian collaboration, and that the original franchise on which it was based was a Japanese export, these material conditions have since acquired the status of factoids, bits of trivia. Yet the very fact that Pokémon's Asian origins could be seen *as* trivial is nothing short of remarkable. For America's nationwide obsession with the game—initially reprising but ultimately eclipsing the "Pokémania" of the 1990s and 2000s, which had been largely restricted to an adolescent audience—points to a strain of Orientalism that seems markedly different from the essentializing, exploitative practice usually discussed in race and postcolonial studies. If, even today, the hint of an "Asian-sounding" name is sufficient to brand its bearer as a "perpetual foreigner," how is it that Pikachu, Ryu, and Pac-Man have been so seamlessly assimilated into American culture, even and especially during periods of rampant anti-Japanese sentiment like the 1980s?[12] As scholars, gamers, and cultural consumers, we all "know" about the Asian origins of Tamagotchi or Yoshi, but why don't we care?

By "care," I mean not so much a lack of global *interest* in the game's Japanese origins—there are whole websites dedicated to exhaustively documenting the Japanese-language equivalents or inspirations for each and every of the 802 Pokémon—but rather the lack of negative impact this knowledge has had on the game's popular reception among international, and particularly American, audiences. As an imported product, the game's being "made in Japan" has had no discernible effect on American consumers' interest in playing the game or purchasing the various products associated with the franchise. In American popular media or culture (with the notable exception of a *South Park* episode discussed below), representations of Pokémon are strikingly devoid of the racial stereotypes that have historically clung to all things Asian in America: if its Asianness signifies at all, it is far more often gently satirized as another example of Japan's "weird" cultural obsession with childish cuteness.

And finally, in scholarship, although many have rightly noted the role played by Nintendo's sophisticated branding strategies in facilitating the franchise's entry into international markets, such efforts on the company's part have on the whole been understood as either wholly ancillary to the game—like an ingenious "localized" translation of the sort Coca-Cola became famous for—or as something that goes no deeper than the level of visual style.

Yet, while Japanese-initiated branding efforts may have helped erase what Koichi Iwabuchi refers to as the foreign "cultural odor" of the Pokémon franchise, Americans have been curiously amenable partners in this venture.[13] Indeed, U.S. disinterest in Pokémon's Japaneseness has at times bordered on selective amnesia. In the second week of *Pokémon GO*'s release, for example, military officials at Pearl Harbor issued a stern public warning to active-duty personnel stipulating that the game was "not authorized for use in restricted areas near [the base] or near entry control points" and promising disciplinary action against those found to be in violation of the policy. When questioned by reporters, the navy spokesperson reassured them that the game posed no "real security threat"; the matter was rather one of establishing behavioral standards befitting the armed forces. Neither in the official press releases nor in the many news stories that reported on the event was there even a trace of ironic recognition that a Japanese game had so suddenly and thoroughly captivated military personnel at the precise location where Japan had unleashed its surprise attack some seventy years before. It was as if the game had erased not only the "scent" of Japaneseness, but the whole history of U.S.-Japan antagonism.

But if the correlation between Pokémon and the events of World War II failed to register for Americans at even a purely coincidental level, this is certainly not because no such correlation existed. In truth, one cannot journey very far into the Pokémon world without exposing the precariousness of that ahistorical fiction. To take one example, many fans know that the original game, and most of its cast of characters, was inspired by creator Satoshi Tajiri's childhood interest in collecting insects. What is hardly ever mentioned in popular or scholarly commentary, yet immediately clear from interviews, is that this idyllic, "universal" picture of childhood dirt digging was in fact deeply inflected by the particularities of the war that had recently concluded—and in particular, the atomic bombs that had hastened its conclusion. Born in 1965 in a suburb of Tokyo, Tajiri's entomological adventures regularly involved crawling through old bomb shelters in pursuit of rare specimens; the mythology surrounding the origin of the "pocket monsters," in turn, speaks tellingly of genetic mutations and alien viruses. Just as the Silicon Valley roots of the later game are clearly important to understanding its seemingly un-gamelike kinship with corporate profiteering, so, too, are the national and historical origins of *Pokémon GO*'s antecedent crucial to understanding Pokémon's politics—which is to say, in the first place, to recognizing that Pokémon *is* political.

The tendency to perceive Japanese video games as not being Asian in the same politically meaningful sense as has historically indexed the racial stigma attached to Asian bodies or spaces is perhaps the reason that Asian American studies has been slow to take up video games like *Pokémon GO*, despite a growing embrace of Colleen Lye's call to consider Orientalism and Asian American racialization as two versions of the same racial form.[14] It is perhaps also why video game scholarship, too, has tended to approach these games in terms of their technological or aesthetic aspects rather than seeing them as expressly "political" in the sense that scholars like Noah Wardrip-Fruin and Ian Bogost have defined that term. Bogost has rightly pointed out that video games are—or at least have the capacity to be—powerful sites of political engagement and critique. This potential lies, for him, in their ability to render visually and conceptually accessible "the Logix that make up a worldview, the ideological distortions and political situations . . . how political structures operate, or how they fail to operate, or how they could or should operate."[15]

Yet the expansive potential for political change which Bogost ascribes to games is, like the theories of game realism we examined in the last chapter, hobbled by an overly narrow yet vague definition of what constitutes a "political game." While Bogost acknowledges that a game's politics go beyond aesthetics and visual representation—thus he excludes from the category of political games those that simply "apply a political skin to existing procedural mechanics"—he remains wedded to a self-determined notion of the political very much like the game-theoretical concept of sovereign choice we saw in chapter 2.[16] For although "not all videogames about politics are political," Bogost's range of examples presumes that all political videogames are in some way "about politics"—where "about" is used to designate an intentional and overt, often visually explicit message immediately grasped by the player.[17] As this chapter reveals, however, political ideologies can inhere in games that don't necessarily see themselves as political. Even more, our analysis of game politics must necessarily extend to the political agendas and uses to which the games are put by those other than the game developers—including, most obviously, politicians. By revealing as politically charged a game like *Pokémon GO* which is deliberately marketed as—and has largely been received as—wholly apolitical, this chapter augments our perspective on the relationship between games and politics at both the visual and the procedural level.

Although *Pokémon GO* was indeed new and different in important ways from the original *Pokémon* franchise—most obviously, in the augmented reality and GPS technology it employed—isolating those technologies from the existing context in which they signified risks fetishizing and dehistoricizing them. Much discussion of augmented reality or pervasive games has taken as axiomatic the notion that they newly blur or dissolve boundaries: between game and reality, play and work, private and public, et cetera. Certainly, as we learned in the last chapter, part of the problem has to do with the false binaries themselves. Yet the binaries persist, for they serve important ideological functions. This chapter explores what some of those functions are by reframing *Pokémon GO*'s marketing and mechanics as the evolution and automation of a much older logic of "location-based" ethnocentrism and a much longer history of "augmenting reality" through the cartographic naturalization of such worldviews. These mapping and marketing efforts collectively create new ways of seeing—or not seeing—Japaneseness and its wartime history, particularly in relation to the conservative nationalist agendas of the present.

Augmenting "Cultural Odor"

In part I of this book, we saw how Asianness in the American context has historically been understood as the biological or cultural feature responsible for the unparalleled efficiency (and cheapness) of Asian American labor. With the rise of Japan as a technology-exporting nation beginning in the 1980s, we see a curious inversion of that narrative. Early game scholars (many of whom, of course, were also consumers) have somewhat optimistically tended to regard Japanese video games like *Super Mario Bros.* and *Donkey Kong* much as business analysts did Sony Walkmans and Toyota sedans: that is, as "culturally neutral commodities whose country of origin has nothing to do with the way that they work and the satisfaction that a consumer obtains from usage."[18] Scholarly appraisals of Nintendo's successful video games have thus often characterized Link, Pac-Man, and Ash Ketchum alike simply as user interfaces, "little more than a cursor that mediates the player's relationship to the story world," as Henry Jenkins puts it.[19]

The complete, cursor-like reliance of such game characters on user input is certainly a central feature of many Japanese video games, distilled to its essence in the 1990s with the Tamagotchi, a helpless digital "pet" requiring constant care and maintenance. Yet claims of video games' Japaneseness as functionally—and thus politically—meaningless ironically attest to the remarkable success of the marketing strategies developed by their creators. These approaches were explicitly intended to "augment reality" by rendering their products *mukokuseki*, which literally means something or someone lacking any nationality, but which is also used to refer to the erasure of racial or religious characteristics and contexts from a cultural product.[20] This erasure can be found throughout Japanese mass culture and especially in cartoons, comics, and video games, where the "look" of Japaneseness is evacuated both by removing the visual markers of human racial difference (hence the huge, jewel-colored eyes and expressive hair of many Japanese animated characters), and by replacing it with the altogether different aesthetic category of cuteness or *kawaii*: that is, not by making the characters "Caucasian," but "cute."

Closely associated with the visual style of internationally popular manga and anime (comics and animated cartoons), *kawaii* is often described in terms of a particular set of physical attributes: namely, large heads and eyes, coupled with small, rounded bodies. The cuteness of creatures like Hello Kitty, Totoro, and, of course, the Pokémon has arguably been central to the erasure of "cultural odor" regarded as essential for their global success in international markets. Indeed, the Pokémon franchise's ambitious and successful expansion from Gameboy games to trading cards and television shows was facilitated by the original's already minimal cultural "odor," with the TV show producers observing that "it appeared easy to produce international versions [because] the setting of the adventure explored looks *mukoku* and religion free."[21]

What Iwabuchi described as the creation of "culturally odorless" products, and Christine Yano as "performing commodity white face," was a complex process that went far beyond mere visual erasure, however. It was part of a broader marketing strategy known as "global localization" in which Japanese companies like Sony and Nomura led the way during the 1980s. "Glocalization," which soon became a part of American business jargon and one of the major marketing buzzwords of the early 1990s, was based on the notion that to succeed simultaneously in a variety of local markets, global companies had to conduct an intricate balancing act: to both "transcend vestigial national differences and to create standardized global markets, whilst remaining sensitive to the peculiarities of local markets and differentiated consumer segments."[22]

In part because the Pokémon universe was composed mostly of nonhuman characters, the Pokémon Company's American marketing sector focused much of their efforts on linguistic rather than aesthetic glocalization. Just as glocalization as a whole, as Tilden emphasized, did not involve "hiding" Pokémon's Japanese origins but rather making the characters "familiar" to American audiences, so linguistic glocalization was understood as something distinct from the sort of translation or dubbing found in traditional textual or filmic Asian imports to the States, where maintaining the semantic meaning of the original is paramount. What linguistic glocalization involved instead, as *Pokémon* TV producer Masakazu Kubo put it, was "erasing Japanese language signs as much as possible"—which, interestingly, meant not wholly translating the characters' names into their semantic English equivalents but rather simply erasing their "Japaneseness" (i.e., their "foreignness").[23] At the same time, it required maintaining the complicated nomenclature and classification system of the Japanese original, which, as Joseph Tobin explains, focused on devising "names that make it easy for children not only to memorize the Pokémon but to understand the relationship of Pokémon both to their evolved higher forms and to their family groups (e.g., water, air, fire)."[24]

The remarkable range of tactics through which this complex process was achieved can be illustrated with just a few examples. In the

English-language version of the Pokémon games and television show, creatures like Fushigibana became Venusaur, Nyarth became Meowth, and the main human character, the Pokémon trainer Satoshi, named after the game's creator, became Ash. The logic behind these "cleverly descriptive" names is, however, different for all three. Fushigibana, in Japanese, roughly translates to "strange flower"; Venusaur, a portmanteau of "Venus" and "dinosaur," effectively captures the connotation of "strangeness," but abandons the sound and denotative meaning of the original.[25] Nyarth is apparently derived from *nya* (ニャー), the Japanese onomatopoeia for the sound a cat makes; hence the English translation to Meowth.[26] Satoshi, a common Japanese name for boys, roughly translates to "intelligent" or "quick-witted"; Ash has no semantic connection, but is rather a combination of three of the letters extracted from the original name (S*at*o*sh*i).

Interestingly, the instances where the original Japanese name was retained—such as Pikachu—were those which the marketing team apparently thought didn't "telegraph" their Japaneseness in quite the same way—meaning, to an American ear, that they not only didn't sound Japanese, but that they didn't sound like words at all. Quite common, in fact, was the assumption of meaninglessness expressed by an English-speaking journalist at *Time* magazine in a 1999 interview with Satoshi Tajiri:

> *Time*: Do the names mean anything or are they just gibberish?
> TAJIRI: They all have meaning. Like Nyarth. It's from a Japanese proverb about a cat with money on his head that doesn't know it's there. It's about understanding the value of money. I don't think they have that concept in the U.S., so the name is different.
> And Pikachu. "Pika" is the sound Japanese say an electric spark makes. And "chu" is the sound a mouse makes. So Pikachu is like an electric mouse.[27]

Although, as Tajiri points out, the original nuances, puns, and culturally specific Japanese references are largely lost in their linguistic glocalization, the very question of what is "lost in translation" in the Pokémon world as a whole is rarely considered in the first place because we tend not to register that what we are encountering is, in fact, a translation.

Figure 5.1. Augmented reality technology in the mobile game *Pokémon GO*. Gameplay screenshot courtesy of *Digital Trends*, www.digitaltrends.com.

We might say, in light of this observation, that glocalization constituted the analog version of augmented reality, fostering the illusion of Pokémon being "local" and "familiar" despite being from Japan. It was in this sense a direct precursor to the digital version of the augmented reality technology found in the later *Pokémon GO* game, which used the smartphone camera to create the illusion of Pokémon existing in the material world (fig. 5.1). While linguistic glocalization was the result of intense imaginative labor on the part of the Pokémon Company, by 2016 that labor had been outsourced—or, rather, mechanized. Now, it was the player's smartphone battery that was taxed in the effort. The constant depletion of power: such is an apt description of the price one paid to play.

Imaginative Geography: A New Techno-Orientalism

Although John Hanke and his San Francisco-based company Niantic have received the lion's share of the credit (and, in later days, the blame) for *Pokémon GO*, the idea for the game as well as the April Fools' Day Pokémon Challenge came from overseas. It was Satoru Iwata and Tsunekazu Ishihara, the CEOs of Nintendo and the Pokémon Company, respectively, who initially pitched the concept to Google; Hanke, at that time a Google employee, was simply the one who "took it seriously"[28] enough to extend it beyond April 1. Iwata, credited with revitalizing the stagnating company upon taking the reins in 2002, had long been interested in mobile and motion control gaming: his visionary leadership resulted in the Nintendo DS, Wii, and Switch. Ishihara, however, was the one who helped broker the eventual collaboration with Niantic, a choice based in part on his appreciation for the company's 2012 mobile title *Ingress*, a sci-fi themed "capture the flag" game with very similar location-based mechanics to *Pokémon GO*.[29]

Ingress, too, had fundamentally relied on the appeal of laminating a second world on top of the first and encouraging the discovery of landmarks that, despite being right in their backyards, Americans may never have noticed. Yet while it attracted significant attention within a particular subset of gamers (including Ishihara), *Ingress* never got close to the mainstream appeal *Pokémon GO* enjoyed. The explanation seems to rest in part on the latter's ability to leverage an established franchise and consumer base: what game writer Ollie Barder has delightfully described as "two decades of Pokémon mindshare."[30] Although the majority of American players of *GO* had never played a single Pokémon game before—the diversity of the demographics was in fact a significant part of what made the game so noteworthy—they were quick to be enraptured by the charming combination of "culturally odorless" and adorably vulnerable creatures that had made the original franchise so successful.

Furthermore, while *Pokémon GO*'s method of changing the way people viewed the world around them also relied, like *Ingress*, on changing their relationships to familiar spaces, its "glocalized" use of augmented reality technology seemed to harmonize far better with the location-based conceit. Whereas *Ingress* used Google Maps to create a futuristic-looking game display, amplifying the difference between "augmented" and everyday reality, *Pokémon GO* was in many ways indistinguishable from the Google Maps interface that had already become an integral part of most smartphone users' daily lives (fig. 5.2). Indeed, if the similarity between *Ingress*'s objective of conquering portals and *Pokémon GO*'s of capturing Pokémon and battling them at local "gyms" made the Nintendo-Niantic collaboration, in Hanke's words, "a perfect match,"[31] so, too, did Pokémon's extraordinarily successful track record of glocalization make it an

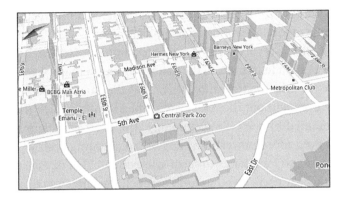

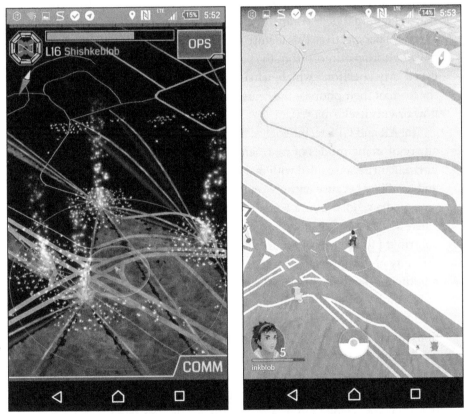

Figure 5.2. Screenshots of real-life locations as seen in Google Maps, the augmented reality mobile game *Ingress*, and *Pokémon GO*. Gameplay screenshots courtesy of Reddit user Inkblob. http://www.reddit.com/r/Ingress/comments/4saih1/two_worlds/.

equally natural fit for a game whose pleasure derived in large part from the mapping of foreign worlds onto familiar ones.[32]

For *Pokémon GO*'s augmented reality technology extended beyond its use of the camera lens: indeed, the battery drain led many veteran users to disable the AR function altogether. That the game could be equally enjoyable even without the AR suggests the extent to which the fiction was maintained by the GPS technology. The latter was, counterintuitively, an even more powerful means of "augmenting reality" because it had become so familiar as to seem self-evident. That is, *Pokémon GO* changed the way users saw the world in much the same way that Google Maps and other navigational apps had done for years: not by adding fanciful landmarks or competitive objectives, but simply by reorienting the user's perspective. This feature had been integrated into the interface of Google Maps almost from the beginning, in the form of a button aptly called "My Location," which, when pushed, literally makes the user—in the form of their phone—the center of the world around which the map now orients itself (fig. 5.3).

The AR and GPS technologies, then, functioned in the game as mutually reinforcing modes of representing the world: as at once exotic and unfamiliar (because filled with magical creatures) and yet completely safe and familiar (because entirely centered around oneself). It underscored new media scholar Laura Kurgan's observation that "maps . . . show us where we are and how to get somewhere else, and in doing so, they can contribute to a sense of security and self-possession. The solidity and certainty of the phrase 'You are here' would be the motto of that identity-reinforcing—and maybe even identity-constitutive—function of maps."[33]

In emphasizing how maps function as a means of representing the world as well as oneself in relation to it, Kurgan builds on the observations of scholars across diverse disciplines—geography, philosophy, new media, and postcolonial studies, in particular—who have compellingly unmasked maps as value-laden, interest-serving fictions whose seemingly neutral choices of content, scale, and perspective disguise the fact that they are "embedded in a history they help construct."[34] *Pokémon GO* is a useful site from which to consider how mapping technology more broadly, and mobile GPS in particular, continues to serve the self-legitimating function of Orientalism that we examined in the previous chapter—what Edward Said dubbed "imaginative geography"—while

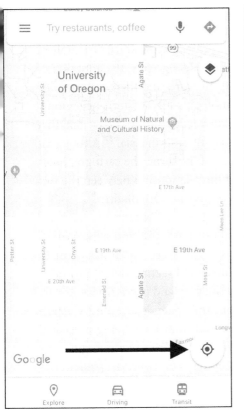

Figure 5.3. "My Location" feature in Google Maps and Apple Maps.

also participating in the late capitalist cultural form that Frederic Jameson, a decade or so after Said, would describe as an "aesthetic of cognitive mapping."[35] Together, they provide a scaffold on which to fashion a historicist account of *Pokémon GO* as it remaps the relation between Japan's imperial past and its nationalist present.

Imaginative geography, Said suggests, "help[s] the mind to intensify its own sense of itself by dramatizing the distance and difference between what is close to it and what is far away."[36] What Said identifies as the dramatic intensity of imaginative geography captures the logic whereby maps—and Orientalist discourse—achieve their implicit authority. As our discussion of Pokémon's glocalization revealed the continuity between marketing tactics and augmented reality technology, so our understanding of the game's location-based, self-orienting technology is incomplete without an account of its Orientalist—or, more precisely, techno-Orientalist—predecessors. Indeed, as critics like John Cheng remind us, Orientalism was always technological, in the sense that "geography, the adoption of international scientific standards for its measure, and their cartographic application were transformative technologies for Western hegemonic modernity, facilitating production of knowledge about 'the Orient' that inverted and assuaged European imperial interests in Asia."[37] Although it has largely receded in our current usage of the term, the cartographic is crucial to understanding the nature of the relationship between the two terms that make up the whole concept of "techno-Orientalism."

David Morley and Kevin Robins coined the term "techno-Orientalism" in 1995 as part of a broader effort to understand how and why, "within the political and cultural unconscious of the West, Japan has come to exist as the figure of empty and dehumanised technological power."[38] They observed that techno-Orientalist imagery and narrative frequently conveyed a sense of Asian threat, yet one that extended beyond Western anxieties about technological advancement that were being projected onto Japan as the creator, and the profiteer, of these technologies. The threat rather coincided with that technology's eastward *migration*, upsetting not simply the technological supremacy historically associated with the West, but the geocentric identity associated with that supremacy: that of being, as the earth itself was long presumed to be, the center of the universe, the world around which all others revolved. In other words, as Asia became, and continues to become, the new center of technological progress, the West is losing its identity as the unmarked, universal point of reference against which the Orient—a term which, as we noted in the last chapter, corresponds not to a specific place but rather a spatial relation—has been constructed as and reduced to a particular, an Other to the West's self. Underlying techno-Orientalism, then, is the broader threat Asia poses to what French philosopher Emmanuel Levinas referred to as "ontological imperialism," in which "human history is seen from the viewpoint of Europe and the West—providing narcissistic forms of self-centered knowledge—philosophy as 'egology,' as Levinas puts it."[39]

Current scholarship on techno-Orientalism tends to understand it in terms of overt and intentional representations (particularly visual and literary) of Asian bodies, landscapes, languages, and other cultural tropes. Yet the "odorless," subtended Asianness of Pokémon is, as we have seen, the result of a painstaking and deliberate *removal* effort: it is, in other words, no more natural or neutral than the seemingly unmarked, objective map of the world it seemingly reproduces. We must, in other words, expand our consideration of techno-Orientalism to include, as Paul Martin does in his inventive reconsideration of the video game *Resident Evil 5*, not solely the game's "ostensible theme"—which is to say, the zombie-killing, world-saving exploits of a white male protagonist and his black female partner in neocolonial Africa—but to the underlying "social imaginary that shapes that theme."[40] Reading *Resident Evil* as a "Japanese game"—not only in the sense of the national and racial identity of its creators, but the extent to which it "obliquely memorializ[es]" the country's colonial history—Martin persuasively argues that the game "transforms a partially suppressed Japanese colonial memory into the performance of a normal [i.e., militarily sovereign] Japanese (inter)national subjectivity" on the global stage.[41] Analogously, it is by recognizing the way the mapping technology of augmented reality games like *Pokémon GO* "obliquely" constructs an Orientalist perspective—which is to say, a means of defining human difference in terms of geographic distance— that we begin to detect in such games the cultural odors which glocalizing efforts so effectively eliminate at the surface level.

In her compelling discussion of "high tech Orientalism" in early cyberspace, Wendy Chun defines that term as a tactic of "navigating by difference," a strategy that "seeks to orient the reader to a technology-overloaded present/future (which is portrayed as belonging to the Japanese or other Far Eastern countries) through the promise of readable difference, and through a conflation of information networks with urban landscape."[42] Written fourteen years before *Pokémon GO*'s release, Chun's emphasis on Asian difference as the product of the lamination of real and virtual spaces provocatively anticipates how the game's "reorienting" appeal relies not simply on making the Pokémon visible but readable; not simply mappable, but collectible (hence the game's slogan, "Gotta Catch 'Em All!").

This "high tech Orientalism" also reworks, for the internet age, the spatial model of political culture that Frederic Jameson discussed in terms of "cognitive mapping." Robert Tally Jr. and others have suggested that Jameson's aesthetic understanding of cognitive mapping was problematically "prefigured" by that of the national allegory as articulated in his deeply controversial essay "Third-World Literature in the Era of Multinational Capitalism." There, Jameson posited that "third-world texts, even those which are seemingly private and invested with a properly libidinal dynamic, necessarily project a political dimension in the form of national allegory: *the story of the private individual destiny is always an allegory of the embattled situation of the public third-world culture and society.*"[43] Aijaz Ahmad, in an early response to Jameson, argued that "there is no such thing as a 'Third World Literature' which can be constructed as an internally coherent object of theoretical knowledge."[44] In short, as Tally notes, Jameson's deployment of the national allegory (and later, of cognitive mapping) functioned as a "renewed or revivified Orientalism, notwithstanding the otherwise good intentions of the critic."[45] Orientalism might then be perceived as a kind of return of the repressed in Jameson's later work on cognitive mapping in his book *Postmodernism*, wherein, as Patrick Jagoda pithily describes it, the term is used to posit a "theoretical way of *knowing* the world without accurately *representing* it."[46] Drawing on Kevin Lynch's *The Image of the City*, Jameson introduced cognitive mapping as an imaginative response to the alienating conditions of (post)modern city life and the vicissitudes of multinational capitalism (and before that, market and monopoly capitalism).[47] In the absence of "traditional" navigational referents such as "monuments, nodes, natural boundaries, built perspectives," the individual struggles to mentally map either themselves or the "urban totality" surrounding them.[48] Jameson is less interested in what cognitive maps might look like, in the neurological sense, than in the ideological function they serve, in the Althusserian sense: as a "representation of the subject's Imaginary relationship to his or her Real conditions of existence,"[49] which, in Chun's account, becomes an explicitly Orientalized representation of the relationship between information networks and urban landscapes.

But who needs cognitive maps when one has Google Maps? Or, to frame it in Chun's terms, what is *Pokémon GO* if not "high tech Orientalism" in app form? For what better representation of the cognitive map's function—what Jameson called "the practical reconquest of a sense of place"[50]—than the *Pokémon GO* interface depicted in figure 5.4, in which the world is nothing *but* a space of conquest—of natives to be captured, "gyms" to be conquered, and "PokéStops" to be raided? And alongside that simulated imperialism, we can speak of the game as a reconquest of a sense of time: a nostalgic return to childhood games of territorial expansion in days when the world was new, each step a frontier.

As we saw in chapters 1 and 3, nostalgia for the closed frontier has guided American cultural production and national imagination since the late 1800s; thus Asian Americans' association with that frontier was crucial in painting them as "pioneering Americans" in the model minority era. The emergence of cyberspace in the mid-1990s gave rise to a reemergence of the frontier trope, with creators and users of the new internet rhetorically framing it as an electronic frontier. As Chun reminds us, "Like all explorations, charting cyberspace entailed uncovering what was always already there and declaring it 'new.' It entailed obscuring already existing geographies and structures so that space becomes vacuous yet chartable, unknown yet populated and populatable. Like the New World and the frontier, settlers claimed this 'new' space and declared themselves its citizens."[51] *Pokémon GO*'s marketing, from the earliest days of the April Fools' video, played explicitly on this idea of a "New World" in which players served as the digital pioneers of twenty-first-century manifest destiny: courageous settlers traveling to the edges of the mappable world (or at least the edges of the cell phone service map), wandering into inhospitable deserts and ascending sheer rock walls to domesticate "monstrous" inhabitants and plant their team flags.

While the newer game's augmented reality and GPS technology helped enhance the visual immersiveness of this fantasy, this simulated imperialism—the goal of collecting all the Pokémon and completing the "Pokédex"—had always been the franchise's core dynamic. Such a convention is arguably not unique to Pokémon, but a central feature of many of Nintendo's most successful games. Speaking of Nintendo games as a form of "New World travel writing," Mary Fuller and Henry Jenkins observe that such games "allow . . . people to enact through play an older narrative that can no longer be enacted in reality—a constant struggle for possession of desirable spaces, the ever shifting and unstable frontier between controlled and uncontrolled space."[52] "When I watch my son playing Nintendo®," Jenkins muses, "I watch him play the part of an explorer and a colonist, taking a harsh new world and bringing it under his symbolic control, and that story is strangely familiar."[53] The very terms in which Jenkins describes the American resonances of these

Japanese-created games—as "strangely familiar"—pithily attests to the remarkable success of Nintendo's glocalization efforts, successfully negotiating the seeming contradiction between "global" and "local" through experiences which, to reinvoke the words of Pokémon's brand manager Gail Tilden, feel "familiar to children all over the world."[54]

Yet, as we saw with the data mining controversy, it is only from a particular perspective that the player appears to be the colonizer; from a broader view, it is the player who is being colonized.[55] Indeed, the conclusions of Stephen Kline, Nick Dyer-Witheford, and Greig de Peuter would suggest that Japanese video games ultimately confirm even as they seemingly resolve American anxieties about Asian invasion: "The microworld colonizer—the player who enjoys exploring the virtual territory of the game—is also the real-world colonized whose imagination is increasingly occupied and shaped into a source of profits for Nintendo. Through identification with Mario the conqueror/explorer/colonist, the player is annexed/invaded/occupied by Nintendo, the company for whom Mario has become conquistador."[56] Kline and colleagues' description of games as "microworlds" adds a further dimension to a historicist approach to game studies. So far, we have focused on historical context mainly in terms of chronology and cartography. To this we can now add the element of *scope*: of micro- and macroworlds, or, in Googlespeak, of "Street View" and "Bird's Eye View." The point here is that a game's ideology functions at the "macro" level as well as the "micro"; however, this is a view that we rarely consider because we instead tend to analyze the game world as the gamer sees it (i.e., at whatever representational scales the game allows: first person, map view, over the shoulder, etc.). But when we zoom out and consider the *Pokémon GO* map from a perspective we would never see within the game because our scale is too limited (for example, the "macro" image depicted in figure 5.4, a user-created map of all the Pokémon gyms in New York City), a different picture emerges of the game itself, not us, colonizing the world.

Beyond the various PokéStops scattered throughout the map—waypoints where players can collect and deploy items to assist them in capturing Pokémon—the game features a series of "Pokémon gyms," at which players can, once they have traveled near enough to the site, train and strengthen their Pokémon by pitting them in combat against

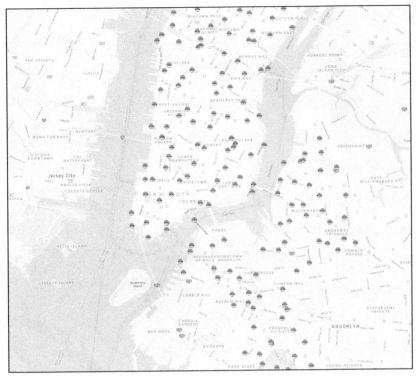

Figure 5.4. Map of *Pokémon GO* gyms in New York City. Image courtesy of the *Observer*. http://observer.com.

a lineup of creatures at the gym. If successful in defeating the reigning champions, control of the gym then falls to whichever of the three teams the player had elected to join during the setup phase of the game. The team controlling the arena is indicated by a prominently colored "flag" on the map; the player whose Pokémon currently reign at the gym receives rewards for each day they manage to maintain control. Above is a "macro" level, user-created map of the gyms in New York City, one which the player themselves would never see in-game because of the physical distance separating gyms (they would likely be able to see at most two or three at a single time from within the game's map view).

Compare the above map with the following one, which appeared in a Japanese propaganda booklet—*A 1942 Declaration for Greater East Asian Co-operation*—used in Japan's Asian and Pacific colonies and occupied

Figure 5.5. A cartoon-like illustration of the Greater East Asia Co-Prosperity Sphere titled "Japan Stood Up" from a wartime propaganda booklet. James Orr, Yayoi Koizumi, and Zeljko Cipris (trans.), "A 1942 Declaration for Greater East Asian Cooperation," Asia-Pacific Journal 6, no. 3 (March 2008): http://apjjf.org.

私タチノ　ダイトウア　ヲ、私

タチノ　手ニ　カヘサウト、

日本ハ　立チ　アガリマシタ。

ソシテ、ツヨイ　日本グンハ、

テキヲ　ダイトウア　カラ

オヒハラヒマシタ。

territories. This map is essentially a visual representation of the foreign policy plan that came to be known in English as the "Greater East Asia Co-Prosperity Sphere" (hereafter GEA): Japan's vision of a pan-Asian military and economic bloc freed of Western imperialist powers and based on a policy, as outlined in a series of official declarations and radio addresses beginning in 1940, of "mutual respect" for each Asian country's "sovereignty and independence."[57]

The visual narrative of racial and spatial unity constructed by this map offers a reflection of how imperial Japan saw the world and its relation to that world: what we might call its cognitive map, if nations can be said to have such things.[58] The map's scale extends not to the entire globe but only to a circumscribed Asian region—with a particular focus on China, Southeast Asia, and the Philippines—within which Japan itself is represented as a literally marginal figure. Such artistic choices, in visually eliminating the "egological ethnocentrism" of Western imperialist cartography—in which one's own nation is depicted at the center of the map—deliberately underscore the image of Japan not as a colonizer but as a regional "friend" and liberator. Although the appearance of Japanese flags makes clear that such "liberation" simultaneously involves a transfer of ownership, the minute size of these flags in comparison to the more prominent ones representing each Asian country constructs an ideal vision of sovereign unity rather than forcible annexation. (Compare this to the depiction of Taiwan and Korea, which are simply filled in with red to communicate their status as geographic extensions of the Japanese landmass.) What we see in this strikingly "cute" cartographic representation is thus the naturalization of the GEA's distorted logic of colonization as liberation: the substitution of individual sovereignty for collective autonomy from the West. The images of the liberated captives are disturbingly reminiscent of the relationship between Pokémon trainer Ash Ketchum and his loyal captive Pikachu—the latter of whom, per Kline and colleagues, might also be understood as a representation of us, the captivated players.

The GEA was framed as an opportunity for broader "co-prosperity" that allowed each individual nation to, as Minister for Foreign Affairs Hachirō Arita put it in 1941, "display their strong points."[59] The plan for unifying so many "peoples of different races," Premier Hideki Tojo argued in 1942, thus involved not forcing them all under a single,

"Japanified" standard, but rather enabling each "to have its proper place and demonstrate its real character."[60] "Developing the creative faculties of each race," the GEA declaration suggested, would collectively "enhance the culture and civilization of Greater East Asia" as a whole.[61] Such, of course, is also the task of the Pokémon trainer and the function of the Pokémon gyms, which involve the strategic construction of a bloc of Pokémon composed of a diverse range of skills to address as many combat contingencies as possible.[62] In other words, the game rhetorically rehabilitates Japan's role from conqueror (or eugenicist) to friendly but demanding personal trainer, developing rigorous, personalized plans for the core strengthening of each individual race.[63]

The point of drawing out these parallels is to recognize how the game's dynamics—its rules and objectives, or what Bogost calls "procedural rhetoric"—make *Pokémon GO* into a "persuasive game," wherein the messy martial realities resulting from the abstract wartime ideals of "racial development" and "social evolution" could be rendered not so much "odorless" as automated and, from the average citizen's perspective, unreal.[64] The wartime policy can in fact be seen more broadly as a source for the game's logic of glocalization. The GEA was ostensibly about maintaining the sovereignty of individual nations and respecting "local cultural differences" through puppet governments—that is, creating a two-part system of Japanese administration on the one hand and "indigenous" national culture on the other. In *Pokémon GO*, we see a conceit that similarly involves the lamination of real and virtual worlds. Yet the GEA illustrates the danger of such conceits: while the doubling of the world can be seen, on the one hand, as an expansion into an exciting frontier of discovery, it can also be seen as the imposition of a newly oppressive set of standards for representing and navigating the world.[65]

Rebranding the Past

Attending to Pokémon GO in terms of the specificity of Japanese imperialism does not diminish earlier insights into its Orientalist functions in the U.S. context—wherein, as we noted, it has been assimilated into a U.S.-specific version of New World manifest destiny. Rather, the multiple national contexts in which the game has successfully functioned attests to the bidirectional and complex possibilities of such reorienting discourses. Indeed, reappropriating Orientalist perceptions into empowering nationalistic rhetoric has arguably been a hallmark of Japanese marketing both at home and abroad. As historian Daniel Sneider notes, despite "the gradual disappearance of the generation that actually experienced the war . . . the younger generation in Northeast Asia seems even more imbued with the ideology of nationalism than those who went through [the war]."[66] Such proxy nationalism has been coincident with Japan's aggressive postwar efforts to rebrand itself in the eyes of the world.

Since the early 2000s, Japan has launched a series of "pop culture diplomacy" campaigns in response to a 2003 Japanese Agency for Cultural Affairs directive, which proclaimed that "in the twenty-first century, 'soft power,' which is the capacity to attract foreign nations by the appeal of lifestyle and culture of the nation, is more important than military power. Japan as the nation rich in attractive cultures is expected to make an international contribution through international cultural exchange and actively display the 21st century model of soft power."[67] "International cultural exchange" was, however, no more a genuine objective than "co-prosperity" was in the GEA. As Koichi Iwabuchi notes, campaigns like "Kūru Japan" (Cool Japan), which pressed characters like Hello Kitty and Doraemon into service as official tourism ambassador and Olympics ambassador respectively, were always conceived of as a one-way street. The intention was never exchange but influence: to, as Iwabuchi puts it, make "other countries more receptive to Japan's positions through the dissemination of the country's cultures and values."[68] "Cool Japan" has been widely discussed in American media and scholarship as an effort to alter Euro-American audiences' techno-Orientalist perceptions of Japan of a late twentieth-century vintage, especially the image of the round-the-clock 1970s Japanese businessman associated with Japan's postwar "economic miracle."[69] Yet, the strategic transformation of the country's national image "from a land that is strange and workaholic to someplace that is humane and cool" was also—as the term "humane" suggests—propelled by a need to soften anti-Japanese sentiment among those East and Southeast Asian countries who had been brutalized by its expansionist ambitions through atrocities that Japan has at times downplayed or even denied.[70]

Video games have played a prominent role in authorizing these acts of national rebranding and historical revisionism. During the closing ceremony of the 2016 Summer Olympics held in Rio de Janeiro, a clever commercial segment featured Japan's prime minister, Shinzō Abe, "morphing" into Super Mario and drilling his way into the Maracanã stadium, emerging from a cartoonish drain pipe clutching a huge red soccer ball reminiscent of those used to capture Pokémon (fig. 5.6). While the majority of American media accounts of the event described it as a "cute" publicity stunt to announce the formal officiation of Tokyo as the 2020 Olympics host, Japanese responses consistently framed Abe's performance as a continuation of the "Cool Japan" campaign, and hence a comment on Japan's past rather than its future. In a much-shared tweet posted after the closing ceremony, a Japanese user edited an image of the classic "warp zone" screen from the Nintendo *Mario Bros.* game, through which players could travel instantaneously to other levels (and, Abe, in the Olympics advertisement, from Shibuya to Rio). The tweeted image was framed as a sort of visual backstory to the Olympics ad, renaming the three drainpipe "portals" as "Prime Minister's Office," "Yasukuni (Shrine)," and "Rio" (fig. 5.6). "Prime Minister, you managed not to make a mistake," the accompanying caption read: a reference to the long-standing controversy over Yasukuni, a Shinto shrine commemorating, among the nation's war dead from the imperial period (1867–1951), over one thousand convicted war criminals. Although Abe has not matched the frequency of personal visits to Yasukuni for which his predecessor, Junichiro Koizumi, received global disapprobation, his biannual *masakaki* (sacred tree) offerings to the shrine have continued to stir up enmity, particularly in South Korea and China.

The tweet, in drawing for its critique of Abe on the same ludic conceit used by the advertising campaign itself to promote him, further draws our attention to the powerful yet often overlooked political intimacies between Japanese video games and Japanese World War II–era history. That is, if the tweet used the Mario game to emphasize parallels between Abe Mario's Rio performance and Prime Minster Abe's conservative attitude toward Japan's wartime past, the Rio performance itself can be understood, in contrast, as an attempt to use the Nintendo franchise to *erase* that wartime connection. Viewed in that light, the spectacular

Figure 5.6. "Abe Mario" August 21, 2016, tweet by @sazanami_kyodai: "Prime Minister, you managed not to make a mistake." Image and translation courtesy of Mokoto Rich, "A Morning Surprise for Japan: Shinzo Abe as Super Mario," *New York Times*, August 22, 2016.

transformation of Abe into Mario functions as a counterpart, rather than a departure from or antidote to, the controversial editing of Japanese history textbooks to revise the narrative of the nation's role in World War II, particularly regarding its treatment of enslaved "comfort women" (efforts with which Abe's conservative party has been closely associated). Like the Pokémon Jigglypuff, whose enchanting voice lulls opponents to sleep, Abe's Rio performance offered an enchanting, sanitized version of himself and of Japan that reassured even his critics: "I hate to admit it," another Japanese Twitter user confessed following the Rio commercial, "but I feel soothed by Abe Mario." Anne Allison notes that "in consuming cuteness, one expresses the yearning to be comforted and soothed."[71] As an embodiment of what Christine Yano calls "Japanese Cute-Cool," Abe Mario thus exemplified the underlying logic not simply of "Cool Japan" but also of the *kawaii* aesthetics so closely associated with the nation and its products.[72]

The absence of Pikachu in the all-star lineup of the Olympics closing ceremony—comprising Pac-Man, Captain Tsubasa, Hello Kitty, Doraemon, and of course Mario—was one which the promo creators later rued. The planning committee had been formed in early 2016, several months before *Pokémon GO* became a global sensation and hence over a decade since the franchise had enjoyed significant overseas success.[73] Otherwise, the adorable Pokémon would have been an obvious choice. Indeed, the franchise's seamless bridging of national and consumer marketing had, during the first wave of "Pokémania" in the late 1990s, already provided the satirical grist for one of the most well-known episodes of the American animated television series *South Park*. In the November 1999 installment, which was later nominated for an Emmy, the fourth-grade protagonists' obsession with the "strange-looking" but adorable "Chinpokomon" is initially dismissed by their parents as a harmless fad . . . until it's revealed that the creatures are part of a nefarious plot by the Japanese government to "once again become a dominant world power" by subliminally converting American children into loyal subjects ready to bomb Pearl Harbor.

The episode is a brilliant example of the show's well-deserved reputation for both pointed and prescient critique. Deliberately written to "skewer the irrational paranoia of American parents" over their children's preoccupation with all things Pokémon, the episode's creators ramped up the perceived malevolence of the franchise by imaginatively inventing sophisticated technology that would not be possible for over a decade—but, essentially, the very technology which would be used in *Pokémon GO*. Thus, in the episode, Pokémon toys serve as vehicles for Japanese nationalist rhetoric—quite literally becoming the plush hosts for tiny speakers and spy cameras embedded within, broadcasting from and streaming back to Tokyo. The satellite technology functions as an analogue to the creatures' disarming cuteness; together, they form a simultaneously political and economic strategy that transforms American

Figure 5.7. "Emperor Hirohito" from *South Park* "Chinpokomon" episode and Shinzō Abe dressed as Mario at 2016 Summer Olympics closing ceremony in Rio de Janeiro. "Chinpokomon," *South Park*, directed by Trey Parker and Eric Stough, written by Trey Parker, broadcast on Comedy Central, November 3, 1999; photo of Abe by Stoyan Nenov.

children into brainwashed robots. The "Chinpokomon training camp" they clamor to attend turns out to be, in fact, a kamikaze flight school. As the children's droning consumerist chant—"I must buy Chinpokomon, I must buy Chinpokomon"—transitions seamlessly to "I must destroy the USA, I must destroy the USA," the episode captures both the absurdity and the sobering reality of the mutually reinforcing mechanisms of nationalist propaganda and entertainment product marketing.

The image of a battle-garbed "Emperor Hirohito," flanked by life-size images of Chinpokomon (fig. 5.7), revealing before an arena of enchanted Colorado schoolchildren his nefarious plans to take revenge on the United States for the "shame" it inflicted on Japan during World War II, acquires an entirely new and disturbing resonance when seen in light of Abe Mario. In the middle of Hirohito's speech, Eric Cartman turns to his friends with a rare look of uncertainty and asks, "Is this cool or not? I can't tell."

The diptych in figure 5.7 above encapsulates what Anne Allison has eloquently described as the mutually constitutive relation between "the products Japan is selling—and using to sell itself."[74] The product we have been examining—*Pokémon GO*—is not simply a product being sold but a story being told, a game being played with national spaces and histories. Satisfying both nostalgia and narcissism, the novel augmented reality and mapping strategies of *Pokémon GO* at once expand and obscure our ability to "place" the origins of, and orient ourselves in relation to, the value-laden representations such technologies implicitly authorize.

Laura Kurgan has suggested that maps "let us see too much, and hence blind us to what we cannot see, imposing a quiet tyranny of orientation."[75] Although Kurgan here echoes postcolonial scholars like Said, Charles Mills, and V. Y. Mudimbe in understanding cartography as a seemingly neutral technology that constructs and legitimizes hegemonic projects of "epistemological ethnocentrism," she also hints at the "localizing" tactics through which maps achieve their aims.[76] Maps both "omit, according to their conventions, those invisible lines of people, places, and networks that create the most common spaces we live in today"—that is, they erase, by failing to represent, the social fault lines or clusters created by nodes of race, class, religion, et cetera—and "blind us to what we cannot see": they erase the very fact of their erasure.[77] Mapping, in this sense, reproduces the logic of glocalized rebranding, wherein the active production of non-Japaneseness as odorlessness has become a telltale sign of Japanese products themselves. *Pokémon GO* becomes a ludic vehicle through which Japan constructs its own magic circle, imaginatively authoring alternative representations of itself whose correspondence to historical reality becomes secondary to their cuteness.

We began this chapter with the kinship between playing and mapping; we end by emphasizing how marketing completes the family portrait. Maps are marketing tools, in the sense that they license (i.e., "sell") a particular version of reality; marketing is also a form of mapping, reorienting one's perspective on the global and the local, the foreign and the familiar, the medium and the message. These processes occur within but also through play: they can give play its pleasure and its form, and vice versa. *Pokémon GO* shatters the illusion of playing, mapping, and selling as discrete, or at least categorically dissimilar, endeavors—and alongside these, the binaries of nations and corporations, world and game, ideology and technology. But what it most effectively demonstrates, in the end, is how the ludic can transform what might appear to be precarious fictions into powerfully enduring worldviews that fundamentally shape the way we perceive—and what we perceive as—reality.

The Catch

Free Labor

6

Game Over?

Internet Addiction, Gold Farming, and the Race Card in a Post-Racial Age

Since the gold farmers started to show,
Don't wanna know what's in the egg roll.
And they keep comin' back cuz you're givin' them dough.
Take one down and I felt inspired,
Corpse camp until this Chinaman gets fired.
That's one farmer they'll have to replace,
Not supposed to be here in the first place.
—"Ni Hao (A Gold Farmer's Story)," a fan-made *World of Warcraft* music video

The shifts we have seen over the last century in conceptions of the ludic, on the one hand, and of Asian bodies and spaces, on the other, are inextricable not only from one another but from broader historical shifts in economic, social, and international relations. Gamification and racialization do not merely reflect, but also shore up and at times subvert, larger projects of nation building, lawmaking, technological development, artistic expression, warfare, and many others, all of which are themselves informed by the value-creating machinery of economic production and consumption.

We should not be surprised, then, to find ludo-Orientalist rhetoric coming to the fore at a moment of national identity crisis: to find, as twenty-first-century Americans struggle to come to terms with their country's eclipsed position in the international arena following China's meteoric rise, portents in popular media of a mass "exodus to the virtual world" and celebrations of online gaming, in particular, as the invigorating remedy for a "broken" reality.[1] At a more abstract level, we take refuge in the presumed superiority of our ludic ideals: U.S. higher education is touted as the international standard for prizing freethinking, creativity, and intellectual curiosity, and hence still the premier destination for Chinese international students raised in a system that prioritizes rote learning and memorization. And when it comes to international relations, we use the language of games to regain the moral high ground, drawing on the magic circle to patch the holes in our fantasies of sovereignty. We may no longer be the star player, but we can still be the referee keeping the new superstar in check. For example, in China, President Barack Obama lamented during his 2015 address on transpacific trade agreements: "The rules are unfair. The playing field is uneven."[2]

The best solution of all, then, is "to make sure America writes the rules of the global economy": to be not just a rule enforcer but a rule maker. He who has the gold, as the saying goes, makes the rules; but the next best thing, when one no longer has the gold, is to make the rules for the circulation and taxation of that gold. Hence the president's curious observation that "when the rules are fair, we win every time." Fairness, in short, becomes America's currency in the ideological economy. Such is the move that Obama promises will keep us in the game, "strengthen[ing] our hand overseas by giving us the tools to open other markets to our goods and services and make sure they play by the fair rules we help write." For he who makes the rules, in the end, determines whether they are fair.

Reorienting ourselves to this new role in the game has, by the now-familiar rules of ludo-Orientalism, also meant re-Orientalizing Asia. If the United States is both rule maker and enforcer, China is now more than ever figured as the rule breaker, the cheater defined by a refusal to play fair: to respect international rules for trade and manufacture as well as those concerning the value of human life in terms of labor laws; or to maintain the presumed sanctity of human rights, particularly regarding free speech and access to information. Chinese, and Asians more broadly, are once again associated with the "dark" side of gaming, with the Chinese government's official designation of "internet addiction" as a mental disorder plaguing adolescent gamers providing an entrée for the United States to rail against the nation's "overreaction" while pathologizing Asians more broadly in just such terms. Since 2008, sensational tales about Asian "web junkies" have become regular fodder for American and British media, who tell of Chinese teenagers allegedly beaten to death at a draconian boot camp for internet addicts; of a South Korean man who played the online game *StarCraft* for five days straight until he dropped dead in his chair; of a Chinese teenager who murdered his parents after they prevented him from going to the internet café.[3]

These tales have not been restricted to mass media, however. In 2010, the American Psychiatric Association released a draft of the fifth edition of the *Diagnostic and Statistical Manual of Mental Disorders* (*DSM-V*), proposing a radical restructuring of the "substance-related disorders" chapters under the new title "Substance-Related and Addictive Disorders." This new chapter would include not only substance dependence and abuse, but "behavioral addictions" like gambling addiction, with the possible addition of a new, separate entry on "Internet Gaming Disorder." Much of the subsequent debate in the medical community centered around the reintroduction of the term "addiction," which struck many as overly stigmatizing and even "potentially harmful" to the future occupational, marital, and financial prospects of any individual so diagnosed. While many critics of the proposed changes further used gaming addiction as a prime example of how "loose" and "indiscriminate" the term "addiction" had become, for the *DSM-V* editors, the driving factor delaying Internet Gaming Disorder from official inclusion was instead that, despite being the focus of "considerable literature [which] does describe many underlying similarities to substance addictions," the disorder yet lacks "a standard [epidemiological] definition" based on "an understanding of the natural histories of the cases."[4]

That the cases in question were at that time almost exclusively young Asian males is a fact the editors made much of, noting that not only had the majority of research been conducted by and about Asians but that "Internet gaming has reportedly been defined as an 'addiction' by the Chinese government." Thus, while "the seemingly high prevalence rates, both in Asian countries and, to a lesser extent, in the West, justified inclusion" in the *DSM-V*, the editors hastily added that since their own description of the condition was adapted from a Chinese study, "conservative definitions ought to be used . . . until the optimal criteria and threshold for diagnosis are determined empirically."[5] Certainly the *DSM-V*'s own brand of conservatism seems clear in the editors' insistent classification of gaming addiction as an "Eastern" disorder, going so far as to note that "it has been speculated that Asian environmental and/or genetic background is [a] risk factor, but this remains unclear."

The *DSM-V*'s interest in tying Internet Gaming Disorder to cultural or even biological differences is a familiar refrain in the longer tradition of racial pathology stretching over two centuries. This has included not only the historical pathologization of race itself as indicative of various social and moral perversions or defects but also the intimate association between substance abuse and minority communities, particularly those latter whose poverty and limited social mobility have been the direct result of long-standing, systemically maintained inequalities. The *DSM-V* yoked Internet Gaming Disorder to "Asianness" in the same terms that crack cocaine use was once yoked to black Americans.[6] And it reflects a similar tactic of racial displacement: despite the *DSM-V*'s suggestion that the "West" trails behind in internet addiction, many American researchers have argued that this apparent disparity merely reflects a comparative lack of government action, not a paucity of American sufferers.[7]

In an effort to settle the controversy, the American Psychiatric Association Substance-Related Disorders Work Group put out a call for research on Internet Gaming Disorder's "prevalence, validity . . . , diagnostic criteria, and cross-cultural reliability and criteria." The most recent and widely cited of these, titled "Internet Gaming Disorder: Investigating the Clinical Relevance of a New Phenomenon," aggregated the results of "the first large-scale studies, to our knowledge, of Internet gaming disorder guided by an open-science approach and grounded in APA criteria."[8] The study's authors found the prevalence rate of the disorder to be quite low, at most around 1 percent in young adults and 0.5 percent among all adults. Many Western players, the authors observed, "may experience a feature of Internet gaming disorder, for example, a preoccupation with a new game that distracts from other responsibilities. Much in the same way a sports fan might feel distracted at work if his or her team reaches the finals, feeling this way may be typical among those for whom gaming is a favored hobby. Such experiences are not necessarily pathological if unaccompanied by significant distress"—or, perhaps, the aggravating risk factor of being Asian. The study ends on a finger-wagging note: "Internet-based games are currently one of the most popular forms of leisure, and researchers studying their potential 'darker sides' must be cautious."[9]

We might offer a similar warning, however, to those researchers who, like the authors of this article, have looked only at the lighter—which is to say whiter—sides of gaming. Whereas the previous studies cited by the *DSM-V* had been overwhelmingly drawn from youth in Asian countries, the four aggregated in this article were composed exclusively of adults from the United Kingdom, the United States, Canada, and—to ensure "cross-cultural robustness"—Germany. Huizinga, no doubt, would have appreciated the study's methodological integrity and its implicit affirmation of the enduring rightness of his conclusions that, despite globalization's border-blurring tendencies, East Asians were still continuing their centuries-long tradition of fun-sucking hyper competitiveness, and "Westerners" in Europe and the United States their well-rounded, healthful sporting traditions. Indeed, if Asians were given only passing mention in the study's conclusion, as a possible disruptor of the overall cross-cultural "stability" of the low prevalence rates, they remain the unnamed negative analogue of this and many other studies, the "pathological" counterpart to the West's ludic "passions."

The New Yellow Peril

Medical professionals' ludo-Orientalist outsourcing of national anxieties over the seductiveness of gaming was only one move in a larger game. In 2005, American media outlets tripped over one another in a race to expose the scandalous existence of an estimated one hundred thousand Chinese "gold farmers": young, poor men (almost always they were men) who made their living playing online games like *World of Warcraft* to acquire virtual in-game currency, which would then be sold for real money to (mostly Western) players looking to accelerate the tedious "grind" of the leveling-up process. By 2009, the number of Chinese gold farmers had swelled to an estimated one million, with Chinese trade in virtual currency valued at nearly $300 million in a single year. "While the Internet has produced some strange new job descriptions over the years," observed technology writer Julian Dibbell, "it is hard to think of any more surreal than that of the Chinese gold farmer," whose very existence was taken as evidence that "something curious has happened to the classic economic distinction between play and production."[10] The dawning mainstream recognition that "play has begun to do real work," for many critics, was unlikely to remain a novelty for long. "Gold farming appears to be anything but a here today, gone tomorrow blip," argued Development Informatics scholar Richard Heeks in 2010. Heeks went so far as to suggest that "gold farming may be a glimpse into a much larger future of international, network-based development where life, work and commerce become ever more immersed in cyberspace. We could be seeing, in short, the emergence of 'development 2.0.'"[11]

Of course, the very invocation of Chinese workers as harbingers of a new world order itself puts us on firm and familiar ludo-Orientalist ground. The twenty-first-century gold farmer in fact bears a remarkable similarity to the nineteenth-century Chinese immigrant laborer, who became in the American imagination what Eric Hayot describes as "a figure for the age, an embodied metaphor for the changes prompted by modernization and the globalized trade and labor networks it permitted."[12] Amid claims in both mainstream and scholarly publications about the seeming newness of gold farming, one finds rhetoric about this twenty-first-century phenomenon that would, as we saw in chapter 1, be equally at home on the floor of Congress during 1870s exclusion debates. By 2007, gold farmers were regularly singled out for in-game harassment and violence by Western players who accused them of ruining the ecosystem. Taking a page from Bill Nye's playbook in Harte's "The Heathen Chinee," fan-made machinima (videos created from gameplay footage) and online forums framed gold farmers as morally reprehensible cheats, as "rats" and "commies" to be exterminated during carefully organized, game-wide "hunt the farmers" days. Indeed, as Nick Yee observes, it is striking how little has changed rhetorically between the physical gold mining of yore and the virtual gold farming of today: the sense of economic injustice and victimization on the part of American gamers; the vilification of gold farmers as cheats and "leeches" who care nothing for fair play; the calls for the game industry to impose stringent sanctions on or eject suspected gold farmers from the game by permanently banning their accounts.[13] In more ways than one, as the front-page New York Times article which broke the story observed, gold farming was simply "yet another new business [being made] out of cheap Chinese labor."[14] And, as it did during exclusion debates, "cheap Chinese labor" here connoted not simply an economic practice but a politically charged ludo-Orientalist discourse inextricable from broader stakes of racialization and national identity.

These stakes are captured in "Anda's Game," a 2004 short story by Canadian-British science fiction writer Cory Doctorow, centered around a bullied, overweight British tween who spends most of her time playing an unnamed *World of Warcraft*-like multiplayer online game. Upon joining "Clan Fahrenheit," a prestigious female game guild, Anda is invited on a series of mysterious missions, where she is paid real money (rather than gold, the in-game currency) for raiding and destroying a series of virtual "sweatshops" filled with gold farmers mass-producing cheap virtual clothing. Initially, Anda is jubilant in her new role meting out justice against those "earning their living by exploiting the game." The way she narrates this heroic charge, and the way her teammate Lucy justifies the killings even when they discover that the gold farmers are impoverished young girls in Mexico, is at once a reprise and a refinement of the self-justifying violence Bill Nye visited on the treacherous but "childlike" Ah Sin in Bret Harte's "The Heathen Chinee." Whereas Ah Sin was breaking the rules of euchre, these gold farmers, Lucy fumes, are "breaking the game." They earn Anda and Lucy's scorn not because they make the game too difficult, but because they make it too easy, allowing wealthy new players ("noobs") "to level-up without all the hard work." As Lucy reminds Anda, "You and me, we would never trade cash for gold, or buy a character or a weapon on eBay—it's cheating. You get gold and weapons through hard work and hard play. But those [gold farmers] spend all day, every day, crafting stuff to turn into gold to sell off on the exchange. That's where it comes from—that's where the crappy players get their gold from! That's how rich noobs can buy their way into the game that we had to play hard to get into."[15]

This raises an important question: if the real cheaters here, as even the most "hardcore" gamers like Anda and Lucy recognize, are not the impoverished gold farmers but rather their Western buyers, then why are the gold farmers the ones who "get it in the face"?[16] Although Doctorow's story makes it clear that gold farming, especially in its early years, was an international phenomenon found in Latin America and eastern Europe as well as Asia, its subsequent encoding in mainstream media as a unique feature of "cheap Chinese labor" harks back to the analogous transformation of gambling that we saw in chapter 1. For now, as then, it is not simply the economic devaluation of "cheap" racialized labor that niggles Anda and her real-life counterparts, but rather the ideological "cheapening" of the game that occurs by pathologizing it—not by making it addictive, but by assigning it economic value (i.e., turning it into work). Thus game publishers, in nineteenth-century exclusionist fashion, have strategically denounced gold farming in ethical rather than baldly economic terms: as the spokesperson for one game being farmed insisted, "Playing games should be fun and entertaining. It's not a way to trade and make money."[17]

The intersection of this ethical rhetoric with a particular racial stereotype of Chinese "heathenness"—redescribed, in the contemporary moment, as a lack of respect for the game's ideals—helps to explain the stigmatization of Chinese gold farmers specifically. As Doctorow's story reveals, hatred for gold farmers, whether Mexican, Chinese, or Romanian, is subtended by a ludic logic. In the short story, when Raymond, an in-game labor organizer, reveals to Anda and Lucy the identity of the human beings behind the generic avatars they are slaughtering, it briefly makes them reconsider their behavior toward these particular children, but not their attitude toward gold farming as a whole. Indeed, Lucy's sympathy vanishes the moment Raymond frames the practice in pragmatic terms of subsistence and economic necessity—"if they don't play, they don't eat"—because it reinforces her conviction that "they don't care about the game. . . . To them, it's just a place to suck a buck out of. They're not players, they're leeches, here to suck all the fun out."

In 2014, "Anda's Game" was adapted into a graphic novel collaboration between Doctorow and Chinese American artist Jen Wang. Titled *In Real Life*, the book reflected the shift that had taken place over the intervening decade since the original short story: now, the gold farmers were not Mexican girls but Chinese teenage boys. And the rhetoric had become more aggressive, as well: now the gold farmers were not just "leeches" but mindless machines to be systematically exterminated. Indeed, *In Real Life* yokes the farmers' systematic, repetitive labor practices to the visual similarity of their generic avatars, merging the racial stereotypes of Asians as "robotic" and "all looking the same" into the figure of the game "bot," a piece of third-party software commonly used to automate gameplay in *World of Warcraft* and other massively multiplayer online games. The graphic novel drives this home far more

36

Figure 6.1. Anda's first in-game encounter with Chinese gold farmers. From *In Real Life* © 2014 by Cory Doctorow. Illustrations © 2014 by Jen Wang. Reprinted by permission of First Second, an imprint of Roaring Brook Press, a division of Holtzbrinck Publishing Holdings Limited Partnership. All rights reserved.

effectively than does the original short story: the gold farmers are represented as a Lilliputian horde of tiny, androgynous humanoids, garbed identically in what seems intended to be read as a "traditional" costume of East Asian origin (light-colored kimono, cloth boots, and a triangular hat; see fig. 6.1). When Anda (now rewritten as an American) cries, "Are you players or bots?" they huddle mutely in response: except for one pathetic creature, who emits a string of encoded characters—等一下! 請不要 . . .—before being eviscerated.[18]

Assuming, from their lack of both verbal and physical response, that the creatures are simply automated software, Anda begins to see herself, in turn, as a living ad-blocker, "fighting spam" for pay.[19] In this version of the story, her self-empowerment as a "soldier" essentially derives from her perception of herself as a glorified American referee of just the sort described at the beginning of this chapter. Blizzard, the American company responsible for *World of Warcraft*, had itself during this same period begun to take an increasingly intolerant stance against botting (the use of bots) as a form of cheating in violation of the game's terms of use. In a May 2016 post on the game's official website, Blizzard announced that it had begun to ban thousands of accounts found to be using bots and encouraged "real" players to report suspected bots. "We're committed to providing an equal and fair playing field for everyone in World of Warcraft," they wrote. "Cheating of any kind will not be tolerated."[20]

In *In Real Life*, the nature of that cheating—the crime that the gold farmers are as guilty of as the buyers—is made far more explicit. From one perspective, gold farmers, as Dibbell and others have noted, simply satisfy a demand created by wealthy players. But from another view—that which we saw taken by Bill Nye during Chinese exclusion debates—gold farmers could arguably be said to have *necessitated* the rule-breaking act of gold buying on the part of Western players. That is, while game publishers condemned gold farmers for "making money" at what should be "fun," the real crime was that they were making money meaningful in what was supposed to be a disinterested space, in the sense Huizinga and Caillois used that term. The magic circle was not simply where "real" money should not be made, but where money itself—at least, what it signified outside the game, "in real life"—should have none of the significance it normally would. This nullification or substitution of value is, indeed, part of what games are supposed to do by transmuting money from a unit of exchange value into a mere functional object (i.e., its utility value). This is simply the flip side of the role of money in gambling games discussed in chapter 3, where money was merely one among many possible options—from matchsticks to one's own life—of stakes for which to play. In the "free" games we have been discussing in part II of this book, likewise, money acquires a different meaning: a quarter becomes not something to be spent but a simple machine for generating randomness and fairness, as in a coin flip, or a substitute for a lost checker or game piece.

By implicitly invoking such "rules of irrelevance," as Erving Goffman has dubbed them, games are thus presumed to enforce their disinterested, meritocratic, level playing field. They nullify the differences between rich and poor: everybody, regardless of how much money or status they possess beyond the game, ostensibly has exactly equal chances of winning. This "imaginary universe," as Pierre Bourdieu described it, is one without "heredity," in which "every soldier has a marshal's baton in his knapsack, and every prize can be attained . . . by everyone."[21] Such a fantasy is, of course, what games are thought to imbue with a material reality: this is, presumably, part of the pleasure we obtain from playing them. But the lived experience can match the imaginary one only so long as economic and social considerations have absolutely no bearing whatsoever on gameplay, and what happens in the magic circle truly stays within the magic circle: which is to say, never. What we learned in chapter 4 about the interdependence of the magic circle and the particular temporal and spatial coordinates of the one defining the magic circle is also true here. To take an example from Goffman's analysis: if one's boss is on the opposing team, the savvy employee is likely to give up an in-game victory in the hopes of currying the employer's out-of-game favor, or at least to diminish the odds of any out-of-game reprisals.

Are We the Gold Farmers?

If traditional parlor games or athletic competitions were played in physical proximity among players with a complex web of relational obligations and constraints, the explosive mainstream popularity of online multiplayer games like *Ultima Online* and *EverQuest* in the 1990s seemed to solve that problem: now, players could remain wholly anonymous and interact with those on opposite sides of the globe. Gold farmers, however, shattered the illusion—for it was, at heart, still just an illusion—of the magic circle as one of the last truly meritocratic realms in modern life. In games like *World of Warcraft*, with their own sophisticated secondary economies, "rich" and "poor"—as defined in terms of a player's in-game gold or the quality and rarity of their equipment—were supposed to correspond to the amount of time the player had invested in playing the game and leveling up their character. "Class" and "race," too, ostensibly did not correspond to their real-world meanings, instead merely distinguishing between a player's choice to play as a Rogue or a Hunter, a Human or an Orc.[22] But gold farmers allowed the economic meaning of class to migrate and signify within the game itself. When Anda visits a Chinese gold farming exchange website, she is agog at the fact that people can buy, for a few hundred dollars, a high-level avatar or in-game item when "people spend *months* trying to earn that much gold. How is this fair?"[23]

What is not fair in the game, of course, is also exactly what is not fair in the world outside the game. But the notion that there is, or at least should be, an inherent difference between the two is part of what keeps us playing both games. For, as digital culture scholar Scott Rettberg points out, games like *World of Warcraft* are designed to offer "players a capitalist fairytale in which anyone who works hard and strives enough can rise through society's ranks and acquire great wealth."[24] Thus has online gaming become the twenty-first-century torchbearer of the American dream, as inextricable from Asian bodies and spaces now as it was a century ago. Asian Americans have been instrumental in maintaining—and equally susceptible to—the myth that American life is a game in the most positive sense, following a mathematic logic where, as science fiction writer Charles Yu put it, "success must be in direct proportion to effort exerted."[25] Chinese gold farmers, in short, were vilified for precisely the same reason that the model minority was celebrated: their role in shaping the national imagination.

This is why the most common explanation for gold farmers' vilification found in game studies scholarship and popular narrative—that of racial scapegoating—is, as Colleen Lye has suggested of scapegoat theories more broadly, of limited use in understanding why Asians, specifically, occupy this role.[26] For Doctorow, what matters about gold farming is not the historical particularity of Asian racialization but the universality of class struggles. The antagonism between gold farmers and "Western" players, from his perspective, is simply the latest episode in the long-running history of "rich assholes" playing "different underclasses off against one another." "Think of how handily Detroit's auto-workers were distracted from GM's greed when they were given Mexican free-trade-zone labor to treat as a scapegoat," he writes in the story's introduction. "The American worker's enemy isn't the Mexican worker, it's the auto manufacturer who screws both of them. They fought NAFTA instead of GM, and GM won."

"Anda's Game" ultimately attempts to resist this ludic logic as well as its racialized outlets by revealing that it's not the adolescent gold farmers but rather their employers, the owners of these "virtual sweatshops," who are "the real enemy"—and, more importantly, a common one. The anagnorisis of the story involves a literal revelation of this commonality: Anda discovers that the funding for her mercenary activities comes not from "some Saudi or Japanese guy or Russian mafia kid who's so rich that . . . he's paying us to mess around with some other rich person," but rather from the owners of rival gold farming factories. Raymond, the authorial proxy, drives the point home: "You're being paid cash to kill [the gold farmers]. . . . You need to play for your money, too. I think that makes you and them the same, a little the same." Seeking to "square up the age-old fight for rights for oppressed minorities in the rich world with the fight for the rights of the squalid, miserable majority in the developing world," "Anda's Game" implores us, like Anda, to see these two endeavors not as antagonistic but interdependent.

Certainly it's true, as we saw in the last chapter, that "Western" players are not exempt from ludic exploitation. Although it rarely unfolds in so overt a fashion as in the story, we arguably perform our fair share of "playbor" (a portmanteau of "play" and "labor") on a daily basis, with ostensibly "free" games like *Pokémon GO* serving as the compensation for the streams of valuable data we provide while playing. Even beyond freemium games and gamified apps like Yelp or Fitbit, one could argue—as Alexander Galloway and many critics in media studies have—that anybody now plugged into a network is performing "digital labor," and that what we are seeing is a problem of "informationalized capitalism," a post-Fordist transformation of "seemingly normal human behavior into monetizable labor."[27] Those at the top—Google, Amazon, the rest of the new GMs—do indeed "spider us and mine us, extracting value from pure information." Hence Galloway's argument that "no longer simply a blogger, someone performs the necessary labor of knitting networks together. No longer simply a consumer, browsing through links on an e-commerce site, someone is offloading his or her tastes and proclivities into a data-mining database with each click and scroll."[28]

This apparently new erosion of the labor-leisure division has, as we've learned, been theorized since the late nineteenth century, although it has drawn especial attention in the postwar years. In the twenty-first century, the concept has taken the name of "gamification," a term that, not coincidentally, entered the vernacular at the very same time as gold farming controversies gained traction. Gamification is characterized as the "dysfunctional perversion" of games, to use Ian Bogost's colorful term, vis-à-vis their conversion into labor and their circulation on the economic market.[29] By emphatically redubbing gamification as "exploitationware"—that is, an insidious marketing strategy to motivate increased consumption and revenue—gamification's opponents have framed their objections in precisely the terms that players have Chinese gold farming. The difference is simply that, rather than seeing either gamification or gold farming as a distinctly "Chinese" malady, these scholars cleave to Doctorow's vision of playbor as a universal form of exploitation of which both "we" and "they" are victims.

But if, as Galloway rightly points out, "we all perform scads of unpaid micro labor," there is something equally troubling about the conclusion he ultimately draws from this premise: that "we are all gold farmers." This is simply a more succinct version of the claim made in "Anda's Game," and thus a narrative that rewards a ludic reading of the sort I have been performing throughout this book—one, that is, which attends to race and game as vehicles for making what is unfair appear fair, or in this case, what is unfair to one appear equally unfair to all. For while, like Charles Yu, Hisaye Yamamoto, and Bret Harte before him, Doctorow uses gaming to expose racially coded economic inequality, he is, like Galloway, too quick to treat racial difference as simply a distraction from the "real" issue of universal exploitation. The result is a series of narrative tactics that "cheapen" race in ways troublingly similar to the hegemonic narratives the story is intended to critique.

The parallels between games and markets, and between the gold farmers and Western players, are in the story refracted not through race but through gender: and specifically, through the figure of the adolescent female body. The game is something the Mexican gold farmers have to play in order to eat: the ultimately unsatisfying, "serious" nature of this play is reflected in the "painfully skinny," sellable bodies of the little girls. Even more disturbing, Raymond informs us, is that the gold farmers are "the lucky ones: the unlucky ones work as prostitutes"; the former merely have their avatars—their virtual bodies—sold on eBay.[30] The money Anda earns as a girl gamer produces an equally deformed corporeality, but in the other direction. Here, the money is used to satisfy a sweet tooth that makes her, in the first place, socially devalued: overweight, completely sedentary, and "unshaggable." But second, and more disturbingly, the game that is allowing Mexican girls just enough food to survive another day is killing Anda by giving her far too much food for her body to handle. Thus, Anda's in-game revelation of the gold farmers' true identity is accompanied by its out-of-game counterpart: her newfound cash has earned her a diagnosis of type 2 diabetes. The symptom? That she is, literally, turning into a colored person: afflicted with acanthosis nigricans, an insulin-related skin pigmentation disorder that involves patches of her skin becoming dark and "dirty."

If this racial parable wasn't clear (or dubious) enough on its own, Anda's subsequent reversal of the process through significant weight loss makes it unmistakable. The weight loss is, on the surface, the result of her parents' intervention: they have confiscated her computer (thereby cutting into her candy budget) and forced her to participate in extra physical education classes. But Anda also has her own reasons for avoiding the sweetshop: "When she thought about sweets, it made her think of the little girls in the sweatshop. Sweatshop, sweetshop. The sweets shop man sold his wares close to the school because little girls who didn't know better would be tempted by them. No one forced them, but they were kids and grownups were supposed to look out for kids. . . . The kids in the sweatshops were being exploited by grownups, too. It was why their situation was so impossible: the adults who were supposed to be taking care of them were exploiting them."[31] One could reasonably suggest that the limitations of this logic are the result of their inventor: a twelve-year-old girl. On the other hand, it seems equally unlikely that a twelve-year-old would also find such homophonic resemblance an opportunity for deep conceptual connections; so it seems relatively safe to surmise that the scene is intended not to showcase the analogy's limitations but its inherent truth. More important than the many important ways in which Anda's sweet tooth is not the same as the gold farmer's sweatshop labor, however, is the way that what initially appears to be a dawning empathy ultimately becomes a vehicle for self-righteous self-pity ("oh, God, she was a fat girl with diabetes"). For while the darkening of Anda's skin reflects the perception of Mexican racial difference as "brown" people, it is not Mexicans but Asians who ultimately facilitate this transition from empathy to self-absorption in the world outside the story. For Asians' oscillation between being cheaters and embodiments of fair play makes them the ideal models through which to articulate Americans' own perceived exploitation.

Galloway is right to point out that the rhetoric of gold farming itself performs "powerful ideological work within contemporary culture."[32] But if that work, in his account, is the work of mystification—to maintain the racialized illusion that "we are the free while the Chinese children are in chains"—his effort to counter this "obscenity" with the revelation that "we are all gold farmers," and this because "in the age of post-Fordist capitalism it is impossible to differentiate cleanly between play and work," must be understood as performing a reductively obfuscating work ultimately analogous to Anda's wordplay. Galloway's conclusion that our being gold farmers is "all the more paradoxical since most of us do it willingly and for no money at all" smacks of questionable logic. In the first place, like sweatshop/sweetshop, it violently flattens the differences in agency, economic context, and working conditions that separate the "invisible" and voluntary, "unpaid micro labor" of Westerners from the micro-remunerated (subsistence-level wage), ruthlessly tabulated labor of Chinese and other gold farmers. It seems to forget, in other words, that, as Nick Yee puts it, "avatars are not created equal even if all are just made of pixels."[33] But beyond that flattening is a further erasure in the form of a strange "reclaiming" of "gold farming" as a term that describes what "we," not they, do: one that Galloway frames as a teleological historical shift of post-Fordism, "migrating from a situation in which users farm for gold, to a situation in which users are being farmed."[34]

I dwell on Galloway here to emphasize how his larger, seemingly universal argument about digital labor, and game studies' claims about the "colorblindness" of technology in general, ultimately depends on a distancing and particularizing of the racialized Other—more specifically, the Asian—in order to make its claims. In flattening the distinctions between us and them—between sweatshop and sweetshop—such rhetoric naturalizes the semantic shift as reflective of a historical truth rather than a forcible annexation: thus the even narrower title of Galloway's chapter, "*We* Are the Gold Farmers." If that reveals disturbing parallels to the cartographic imperialism of the previous chapter, it also points to the broader continuity of ludo-Orientalist epistemologies in game studies that span the analog/digital gap. For "we are all gold farmers," in the end, looks an awful lot like Huizinga's comment that "all people play, and play remarkably alike; but their languages differ widely . . . conceiving it neither as distinctly nor as broadly as modern European languages do."[35] Whereas "all people," in Huizinga's account, ultimately turns out to mean Other people, in Galloway's "all" is used to exclude those non-European Others from the seemingly universal "we" (because otherwise, why would the term "all" be needed?). That is, the implication is that "we" means the West, not "all of us": "all" functions as an additive to modify the existing "them" of the gold farmers. Together, they illustrate how seemingly disparate ludic means can be made to serve analogously Orientalist ends.

In short, we see here yet another instance of Asians functioning as both peril *and* model, with the figure of the Chinese gold farmer symptomatic of a broader tendency in postmodern theories to use race as a kind of template or meme to articulate an ostensibly universal condition of exploitation. As Philip Brian Harper first observed in 1994, "The experiences of socially marginalized groups implicitly inform the 'general' postmodern condition without being accounted for in theorizations of it."[36] In the digital realm, this tendency produces an analogously silencing effect, a sense that Lisa Nakamura describes as "if we are all marginalized and decentered, or if we are all equally 'virtual' when we are in cyberspace, what need is there to refer to race at all in discussions of identity online or in a postmodern world?"[37] Nakamura rightly points out that these "racial identity plays stand as a critique of the notion of the digital citizen as an ideal cogito whose subjectivity is liberated by cyberspace. On the contrary, only too often does one person's 'liberation' constitute another's recontainment within the realm of racialized discourse."[38] While Nakamura's focus is on the Orientalized avatars and online worlds through which Western players are invited to indulge in a kind of "identity tourism," literary artifacts like "Anda's Game" further demonstrate how cybertypes like the Chinese gold farmer allow other marginalized groups, such as female game players, to experience not liberation from the constraints of their "real-life" gender but rather an empowering sense of pride in their identities as "girl gamers."

In a dynamic that harks back to early American abolitionist and suffrage movements, white American women in *In Real Life* are depicted as possessing a "double consciousness" of their own. Like the Chinese male gold farmer, Anda is seen as analogously marginalized—as a female, and specifically as a female gamer—but also analogously constrained, being a minor subject to the whims of her parents, who hold both the purse strings and the key to her computer. Thus, in a plea to earn the gold farmers' trust, she tells them, "I don't know what it's like to live in China . . . and I don't know what it's like to be a gold farmer. But I do know what it's like to be a kid who loves video games."[39] At the same time, being an American, Anda is seen as more fortunate than her gold farming counterpart Raymond, who in the graphic novel suffers from chronic pain due to strenuous factory labor but fears incurring debt and being fired from his job if he seeks medical treatment. Anda is not only made aware of how "lucky" she is to live in a country with child labor laws and access to health insurance, but further comes to see the "liberation" of Raymond and his co-workers as a sort of white American woman's burden, not only her privilege but her duty.

The simultaneous kinship and distance Anda shares with Raymond is rendered visually explicit in the graphic novel's depiction of her adoption of a second in-game avatar following the guild's banning of her first (fig. 6.2). Anda is now, essentially, identical to the gold farmers, but with a few important differences: namely, the more obviously gendered signs of a large bun-like hairstyle/headpiece, bared arms, and colorful scarf or necklace. In her new, low-level guise, she is able to approach a gold farmer whom she initially mistakes for Raymond and discovers that her friend, upon following Anda's advice to organize and strike, has been fired and blacklisted for "instigat[ing] other employees to engage in violating company regulations"—in short, for breaking yet another set of rules. The bearer of this bad news, one of Raymond's co-workers, indulges in a rare moment of angry volubility: "Nice job, American," he spits. "You don't know anything about us. Next time stick to your own game."[40]

Figure 6.2. Anda's female "gold farmer" avatar. From *In Real Life* © 2014 by Cory Doctorow. Illustrations © 2014 by Jen Wang. Reprinted by permission of First Second, an imprint of Roaring Brook Press, a division of Holtzbrinck Publishing Holdings Limited Partnership. All rights reserved.

What we are witnessing here is the way that visual representation, narrative, and ludic theory mutually reinforce one another's racializing logic. While numerous works of scholarship in the field focus on racial representation in games—that is, the way games depict race through visual, linguistic, or behavioral signs and stereotypes—many game studies scholars have tended to flatten racial differences by understanding them as at worst distractions from and at best a sort of ventriloquist dummy for articulating the "real" issue of economic exploitation (which brings us back to the artificial binary of race and class discussed at length in chapter 3).[41] Galloway's description of the Chinese gold farmer as, essentially, a "flat" character—"an allegorical portrait for how identity exists online, a portrait not so much of the orientalized other, but of ourselves"[42]—is meant to hark back to his larger claim, developed across three monographs he collectively refers to as *Allegories of Control*, that software serves not merely as an ideological vehicle but the form through which "the ideological contradictions of technical transcoding and fetishistic abstraction are enacted and 'resolved.'" Taking a methodological cue from Frederic Jameson, Galloway's approach to allegorical interpretation valuably attends to the shifting relations and dynamic meanings that, as Jameson points out, have the potential to move us beyond traditional reading practices and "our stereotypes of some static or medieval or biblical decoding."[43] Yet Galloway's framing of race as allegory—as ideological software—also risks uncritically reproducing the ethnocentric assumptions and reductive reading practices implicit in Jameson's controversial approach to "Third World texts" as "national allegories." "Allegory" is thus an ostensibly universal—that is, abstract—critical theory about "how identity exists" today, except that this identity is implicitly coded as Western.

Gaming technologies allow us to flatten not only racial differences but the difference between different kinds of unfairness by tyrannically imposing the same definition of fairness for every situation. That is, if Chinese gold farmers initially seemed to *create* the problem by making the game unfair for all, they also provided the discursive vehicle for us to resolve that problem: first, by making it *our* problem—*We* are the gold farmers—and second, by imposing the kind of ludic soft power at work in President Obama's speech about transpacific trade: by making what is fair for us appear to be fair for everybody. (Hence Anda's naïve presumption that what worked for American auto workers would, by definition, also work for Chinese gold farmers.) Internet addiction and gold farming thus ultimately emerge as two halves of the same racialized, ludo-Orientalist coin—one used in and out of game, in fields as diverse as psychiatry, international commerce, and creative writing, to racialize Asians in terms of their abnormal relation to play, and reorient ourselves accordingly. Together, these scenes form a familiar picture of Asia less as a specific place than, as with Orientalist portraits more broadly, a particular, antipodal relation: in cyberspace, to "normal" gameplay, and in the global arena, to the political, economic, and ethical standards of the "West." They are, in other words, a dyad exemplary of the game-nation intersection that this book has tracked from the side of ludic as well as national discourses. Gold farming and internet addiction underscore how nation making and race making play out in seemingly colorblind, global digital spaces, and how the allegorical logic that governs these virtual worlds, in turn, works to shore up the compelling fictions through which the "real world" maintains its identity and its authority.

ACKNOWLEDGMENTS

```
F   A   R   V   B   N   A   L   A   H   W   U   C   E   S
A   R   E   A   D   E   R   S   R   Y   U   K   L   I   D
N   Z   Z   Z   L   X   L   E   E   Q   S   H   B   D   M
U   R   T   Q   A   N   N   L   L   T   Y   F   C   U   J
Y   U   L   U   W   N   G   R   E   B   N   E   S   O   R
A   N   E   E   I   I   N   F   E   T   L   E   M   G   F
Q   N   S   Z   U   H   A   O   H   C   T   B   C   N   J
T   A   O   Q   O   N   H   R   W   T   A   O   O   A   S
C   M   T   S   S   L   C   D   C   D   R   S   W   K   A
S   L   R   U   G   C   M   F   Y   B   R   O   W   N   A
D   I   I   S   S   N   I   K   N   E   J   M   N   H   A
M   N   P   H   X   C   O   S   T   A   N   T   I   N   O
G   G   I   P   K   W   U   T   M   A   C   I   A   K   E
O   H   N   L   E   S   A   U   N   D   E   R   S   M   M
C   H   E   N   G   P   O   K   E   L   L   Y   Q   T   S
```

Solution on page 201.

ACKNOWLEDGMENTS (SOLUTION)

AAASJFR (Association for Asian American Studies Junior Faculty Retreat)

ARC (Americanist Research Colloquium, UCLA)

Steven BELLETTO

Kirby BROWN

CAS (College of Arts and Sciences, University of Oregon)

Roy CHAN

Edmond CHANG

Tina CHEN

Mai-Lin CHENG

Kandice CHUH

Jesús COSTANTINO

David ENG

Everyone at FBI (First Book Institute)

Marvin FICKLE

Karen FORD

Sean X. GOUDIE

Henry JENKINS

Laura Hyun Yi KANG

Daniel KIM

Rachel C. LEE

Jinqi LING

Phil MACIAK

Anita MANNUR

Mark MCGURL

MELT (Modernist/Experimental Literature Colloquium, UCLA)

Michael NORTH

Brendan O'KELLY

OHC (Oregon Humanities Center, University of Oregon)

Dolma OMBADYKOW

Chris PATTERSON

Paul PEPPIS

Mark QUIGLEY

My two anonymous READERS

Dan ROSENBERG

Ben SAUNDERS

Mark SELTZER

Shu-mei SHIH

Stephen SOHN

Brian Kim STEFANS

Marina SUING

Karen TONGSON

David VAZQUEZ

Priscilla WALD

Sarah WALD

Mark WHALAN

Betsy WHEELER

Eric ZINNER

NOTES

INTRODUCTION

1 Omari Akil, "*Pokémon GO* Is a Death Sentence If You Are a Black Man," *Medium*, July 7, 2016, www.medium.com. See also the October 21, 2016, special issue of *In Media Res* devoted to scholarly appraisals of the game.

2 Schiller, *On the Aesthetic Education of Man*, 107.

3 This shift is indicative of a dialectical movement regarding the issue of representation in game studies over the last dozen years. Recently, one has witnessed an interesting return to issues of identity and representation in video games, following a shift toward game actions and procedural rhetorics at the end of the first decade of the twenty-first century, itself arguably part of a broader interest in interface and hardware and software studies taking place in the field of media studies (see Anna Everett's foreword to *Gaming Representation* for a valuable historical account of these developments). Unfortunately, the shift in game studies from visual (as well as textual and auditory) on-screen representations to in-game player actions and game worlds, while deeply generative from a (neo-)formalist standpoint, has in many cases led to an increasingly abstract focus on issues of realism and rhetoric at the expense of more concrete investigations of how, precisely, race is "transcoded" (Lev Manovich's term) into game actions rather than merely represented within game worlds. As Everett, in her foreword, asks, "Has the trend towards code analysis and platform studies inadvertently worked to silence, marginalize, or dismiss representational analysis in the field? . . . Are we at a moment when 'representation,' 'diversity,' and 'identity' have become dirty words in game studies?" (1). For earlier examples, see Šisler, "Digital Arabs"; Shaw, *Gaming at the Edge*; Taylor, *Play between Worlds*; and Kafai et al., *Beyond Barbie and Mortal Kombat*. See also Everett's aptly titled chapter "Serious Play: Playing with Race in Contemporary Gaming Culture" in *Digital Diaspora*.

4 See Nakamura, *Cybertypes*, for a compelling discussion of how this racialized experience of disorientation has been reappropriated to construct a portrait of the internet user in the postmodern age. See also Harper, *Framing the Margins*, for a broader theorization of this "e-racing" tendency in postmodernist notions of culture and knowledge formation.

5 The presence of Asians in video games, which has historically been analyzed in terms of exotifying stereotypes of racial Others, is discussed in detail in part II of this book. For a discussion of how Asian diasporic identity and racial dynamics

have functioned in cyberspace more broadly (i.e., the internet as a whole beyond the subset of online gaming), see the rich tradition of scholarship set in motion by Lisa Nakamura's *Cybertypes*, *Digitizing Race*, and *Race after the Internet* (with Peter Chow-White); Rachel C. Lee and Sau-Ling Cynthia Wong's edited collection *AsianAmerica.net*; and Wendy Chun's *Control and Freedom*.

6 See Lye's *America's Asia* and "Racial Form."

7 Chang, "Queergaming." See also discussions of "voice-activated racism" in Nakamura, "It's a Nigger in Here! Kill the Nigger!"; Shiu, "What Yellowface Hides"; Gray, *Race, Gender, and Deviance in Xbox Live*.

8 Leonard, "Not a Hater, Just Keepin' It Real," 83.

9 Hayles, "Print Is Flat, Code Is Deep."

10 Wark, *Gamer Theory*, paragraph 21. For a discussion of how this notion of a world coterminous with a gamespace has been invoked in Asian American literature, see Fickle, "American Rules and Chinese Faces," esp. 73–76.

11 Nakamura, "Afterword," 4.

12 Nakamura, 2. The term "cruel optimism" comes from Lauren Berlant's book of the same name.

13 See also Edmond Y. Chang, "Gaming Writing: Teaching (with) Video Games" (Prezi presentation, TYCA-PNW Conference, Highline Community College, Des Moines, WA, 2012), http://prezi.com. For a fascinating dissection of this methodological paradigm as it has become canonized (and subsequently critiqued) in game studies, see Murray, "Work of Postcolonial Game Studies in the Play of Culture."

14 Simmel, *Sociology of Georg Simmel*, 49.

15 Mills, *Racial Contract*, 42.

16 Bogost, *Persuasive Games*, 4.

17 Mills, *Racial Contract*, 51.

18 Beyond offering a new lens through which to read Asian American literature, then, this book uses the ludic to provide a fresh perspective on Asian American racialization as a form of *gamification*. To see race as gamified is, ultimately, to become aware of the underlying ludic logic that allows race to persist not in spite but because of its arbitrariness: that is, its socially constructed rather than biologically essential nature. The historical invention of "race" during the Enlightenment can itself be understood as a gamified process, in which certain arbitrary distinctions like skin color were perceived and thus transformed into meaningful—and legally enforceable—differences between human beings. By the late twentieth century, the reaffirmation of race's inherent arbitrariness—its status as social fiction rather than biological fact—provided the counterintuitive justification for its continued relevance in American life, with both the right and the left using such fictionality as grounds for dispensing with, or conversely augmenting, policies intended to construct a "level playing field" for those historically excluded from the game. The twenty-first century's "rediscovery" of race's biological reality in the form of genetics rather than blood quantum, while initially predicted to transform both the study of race and its social meaning, has in fact had surprisingly

little effect on either—perhaps because, like gamified structures more broadly, race is not only a fiction but a feedback system: a self-perpetuating means of recording, comparing, and motivating human beings, both in literal, quantitative terms like quotas and censuses and through the far more abstract, qualitative mechanisms of perception and affect. Gamification thus names both a critical approach to, and the existing historical phenomenon of, race as a form of social engineering.

19 For a discussion of neoliberalism in the context of video games, see Baerg, "Governmentality, Neoliberalism, and the Digital Game"; and Rey, "Gamification and Post-Fordist Capitalism." For an important discussion of this dynamic in terms of "gender uplift" in video games, see Stabile, "I Will Own You."

20 See Christopher T. Fan's recent work for an important critique of, and potential corrective to, the "antinomic Orientalism" that he sees as symptomatic of contemporary in-field discussions of techno-Orientalism. In "Techno-Orientalism with Chinese Characteristics," Fan traces how techno-Orientalism, far from being a static phenomenon or one forever "looking back" toward yellow peril–era imagery and tropes, has shifted in relation to world events, particularly the late twentieth-century trajectory of "U.S.-China interdependency," and how this evolution is evinced in an analogous shift from cyberpunk aesthetics' own "post-" turn after 1984. Finally, see Thomas Foster's incisive observations on the relationship between "technicity" and ethnicity in "Faceblindness, Visual Pleasure, and Racial Recognition."

21 Patterson, "Asian Americans and Digital Games."

22 Rivera, "Do Asians Dream of Electric Shrieks?" 67. More recently, in an important continuation of Lisa Nakamura's work on the "cybertype," Rivera examines the techno-Orientalist dynamics of World of Warcraft and considers the implications of "deriving ludic pleasure from [racial] essentialism" and the immersive ludic potential of biopower. See Rivera, "Orientalist Biopower in World Of Warcraft: Mists Of Pandaria."

23 Chun, "Introduction," 7.

24 Nick Dyer-Witheford and Greig de Peuter get at this when they eloquently describe game consoles as "not just hardware but techno-social assemblages that configure machinic subjectivities" (Games of Empire, xxxi; italics in original).

25 See Jenkins, "Game Design as Narrative Architecture"; and Aarseth, Cybertext.

26 See Castronova, Exodus to the Virtual World; and Baudrillard, Seduction.

27 Caillois, Man, Play, and Games, 11.

28 Ehrmann, "Homo Ludens Revisited," 43n4.

29 See Tuan, Forever Foreigners or Honorary Whites?

30 See also Kim, "Racial Triangulation of Asian Americans."

31 Lye, "Racial Form," 92.

32 Chan et al., Big Aiiieeeee! 2.

33 Chiang, Cultural Capital of Asian American Studies, 87.

34 Chiang, 89.

35 The basic version of the game goes like this: a writer who is by whatever means recognized as Asian American writes a novel, usually featuring an Asian cast. The novel is well received among mainstream reviewers and the general reading public. An Asian American critic writes an article that excoriates the book for its variously racist, inauthentic, factually incorrect, exotifying, self-Orientalizing, man- or woman-hating, "fake" representations of a character, place, cultural practice, et cetera. Other critics, perhaps even the writer him- or herself, mount a defense, usually one hinging on the distinction between literature and nonfiction, the meaning of artistic license, and so forth. More critics and writers join in. The winner is not usually decided until later, after the controversy has become the set piece for critical monographs published in the field over the next several years.

36 Chiang, 28.

37 For a detailed exploration of this phenomenon, refer to Ludwig Wittgenstein's discussion of language games in *Philosophical Investigations*.

38 "Rules of irrelevance" is a term Goffman first introduces in "Fun in Games," a chapter in *Encounters*.

39 See, for example, Gayatri Spivak's discussion of how feminist projects have strategically deployed the fiction of gender in Danius, Jonsson, and Chakravorty Spivak, "An Interview with Gayatri Chakravorty Spivak."

40 Huizinga, *Homo Ludens*, 10.

41 Bateson, *Steps to an Ecology of Mind*, 188.

42 Bateson, 187–88.

43 Kingston, *Woman Warrior*, 6. See also Wong, *Reading Asian American Literature*; and Ling, *Narrating Nationalisms*. Wong makes the point that that art has historically been "perceived as antithetical to self-justifyingly 'serious' activities, which, in the Asian American context, we have come to understand as the business of survival" (166).

One would expect the field's recent interest in formalist approaches to Asian North American literature—which has valuably drawn our attention to the sophisticated language games of avant-garde poets like Myung-mi Kim, Fred Wah, and John Yau and experimental works like Theresa Cha's *Dictee* and Pamela Lu's *Pamela*—to have had a salutary effect on our historical ludic disinterest. Yet they have, ironically, exacerbated the problem: for in critical discussions of these formally innovative texts, "gaming" essentially never escapes the quotation marks. What marks a "turn" for Asian American literary studies away from historical instrumentalism, that is, also marks a turn toward the long-standing tradition in literary criticism of using the ludic to refer to a stylistic quality of diction or syntax, particularly in the postmodernist sense of the "freeplay" of endless chains of resignification. The interest in Asian American "form games," then, has been negatively correlated with an interest in games at the level of literary content (see Fickle, "English before Engrish"). The strategic force of such language games have, in short, often been grasped at the level of the sentence or paragraph: in the jocular tone a critic adopts, the turns of phrase they use, the deliberate repetition-with-a-difference of a certain string of words, or even an intentionally abstruse use of language that the reader is meant to encounter as a kind of riddle or puzzle. The term "form game" comes from Baecker, "Form Game."

44 Chua, *Battle Hymn*, afterword.

45 See Harryette Mullen's discussion of poetry and identity in *The Cracks between What We Are and What We Are Supposed to Be*.

46 Huizinga, *Homo Ludens*, 10; Kingston, *Woman Warrior*, 11.

47 Kingston, 201.

48 Wong, *Fifth Chinese Daughter*, x.

49 Yang and Pham, *Level Up*, 120.

50 Moulthrop, "Preface," xxi.

51 Literary representations of games provide an opportunity to reconsider the equivocal status of literary games more broadly. For game outcomes are, by definition, uncertain until the very end, almost always involving a degree of chance or luck—whether explicitly, as in roulette, or incidentally, as when the first-place competitor in a race accidentally trips, falls, and ends up in second. But novels are, at least according to the general definition, never undetermined. Not only are their endings usually written long before we read them, but the events in the book are determined by precisely the sort of absolute authorial license mentioned above. Hence literary critic Leland Monk's conclusion that "it is in the nature of narrative to render chance as fate so that 'what happens' in a story becomes indistinguishable from the more evaluative 'it was *meant* to happen'" (*Standard Deviations*, 8) This is, on the one hand, a pithy explanation of how racialization works more broadly: by assigning an individual's actions or qualities the status of deterministic causality, as that which does not occur by chance or accident but because of—that is, by the *design* of—one's race. But Monk's unintentional comparison of contingency to minority identity—his observation that "chance is the unrepresentable Other of narrative" (23)—suggests that, for an already Othered writer who wishes their representations to be read as nonrepresentative, there may be some critical potential to be grasped in the very attempt to represent chance events—that is, events which, like the outcome of a lottery, *cannot* be read as representative either of the winner's merit or the future of the next jackpot.

52 Wong, *Fifth Chinese Daughter*, 20. For an expanded discussion of this point, see Fickle, "Family Business."

53 Wong, 20–21.

54 Tan, *Joy Luck Club*, 33.

55 Tan, 94. Those few critics that do attend to ludic scenes like these have overwhelmingly read them as at best an extended metaphor for the intergenerational and cross-cultural conflicts that remain a hallmark of the genre, and at worst a superfluous distraction of the very sort scorned by the characters within the texts themselves. When Asian American writers *represent* games,

however, what is occurring is not a trivial flattening but in fact a *doubling* of the broader "game of representation" that Chiang describes.

56 Six-sided die are used in a range of games across the world, especially in the games of East and West: in mahjong, craps, chō-han, Yahtzee, or the Chinese game sic bo and its English variant, chuck-a-luck. But while these games all employ dice with the same number of faces that follow the same rule of opposite sides adding up to seven, there is a fundamental difference between the dice used in mahjong or sic bo and those in Yahtzee and craps: the position of the 3 and 4 faces. This difference refers to the chirality of six-sided dice, the asymmetry that distinguishes a "right-handed" die (in which the faces are arranged counter-clockwise around the vertex shared by the 1, 2, and 3) from a "left-handed" die (in which faces are arranged clockwise), in the same way that one's left hand is distinguished from one's right hand. These arrangements are, at one level, simply two different ways of maintaining the structural coherence of a six-sided die. They are, in that sense, the very same die, used to produce the same odds; and in fact, no casual player would likely ever notice the difference. But they correspond, very systematically, to enormously significant spatial and racial differences: "Western dice," as they are known, are normally right-handed; what are called "Chinese dice," on the other hand, are almost always left-handed. This "cultural" chirality has its analogue at the biochemical level, with the polarity or "handedness" of a given isomer accounting for the divergent odor and taste of foods like lemons and oranges, or caraway and mint. And it is these sorts of seemingly minor but in fact major differences that chapters 3 and 4, and indeed the whole ludic arrange-ment of the book's chapters, are intended both to illustrate and to work through by thinking about how race becomes a difference that *makes* a difference, how the seemingly irrelevant alteration of a sequence of numbers—or chapters, or mol-ecules, or zeroes and ones—can make the difference between sense and nonsense, between winning and losing in the games of life.

57 My use of "algorithmic" here and throughout cleaves to the methodological prec-edents established by scholars like Alexander Galloway, Wendy Chun, and Brian Kim Stefans, who emphasize the formally strategic logic of gaming, aesthetics, and/or racialization. See also my discussion of this term above vis-à-vis the work of Lisa Nakamura and McKenzie Wark, as well as in chapter 6.

CHAPTER 1. EVENING THE ODDS THROUGH CHINESE EXCLUSION

1 Brown, *How to Win at Poker*, 102.
2 *Report of the Joint Special Committee*, 223, 646, 228. In this document, discussions of gambling appear on twenty-eight separate occasions throughout the testimony of the 130 witnesses, who ranged from police chiefs to labor union representatives to manufacturers.
3 Brown, *How to Win at Poker*, 102.
4 I have borrowed the phrase "negative analogue" from Fabian, *Card Sharps*, 4.
5 Zorbas, *Banished and Embraced*, 98.

6 Perhaps due to the combination of the Gamblers Unions, which promised to shield its members from legal prosecution, and the prevalence of Chinatown "specials"—city police officers assigned specifically to, and paid by, Chinese American communities—the number of Chinese Americans actually arrested on gambling charges was quite low, on the order of around six over six months in 1876 San Jose; however, such laxity seemed to extend to white Americans as well, as only four were arrested on gambling-related charges in the same period. For historical accounts of early Chinese American gambling, also see Capron, *History of California*.

7 Seligman, *Tong Wars*.

8 The advent of such anti-gambling laws led to a sharp racial stratification in the gambling scene, mostly into the camps of "white" and "Chinese" gambling dens that catered almost exclusively to their own racial clientele.

9 *Report of the Joint Special Committee*, 58.

10 Culin, *Gambling Games of the Chinese*, 15.

11 Fabian, *Card Sharps*, 10.

12 *San Francisco Illustrated Wasp*, February 8, 1879, 439.

13 Fabian, *Card Sharps*, 9.

14 Kanazawa, "Immigration, Exclusion, and Taxation."

15 See the work of Shirley Hune, particularly "Politics of Chinese Exclusion."

16 Lears, *Something for Nothing*, 2–3.

17 This is true of otherwise excellent and comprehensive works like Lears's *Something for Nothing*, Fabian's *Card Sharps*, and Oriard's *Sporting with the Gods*. It is, interestingly, less the case in Canadian scholarship on Chinese immigrants; see, for example, Morton, *At Odds*, esp. 108–34.

18 *Report of the Joint Special Committee*, 823.

19 Oriard, *Sporting with the Gods*, xiii.

20 Mills, *White Collar*, 219.

21 Gleason, *Leisure Ethic*, vii.

22 Mills, *White Collar*, 236, 238.

23 *Report of the Joint Special Committee*, 1042. Thus, in various arguments against Chinese labor raised in the years leading up to exclusion, various exclusion proponents analogized Chinese labor to the black slave labor on which the South was built, the economic and moral problem over which the Civil War had been ostensibly fought. However, Chinese coolie labor was also distinguished, in important ways, from the history of African American slavery. See Phan, "Race So Different."

24 As one witness put it in the *Report of the Joint Special Committee*, "In the great struggle for existence the Chinaman will come to the top every time if left to free and equal competition" (1054).

25 *Report of the Joint Special Committee*, 251.

26 Fabian, *Card Sharps*, 3.

27 A Chinese "special" was a city police officer assigned specifically to, and paid by, Chinese American communities.

28 *Report of the Joint Special Committee*, 224, 227.

29 Culin, *Gambling Games of the Chinese*, 15.

30 Culin, 15.

31 Cong. Globe, 41st Cong., 3d Sess. 354–55 (1870).

32 Hayot, "Chinese Bodies." For a fascinating discussion of popular ludic discourses and beliefs regarding racialized "styles" of play, see Leonard, *Playing While White.*

33 See Mason, *Melodrama and the Myth of America*, 150; and Scharnhorst, "Ways That Are Dark," 377.

34 While rarely played these days, euchre was, at the time of the poem, essentially America's national card game, responsible for introducing the joker into modern card packs.

35 In earlier versions of the poem, these quoted lines read "Henceforth I'm opposed to cheap labor" and "twenty-four packs [of cards.]" Margaret Duckett discusses the publication and reception history of the poem in "Plain Language from Bret Harte."

36 Scharnhorst, "Ways That Are Dark," 377.

37 Caillois, *Man, Play, and Games*, 115.

38 Lye, *America's Asia*, 65.

39 See Brown and Fletcher, *New England Farmer*, 467, 510.

40 Chapleau and Gray, *Report of the Canada Royal Commission on Chinese Immigration*, 181.

41 See Consalvo, *Cheating*; and Josh Bycer, "Cheating vs. Exploiting in Game Design," *Gamasutra*, January 4, 2015, www.gamasutra.com.

CHAPTER 2. JUST DESERTS

1 Myer, *Uprooted Americans*, 55.

2 Transcript, "Conference in Office of General DeWitt," January 4, 1942, file 014.31, box 7, RG 338, Records of the Western Defense Command and Fourth Army, National Archives.

3 Tolan Committee testimony transcript, February 1942, quoted in Weglyn, *Years of Infamy*, 38–39.

4 At least, not in the official discourse; anti-Japanese journalism, particularly in publications owned by W. R. Hearst, explicitly argued that Japanese were racially incapable of loyalty to the United States. See War Relocation Authority, *WRA*, 9.

5 DeWitt, *Final Report*, 9.

6 Belletto, "Game Theory Narrative," 333.

7 Quoted in Poundstone, *Prisoner's Dilemma*, 6.

8 Quoted in Nakamura, "Introduction," in *Treadmill.*

9 Okada, *No-No Boy*, 65; Nakamura, *Treadmill.*

10 McCain, *Game Theory and Public Policy.*

11 Von Neumann, "On the Theory of Games of Strategy."

12 Poundstone, *Prisoner's Dilemma*, 39. The theory would later be expanded to include non-zero-sum games.

13 Cagle, "Elegant Complexity," v.

14 See, for example, Booker, *Monsters, Mushroom Clouds, and the Cold War*; Grausam, *On Endings*; and Piette, *Literary Cold War*.

15 Morgenstern, "Game Theory," 267.

16 Richard Ernest Bellman, David Blackwell, and J. P. Lasalle, "Application of Theory of Games to Identification of Friend and Foe," RAND RM-197-PR, July 1949, 1.

17 Bellman, Blackwell, and Lasalle, 1.

18 Bellman, Blackwell, and Lasalle, 1.

19 Bellman, Blackwell, and Lasalle, 3.

20 Seltzer, "Parlor Games," 101.

21 Luhmann, *Observations on Modernity*, 47.

22 Luhmann, 45, 48.

23 Interestingly, this latter type of loyalty, which Japanese Americans were presumed to possess toward Japan, is essentially the model on which late twentieth-century notions of consumer loyalty to a brand, or of fan loyalty to a sports team, television show, book series, et cetera, would be founded.

24 Nakamura's use of bridge, in particular, as a site for his formal experiments with parataxis, set up the nonlinear and noncausal relationship between individual and choice that becomes the basis for his depiction of the loyalty questionnaire as a dilemma game.

25 Cherstin Lyon, "Loyalty Questionnaire," *Densho Encyclopedia*, May 2014, http://encyclopedia.densho.org.

26 Nakamura, *Treadmill*, 61.

27 Nakamura, 154. DeWitt was a vocal opponent of the loyalty questionnaire, arguing that it was not only "a sign of weakness" but, indeed, impossible to determine the loyalty of a Japanese. See General DeWitt and John J. McCloy, Telephone Conversation, January 18, 1943, Hoover Institution Digital Collections. See also General DeWitt and General Gullion, Telephone conversation, January 14, 1943, CWRIC Records, reel 7, p. 8218, quoted in Muller, *American Inquisition*.

28 Nakamura, *Treadmill*, 197.

29 See von Neumann and Morgenstern, *Theory of Games and Economic Behavior*, 176; as well as Morgenstern's "Theory of Games," 24, which uses a scene from Arthur Conan Doyle's "The Adventure of the Final Problem" to illustrate the "endless chain of reciprocally conjectural reactions and counter-reactions" underlying dilemma games.

30 Nakamura, *Treadmill*, 138, 180.

31 Nakamura, 195.

32 DeWitt, *Final Report*, vii.

33 One recognizes the true gravity of Bob's situation upon realizing that by answering no-no he will essentially become, like John Okada's Ichiro Yamada, a postwar social pariah both within his own ethnic community and, in large part, to the rest of United States for being a "draft dodger" and an ex-convict.

34 Nakamura, *Treadmill*, 153.

35 Nakamura, 165.
36 Nakamura, 5.
37 Nakamura, 27.
38 Nakamura, 52.
39 Williams, *Compleat Strategyst*, ix, 11.
40 Poundstone, *Prisoner's Dilemma*, 2.
41 Poundstone, 2.
42 Also called a puzzle box, this term is used in social philosophy and behavioral psychology to refer to self-enclosed puzzles often requiring the manipulation of levers, buttons, et cetera, to produce the desired solution; the concept has also spawned its own genre of "room escape" video games.
43 Williams, *Compleat Strategyst*, 13.
44 Murayama, *All I Asking for Is My Body*, 65.
45 Poundstone, *Prisoner's Dilemma*, 48.
46 For a compelling discussion of the internment's transnational dimensions, see Chuh, *Imagine Otherwise*, wherein she notes that "Asiatic racialization may be understood as the technology of the production of an imagined transnationality ascribed to Asian-identified individuals and groups" (61), a mechanism she connects to the concept of Derridean undecidability to trouble the stability of an identificatory term such as Asian American.
47 DeWitt, *Final Report*, 34. Chuh's discussion of internment undecidability, in which "loyalty and disloyalty are possibilities in the determination of what race means" (*Imagine Otherwise*, 70), further clarifies the ways game theory intersects with transnational discourse to construct Asiatic racialization vis-à-vis (extra)national forms of affiliation.
48 Murayama, *All I Asking for Is My Body*, 44.
49 Murayama, 45, 84.
50 Murayama, 98.
51 See Ling, *Narrating Nationalisms*, esp. 22–25.
52 Whether the reader is meant to take this scene as an explicit invitation to seek his own fortune at craps, or whether Murayama simply wanted to draw a stronger connection between Kiyo's craps victory and the young man's ingenuity, remains a source of critical debate. In *And the View from the Shore*, Stephen Sumida reads Kiyo's decision to send the money home as evidence of his ultimate reaffirmation of the Japanese familial institution and its cultural values, while others have argued that it serves as a deus ex machina that shores up Kiyo's faith, however misguided, in the transformative potential of America's democratic ideals (see, for example, Chang, "Social Stratification"). Disagreeing, ultimately, only over which nation's values are eventually endorsed, neither approach takes much critical interest in Murayama's choice to dramatize that ideological conflict through a *game*.
53 Murayama, *All I Asking for Is My Body*, 101.

54 Murayama, 103. This scene is strongly reminiscent of gambling scenes found throughout Carlos Bulosan's *America is in the Heart*, which reflects on gambling as an "art" and the extent to which cheating becomes "an imperative of the game."

55 Murayama, 103.

56 Murayama, 82.

57 Okada, *No-No Boy*, 40.

58 Okada, 241–42.

59 Seltzer, "Parlor Games," 108; italics added.

60 Okada, *No-No Boy*, 121. This contradiction was also central to arguments made by interned Nisei men of the aptly named Heart Mountain Fair Play Committee when the loyalty questionnaire was distributed.

61 Okada, 134.

62 Hence, critics too numerous to list here have attributed Ichiro's fragmented psyche to an "identity crisis" produced by the "liminality" of his Japanese American subject position; or, even more explicitly, by his failed "attempt to claim an identity as an American." See Yogi, "You Had to Be One or the Other," 64.

63 Kim, "Once More, with Feeling."

64 Okada, *No-No Boy*, 163.

65 Okada, 104.

66 Okada, 53.

67 Critics have, in the last decade or so, explored *No-No Boy*'s gendered dimensions mainly by reading the novel's two major female characters—Ichiro's mother and his lover, Emi—through a historicist lens. Jinqi Ling, for example, suggests that Emi represents Okada's strategic attempts to use established generic models of sentimentality and romance to negotiate with a hostile. From a slightly different angle, Daniel Kim and Viet Nguyen have recently argued that Mrs. Yamada reflects a prevailing Cold War culture ideology dubbed "momism." See Ling, "Race, Power, and Cultural Politics"; and Kim, "Once More, with Feeling"; and Nguyen, *Race and Resistance*.

68 This story is a much-cited example in game theory literature. See Williams, *Compleat Strategyst*.

69 Okada, *No-No Boy*, 19. The rhetorical coincidences here, too, make it almost irresistible to define Mrs. Yamada as a "tiger mother" in the most literal of senses. It is a bit too convenient to read Emi as the "lady" who promises Ichiro salvation, however; she is, in the first place, already married, and even if she were not, she is obviously in love with Kenji.

70 Okada, 23.

71 See David Palumbo-Liu's important discussion of racial physiognomy in *Asian/American*, esp. 81–115.

72 Wimsatt and Beardsley, "Intentional Fallacy," 469.

73 Wimsatt and Beardsley, 477. See also Cleanth Brooks's discussion of authorial intention and the "defensible strategy [of the] ideal reader" in "Formalist Critics."

74 Daase and Kessler, "Knowns and Unknowns," 412.
75 "DoD News Briefing: Secretary Rumsfeld and Gen. Myers," U.S. Department of Defense, February 12, 2002, http://archive.defense.gov; "Press Conference, NATO Headquarters, Brussels," June 6, 2002, http://www.nato.int.

CHAPTER 3. AGAINST THE ODDS

1 Lowenthal, *Literature and Mass Culture*, 220.
2 Mills, *White Collar*, 284.
3 Mills, 284. This closely anticipates Roger Caillois's theory of games of chance, as discussed in chapter 4.
4 Lowenthal, *Literature and Mass Culture*, 220; Michaels, *Trouble with Diversity*, 135–36.
5 Michaels, 7.
6 Michaels, 201.
7 For an extended discussion of the work-play dialectic as it has played out in Asian American literature, see Fickle, "Family Business."
8 For an especially strong recent example of this counter-discourse, see Chen, "Limit Point of Capitalist Equality." Michael Omi and Howard Winant were among the first to articulate and challenge this epiphenomenal discourse in *Racial Formation in the United States*.
9 See, especially, Michaels's recent contribution to *The Cambridge History of the American Novel*, "Model Minorities and the Minority Model," and Colleen Lye's discussion of it in "Unmarked Character."
10 Michaels.
11 Wu, *Color of Success*, 3.
12 See Wu, *Color of Success*; Bascara, *Model Minority Imperialism*; and Wu, *Yellow*.
13 See the appendix of Palumbo-Liu's *Asian/American*.
14 Lowenthal, *Literature and Mass Culture*, 208.
15 William Petersen, "Success Story, Japanese-American Style," *New York Times Magazine*, January 9, 1966; Jack Jones, "Now Millionaires: Japanese American Comeback on West Coast Spectacular," *Boston Globe*, November 25, 1965. The notion of a post-internment "comeback" played an especially important role in elevating Asian Americans to a degree of racial celebrity status. This curious tendency to consider an entire racial group celebrities persists in such works as Malcolm Gladwell's *Outliers*, where, alongside chapters dedicated to Bill Gates and Robert Oppenheimer, one finds a chapter simply devoted to "Chinese people" ("Rice Paddies and Math Tests").
16 Wu, *Color of Success*, 1.
17 Michaels, *Trouble with Diversity*, 75.
18 Team Coco, "Bo Burnham's Inspirational Advice: Give Up Now—CONAN on TBS," YouTube video, 1:32, June 28, 2016, http://youtu.be/q-JgGoECp2U.
19 Lye, *America's Asia*, 4–5.
20 Wu, *Color of Success*, 182. As Lisa Nakamura reminds us, "In a viciously neoliberal economy, gaming feels like a virtuous pleasure, for games reward player labor,

while, in contrast, labor in the real world is often undervalued, often treated as surplus or even as worthless" ("Afterword," 4).

21 Gold Mountain was a toponym frequently used by early Chinese immigrants for California and the Western United States more broadly, in reference to the gold found there. See Hsu, *Dreaming of Gold, Dreaming of Home*.

22 Wu, *Yellow*, 50.

23 Wu, 57.

24 Fabian, *Card Sharps*, viii.

25 "The World's Biggest Gamblers," *Economist*, February 9, 2017, www.economist .com.

26 Lears, *Something for Nothing*, 6.

27 *OED Online*, 3rd ed., s.v. "gamble," www.oed.com.

28 Clark et al., "Gambling Near-Misses."

29 Quoted in Sam Louie, "Asian Gambling Addiction: More Than Just Chance," *Psychology Today*, July 10, 2014, www.psychologytoday.com. See also Fong, "Vulnerable Faces of Pathological Gambling," 34.

30 Bourdieu, "Forms of Capital," 246.

31 Bourdieu, 246. This view is importantly complicated, as Julian Stallabras reminds us, by Walter Benjamin's writing about gambling. As Stallabras explains in his own discussion of computer games as an "ideal image of the market system," "Part of the point behind Benjamin's writing about gambling was his assertion that in games of chance, the player empathizes directly with the sums bet, paving the way for an empathy with exchange value itself" ("Just Gaming," 103).

32 Mills, *White Collar*, 34, 219.

33 Petersen, "Success Story," 36, 38.

34 Petersen, 36, 38.

35 Martin, *Empire of Indifference*, 18.

36 Martin, 37. For earlier discussions of this topic, on which Martin draws for his observations of race and risk, see Hilferding, *Finance Capital*, esp. 335.

37 Martin, 8, 14, 21. See also Rey Chow's illuminating reflections on this process in *The Protestant Ethnic and the Spirit of Capitalism*.

38 Petersen, "Success Story," 43.

39 Petersen, 43.

40 Petersen, 37.

41 Petersen, 21.

42 Charles Michener, "Success Story: Outwhiting the Whites," *Newsweek*, June 21, 1971.

43 Petersen, *Japanese Americans*, 101.

44 Oriard, *Sporting with the Gods*, 71.

45 Oriard, 77. Articles in the *New York Post* like Beckett's "Why Chinese Kids Don't Go Bad" continually refer to gambling as a bygone practice for which the current generation had not the least appetite. "Although it is true that in the past, gambling has been the traditional Chinese vice," the Reverend Paul Chang tells

us, yet "the younger generation is disgusted by [gambling], knowing how families have been impoverished" (5669). Other sources argued that accounts of turn-of-the-century Chinese gambling had been entirely "exaggerated by the press" (5671); in fact, they claimed, gambling had been limited to a fringe minority of the immigrant community: "The big gamblers were mainly seamen, without wives, on shore leave" (5670).

The sheer amount of effort and ink expended to rhetorically abolish gambling as a minor element of an earlier epoch, however, could not fully erase either its past or its continued significance. Indeed, gambling, in this article especially, turns into the return of the repressed, becoming an index of Asian Americans' incomplete and asymptotic relationship to whiteness and maintaining their status as what Ellen Wu calls "assimilating Others" in *Color of Success*, 9. "And still Chinatown is not perfect," the article concludes. "As recently as last August, police broke up a $1 million lottery ring" (5672).

The reigning assumption that the model minority stereotype involved a rhetorical erasure of the "Asian" affinity for gambling and the other moral vices invoked during the yellow peril era, celebrating instead the group's penchant for hard work and frugality, thus inadvertently risks becoming complicit with what Garrett Hongo, in his introduction to Wakako Yamauchi's *Songs My Mother Taught Me*, derides as the "readily available, politically coercive, and quite corny story" of the model minority that has traditionally been the target—and most important rallying cry—of Asian Americanist critique (6).

46 Goffman, *Interaction Ritual*, 267–68.

47 Okihiro, *Margins and Mainstreams*, x, ix.

48 Okihiro, 175, ix–x, 151.

49 Goffman, *Interaction Ritual*, 218–19.

50 See also Mark Chiang's discussion of Asian American identity as cultural capital in *The Cultural Capital of Asian American Studies*.

51 For a compelling discussion of this phenomenon as it has functioned in the age of neoliberalism, see Koshy, "Neoliberal Family Matters."

52 Palumbo-Liu, *Asian/American*, 156.

53 See Beckett, "Why Chinese Kids Don't Go Bad"; and "Americans without a Delinquency Problem," *Look*, April 29, 1958, 22, 75–81, quoted in Wu, *Color of Success*, 197.

54 Barbara Humphrey, "Looking for a Hobby? Try Model Building," *Today's Health* 36, February 1958, 37, 54, quoted in Gelber, *Hobbies*, 264.

55 "From Toys to Hobbies: Way to Men's Hearts," *Businessweek*, January 28, 1956. Interestingly, the mid-century popularity of modeling extended to airplanes, cars, boats—but far less often to trains. Model railroad building required significant space, expense, and electrical know-how, limiting the hobby to a small but dedicated community. Yet model railroading, even more than model airplanes, embodied the nostalgic vision of the open frontier that the hobby satisfied for those able to spare the floor space. In a curious prequel to the model minority scene, white Americans had by the 1930s begun modeling their leisure time after

nineteenth-century Chinese American labor by re-creating, in miniature, the railroad systems the yellow peril had been instrumental in completing.

56 William McIntyre, "Chinatown Offers Us a Lesson," *New York Times Magazine*, October 6, 1957.

57 McIntyre.

58 "Why Chinese Kids Don't Go Bad," 84th Cong., 1st Sess., Congressional Record 101 (August 2, 1955), A5668–72 (originally cited in Sung, *Mountain of Gold*).

59 As Steven Gelber observes in his ranging account of hobbies in late nineteenth- and twentieth-century America, "Hobbies gained wide acceptance because they could condemn depersonalized factory and office work by compensating for its deficits while simultaneously replicating both the skills and values of the workplace" (*Hobbies*, 2). This "disguised affirmation," as Gelber calls it, "allows participants to think about an activity as leisure-time recreation while it functions as a form of ideological re-creation" (2). Whereas model airplane kit manufacturers like Airlane enticed would-be buyers with the triple threat of affordability, reliability, and verisimilitude—"Value and performance above all!" "Flies like a real airplane!"—model minority discourse sold Asian Americans as what Mia Tuan in *Forever Foreigners or Honorary Whites?* memorably dubbed "honorary whites": trustworthy, "economically efficient" citizens. See also Ellen Wu's discussion of Asian Americans as "assimilating Others" in *Color of Success*.

60 "100% Americans," *60 Minutes*, January 9, 1972, quoted in Wu, *Color of Success*, 249.

61 Kingston, *Woman Warrior*, 339. It is difficult to decide which is the stranger aspect of the scene: that the narrator thinks of gambling as an occupation rather than its antithesis, or that she believes such an "admission" could retroactively undo the legitimacy of her parents' immigration status and her own citizenship.

62 John M. Glionna, "Gambling Seen as No-Win Situation for Some Asians," *Los Angeles Times*, January 16, 2006.

63 American Psychiatric Association, *DSM-5*, 587.

64 I thank Stephen Sohn for this valuable phrase.

65 As much as they may seem to install equality and fairness, games, Michael Oriard argues, do not actually "disturb power arrangements. . . . Playing well in itself confirms the legitimacy of power" (*Sporting with the Gods*, 26).

66 Lee, *Semblance of Identity*, 144.

67 Nguyen, *Race and Resistance*, 144.

68 Goffman, *Interaction Ritual*, 170

69 Chin, "Come All Ye Asian American Writers."

70 Crow and Yamamoto, "*MELUS* Interview," 76.

71 The story was not published until 1994 in the collection *Songs My Mother Taught Me*. In a 1998 interview, Yamauchi says it began life as a short story in a correspondence class she took shortly after trying to get *And the Soul Shall Dance* published, which suggests it was written in the 1960s. See Osborn, Watanabe, and Yamauchi , "*MELUS* Interview."

72 The narrator dates the first encounter "along"—sometime around—1949–52 (*Songs*, 105).

73 In "The Brown House" (1951), the father, Mr. Hattori, is a compulsive gambler who frequents a Chinese-run poker house in southern California, and "Seventeen Syllables" (1948), Yamamoto's most widely anthologized story, makes reference to a Japanese American family's nightly game of flower cards, also Las Vegas Charley's game of choice.

74 Yamamoto, *"Seventeen Syllables,"* 79.

75 Yamamoto, 70.

76 See Lye, *America's Asia*, esp. chap. 4.

77 Yamamoto, *"Seventeen Syllables,"* 71.

78 Yamauchi, *Songs*, 103. In a foul mood after her own streak of bad luck at the casino, the narrator responds with a curt reminder to her husband of the fact that, given the impoverished fortunes of postwar Japan, Japanese beggars were by no means a rare sight: "Why, there must be thousands begging on the streets of Tokyo, or Hong Kong, or wherever" (104). But not in Las Vegas—and so Jim, heedless, keeps repeating, "I can't believe it. Begging . . ." (104).

79 Yamauchi, 104.

80 Yamamoto, *"Seventeen Syllables,"* 79.

81 Yamamoto, 80.

82 Yamamoto, 71.

83 Yamauchi, *Songs*, 108.

84 Goffman, *Interaction Ritual*, 195.

85 Yamauchi, *Songs*, 101, 104.

86 Oriard, *Sporting with the Gods*, 72.

87 Michener, "Success Story."

88 Yamamoto, *"Seventeen Syllables,"* 80.

89 Yamamoto, 72.

90 Yamamoto, 82.

91 Caillois, *Man, Play, and Games*, 17.

92 Caillois.

93 See Hirabayashi, "Wakako Yamauchi's 'the Sensei'"; and Garrett Hongo's introduction to Yamauchi's *Songs*.

94 Yamamoto, *"Seventeen Syllables,"* 84–85.

95 McClanahan, *Dead Pledges*, 1; Lazzarato, *Making of the Indebted Man*, 11; Joseph, *Debt to Society*, xi.

96 Hoberek, *Twilight of the Middle Class*, 11.

97 Lazzarato, *Making of the Indebted Man*, 11; McClanahan, *Dead Pledges*, 4.

98 Melamed, *Represent and Destroy*, 13.

CHAPTER 4. WEST OF THE MAGIC CIRCLE

1 For a useful overview of earlier ludic scholarship, see Sutton-Smith, *Ambiguity of Play*; and Levinovitz, "Towards a Theory of Toys and Toy-Play."

2 Huizinga, *Homo Ludens*, 13.

3 It is important to note, however, that some recent critics have revisited these largely celebratory accounts of Huizinga and the magic circle. See especially Dyer-Witheford and de Peuter, *Games of Empire* (with a specific discussion beginning on p. xxxiv); and Ian Bogost's discussion of the "gap in the magic circle" (135) in *Unit Operations*.

4 Huizinga, *Homo Ludens*, ix.

5 As Caillois put it, "The spirit of play is essential to culture, but games and toys are historically the residues of culture" (*Man, Play, and Games*, 58).

6 Ehrmann, "*Homo Ludens* Revisited," 55.

7 Caillois, *Jeux et sports*, vii, quoted in Ehrmann, 46.

8 Ehrmann, 48. See also Caillois's observation that, although property might be exchanged between players, "nothing has been harvested or manufactured, no masterpiece has been created, no capital has accrued." (*Man, Play, and Games*, 5). Ehrmann's account of Huizinga and Caillois could be paraphrased as saying that what Huizinga and Caillois did not register in their own theories was that they were inherently political. As Said has observed, cultural structures that produce oppositions between the familiar and the strange are inevitably political and tend to metastasize around physical geographies and human groupings in ways that eventually come to seem natural. Among the most fundamental of these is, of course, the East/West dyad.

9 See, for example, Omi and Winant, *Racial Formation in the United States*; and HoSang, LaBennett, and Pulido, *Racial Formation in the Twenty-First Century*.

10 Ehrmann, "*Homo Ludens* Revisited," 49.

11 Said traces the phenomenon back to classical antiquity, but dates modern Orientalism to at least before the turn of the nineteenth century.

12 *OED Online*, 3rd ed., s.v. "orient," www.oed.com.

13 See, for example, Reichmuth and Werning, "Pixel Pashas, Digital Djinns"; Höglund, "Electronic Empire"; and Šisler, "Digital Arabs." Soraya Murray pithily describes the latter as "another seminal example of an Edward Said style critique of representational problematics within a larger culture that vilifies the Arab as a kind of twenty-first century political boogeyman" ("Work of Postcolonial Game Studies," 13). For an illustration of alternate methodological possibilities vis-a-vis a "postcolonial game studies," see Mukherjee, "Playing Subaltern"; and Murray, "Work of Postcolonial Game Studies." For an earlier, "analog" discussion of this intersection between the ludic and the colonial, see Mangan, *Games Ethic and Imperialism*.

14 Said, *Orientalism*, 2. Indeed, Huizinga's and Caillois's use of the term "culture" can be understood, in fact, partially as a response to what seemed to these twentieth-century writers an embarrassingly antiquated binary of "primitive" and "civilized." We find throughout that both texts express authorial attempts to distance themselves from primitivist discourses, with both frequently adding the [modifier] "so-called primitive societies" in discussions of African and other "indigents" and

Caillois renaming the traditional "civilized"/"primitive" hierarchy (he renames the poles as "rational" versus "Dionysian"). Caillois's aim, made explicit partly through the book, is to extend Huizinga's theory of culture-as-play to use games, rather than the more familiar valences of genetic or intellectual inferiority, to provide an even stronger rationale for the fictions of ethnocentrism. He notes that, "in societies conventionally called primitive as against those described as complex or advanced, there are obvious contrasts that in the latter are not exhausted by the evolution of science, technology, industry, the role of administration, jurisprudence, or archives, theoretical and applied mathematics, the myriad consequences of urbanization and imperialism, and many others with consequences no less formidable or revocable. It is plausible to believe that between these two kinds of society there is a fundamental antagonism of another order, which may be at the root of all the others, recapitulating, supporting, and explaining them" (86). Here, games, as that "fundamental antagonism," provide a "new set of labels or general concepts" (86) and justifications for a very old ethnocentric project of hierarchical classification, ensuring its "metaphysical" continuation long after the so-called scientific evidence of genetic difference had been revealed as a fiction.

15 Huizinga, *Homo Ludens*, 3.
16 Burckhardt, *Greeks and Greek Civilization*, 162.
17 Burckhardt, 162–63.
18 Victor Ehrenberg, *Ost und West*, 93–94, quoted in Huizinga, *Homo Ludens*, 72. While Ehrenberg had "condescended to recognize the agonistic principle as universally human" (Huizinga, 72), this recognition served not to elevate but denigrate the significance of play more broadly, for its extension to other cultures was based on the assumption that it was "historically uninteresting and without significance"; hence there was little at stake in extending it to the rest of the non-Greek world. Huizinga, then, was faced with a curious set of rhetorical assumptions: that if play was also found in Asiatic culture, it was trivial; and if it was significant, then it was uniquely Greek.
19 Huizinga, 53.
20 Huizinga, 54.
21 Morley and Robins, *Spaces of Identity*.
22 The seemingly contradictory dynamic we saw in part I of this book—where gambling's racialization as an essentially Asian passion produced conflicting yellow peril and model minority stereotypes—can thus be seen here in game studies' Orientalization of play, wherein Asia is framed as at once the West's ludic equal and its degraded antithesis.
23 Said, *Orientalism*, 2–3.
24 Huizinga, *Homo Ludens*, 66.
25 Quoted in Said, *Orientalism*, 52.
26 Said, 40.
27 Huizinga, *Homo Ludens*, 10; italics added.
28 As Huizinga notes, "illusion" literally means "in-play" (11).

29 Huizinga, 10.

30 Huizinga, 9.

31 Said, *Orientalism*, 43.

32 Ehrmann, "*Homo Ludens* Revisited," 55.

33 Bogost, "Gamification Is Bullshit."

34 The term was first defined in Deterding et al. "From Game Design Elements to Gamefulness."

35 Seltzer, "Parlor Games," 103.

36 Juul makes this even more explicit in his attempt to compare real time to game time in explicitly circular/rectilinear terms. See Juul, "Introduction to Game Time." Note also how the theory of "game as whole world" is a reproduction of Huizinga's earlier characterization of the "puerilism" of China.

37 Ehrmann, "*Homo Ludens* Revisited," 56.

38 Galloway, *Gaming*, 78.

39 Salen and Zimmerman, *Game Design Reader*, 122.

40 Caillois, *Man, Play, and Games*, 83.

41 Caillois, 67.

42 See, for example, Dennis, "Social Darwinism"; Palumbo-Liu, *Asian/American*; and Balibar, "Is There a 'Neo-Racism'?"

43 Caillois, *Man, Play, and Games*, 86, 84.

44 Caillois, 33.

45 Hongming, "Great Sinologue"; Parker, "Notes."

46 These include *wan, jeou-nao, tchouang, hsi, choua (shua), teou (tou), ton (tu)*, and other variations.

47 Caillois, *Man, Play, and Games*, 27.

48 Caillois, 35.

49 Said, *Orientalism*, 2.

50 Caillois, *Man, Play, and Games*, 65.

51 This system appeared in the tenth edition of *Systema Naturae* (1758). For further discussion of this classification, see Marks, "Long Shadow of Linnaeus's Human Taxonomy"; Gould, "Geometer of Race"; and Krenn, *Color of Empire*.

52 These translations are Gould's.

53 Caillois, *Man, Play, and Games*, 74.

54 Caillois, 114.

55 Caillois, 47.

56 Caillois, 150–51. Caillois renders this term for the "Chinese charade" as *Riffa Chifa*.

57 Caillois, 127.

58 Caillois, "Circular Time," 13, 2. See also his discussion of the "fundamental relationships" between *agon-alea* and *mimicry-ilinx* in *Man, Play, and Games*, particularly chap. 6, "An Expanded Theory of Games."

59 Caillois, "Circular Time," 7, 13.

60 Caillois, 13.

61 Caillois, *Man, Play, and Games*, 17.

62 Caillois, "Circular Time," 8, 7.
63 Caillois, 12.
64 Derrida, "Structure, Sign, and Play," 228.
65 Derrida.
66 Aarseth, *Cybertext*.
67 Ehrmann, *Homo Ludens* Revisited," 55.

CHAPTER 5. MOBILE FRONTIERS

1 Within a few years, the stunt had become so well-known—and widely anticipated—that Google would deliberately use the annual occasion to blur the fiction/reality bounds and turn users' expectations on their heads. For example, on March 31, 2004, the company announced the release of an email service called Gmail that offered an inconceivable 1GB of free storage space (Hotmail at that time offered 2 MB, or 0.002 GB)—and which many users initially mistook for an April Fools' joke.

2 Google Maps, "Google Maps: Pokémon Challenge," YouTube video, 2:33, March 31, 2014, http://youtu.be/4YMD6xELI_k. For a germane reflection on the divergence between the "wilderness" presented here and the actual game's "ongoing neglect of rural environments" as reflective of continuing "digital divides," see Alenda Chang, "Where the Wi-Fi Ends," *In Media Res*, October 15, 2016, http://mediacommons.org.

3 "Become a Pokémon Master with Google Maps," *Google Blog* (blog), March 31, 2014. http://blog.google.

4 Google would receive widespread disapprobation for a 2016 prank that was seen as not only "not funny" but a massive misappropriation of company resources. See Ivana Kottasova, "Google April Fool Prank Backfires," *CNN Tech*, April 1, 2016, http://money.cnn.com.

5 For an important account of Google's social hegemony and how it benefits from the "labortainment" of its users, see Noble, *Algorithms of Oppression*, esp. 36–38. See also chapter 1 of Dyer-Witheford and de Peuter, *Games of Empire*, for "a short history of the video game from the perspective of immaterial labor" (5).

6 Adam Reeve, "Pokemon Go Is a Huge Security Risk," *Adam Reeve* (blog), July 9, 2016, http://adamreeve.tumblr.com/post/147120922009/pokemon-go-is-a-huge -security-risk. See also Joshua Axelrod, "Franken Concerned About 'Pokemon Go' Data Mining," *Washington Examiner*, July 12, 2016, www.washingtonexam iner.com. For one example of the ambiguous definition of "consent" in electronic end-user agreements and smart contracts, see the cogent points made by Dennis Tenen in *Plain Text*, particularly chap. 3, "Form, Formula, Format."

7 "How Is Pokémon Go Collecting Data on Its Users?" NYU Center for Data Science, July 28, 2016, http://cds.nyu.edu.

8 See Wendy Chun's *Control and Freedom* for an important discussion of this eponymous dialectic, particularly chapter 4, "Orienting the Future."

9 This is a question that Sau-ling Wong also addresses in her chapter on the "Asian American Homo Ludens" in *Reading Asian American Literature*. Wong, in her examination of aesthetic play in several canonical Asian American literary works, concludes that despite the appearance of a "'universal' paradigm of play, certain recurrent themes in Western ludic discourse are noticeably absent or de-emphasized by the Asian American authors, or are otherwise inapplicable to them" (183–84).

10 Hatakeyama and Kubo, *2000 Pokémon Story*, 421–22. We might say that the "not hidden" residue of the "Japaneseness" of Pokémon can be understood to reside in the very act of its apparent erasure in the form of "localized" resignification. That is, the very appearance of "odorlessness" or global appeal becomes a sign of the product's Japanese origins—but without any of the stigma that such evidence might normally bring.

11 Yano, *Pink Globalization*, 17.

12 The label of "perpetual foreigner" was coined by Mia Tuan alongside her brilliant discussion of Asian Americans as "honorary whites."

13 Iwabuchi, "How 'Japanese' Is Pokémon?" 57.

14 Lye, *America's Asia*, 5.

15 Bogost, *Persuasive Games*, 75.

16 Bogost, 94.

17 Bogost, 90.

18 Hoskins and Mirus, "Reasons for the US Dominance of the International Trade in Television Programmes," 503. For a discussion of Japanese managerial culture and U.S. corporate management theory as it relates to the techno-Orientalist dynamics referenced here, see Victoria's discussion of "corporate Zen" in *Zen at War*, 186; and Williams, *Buddha in the Machine*, specifically the chapter on "*Technê*-Zen and the Spiritual Quality of Global Capitalism." For a discussion of this phenomenon in terms of digital games, see also Anthony Sze-Fai Shiu's analysis of the game *Shadow Warrior*, the putative sequel to *Duke Nukem 3D*, which not only allows but requires the player to "prevent the spread of corrupt Japanese capital" in the guise of a robotic samurai controlled by a Japanese businessman in order to win the game ("What Yellowface Hides," 113).

19 Fuller and Jenkins, "Nintendo® and New World Travel Writing," 59.

20 Aksoy and Robins, "Hollywood for the 21st Century," 18.

21 Kubo Masakazu, "Sekai wo haikaisuru wasei monsutā Pikachū" (Pikachu wandering over the world), quoted in Iwabuchi, "How 'Japanese' Is Pokémon?" 68.

22 See Robertson, "Glocalization," 38. It is interesting to note that, although glocalization, the word is attributed to Japan etymologically, being "modeled on Japanese *dochakuka* (deriving from *dochaku* 'living on one's own land'), originally the agricultural principle of adapting one's farming technique to local conditions, but also adopted in Japanese business for global localization, a global outlook adapted to local conditions." See also Tulloch, *Oxford Dictionary of New Words*.

23 Masakazu, "Sekai wo haikaisuru wasei monsutā Pikachū," quoted in Iwabuchi, "How 'Japanese' Is Pokémon?" 68.

24 Tobin, *Pikachu's Global Adventure*, 265–66.

25 Howard Chua-Euan, "PokéMania," *Time*, November 22, 1999.

26 Many of these explanations are the result of the exhaustive labor and etymological research conducted by "hardcore" fans on sites like Bulbapedia (http://bulbapedia .bulbagarden.net), which bills itself as "the community driven Pokémon encyclopedia." The game's producers have been somewhat tight-lipped about how the majority of the translations came about.

27 Tim Larimer, "The Ultimate Game Freak," *Time Asia*, November 22, 1999.

28 Takashi Amano, "Pokémon GO Was April Fool's Joke before It Became a Huge Hit," *Bloomberg Technology*, July 11, 2016, www.bloomberg.com.

29 Indeed, the *Pokémon GO* game was essentially laminated on top using existing *Ingress* infrastructure; the landmarks first created in *Ingress* later became the sites of PokéStops and gyms. Nicole Carpenter, "How AR Game *Ingress* Directly Led to *Pokémon GO*," *IGN*, December 20, 2015, www.ign.com.

30 Ollie Barder, "'Pokémon GO' Conceived as an April Fool's Joke but Has since Secured Satoru Iwata's Legacy," *Forbes*, July 12, 2016, www.forbes.com.

31 Carpenter, "How AR Game *Ingress* Directly Led to *Pokémon GO*."

32 Just as the glocalized background of *Pokémon GO* was crucial to understanding why it succeeded where *Ingress* did not, the mapping technology developed by Google is crucial to understanding why *GO* succeeded among such a wide variety of Americans whereas the original Gameboy games did not, allowing it to break out of the "kid" audience the original franchise had targeted—and even beyond the grown-up kids for whom pure nostalgia provided sufficient initial lure.

33 Kurgan, *Close Up at a Distance*, 16.

34 Wood and Fels, *Power of Maps*, 28.

35 Jameson, *Postmodernism*, 51. See also Jameson, "Cognitive Mapping."

36 Said, *Orientalism*, 55.

37 Cheng, review of *Techno-Orientalism*, 384.

38 Morley and Robins, *Spaces of Identity*, 172. As Stephen Hong Sohn notes, however, "the term techno-Orientalism seems to have a two-fold origin. While Morley and Robins first defined it in print, [Lisa] Nakamura cites Greta Aiyu Niu's paper presentation at Duke University in 1998 as her model for the definition." See Sohn, "Introduction," 19n5.

39 Quoted in Morley and Robins, 207. Also see Toshiya Ueno's influential account of techno-Orientalism in "Techno-Orientalism and Media-Tribalism." For contemporary accounts of Orientalism in the sinological context, see Vukovich, *China and Orientalism*; and Chen, *Occidentalism*. Vukovich discusses the Orientalizing practices of contemporary Western scholarship (specifically in Chinese studies) as a shift from hegemonizing discourses of China guided by "a logic of 'essential difference' to one of 'essential sameness' or general equivalence" (1). Such representations of China focus on its "becoming-the-same"—that is, becoming "like

us," a phenomenon that reflects a certain "capitalist complicity" with neoliberalism (127, 143).

40 Martin, "Race, Colonial History and National Identity," 15.

41 Martin, 1, 4. In suggesting that "it seems plausible that the constellation of expectations about this kind of Digital Asia in popular culture includes experiential, gamic elements in addition to the more conventional aesthetic qualities that we associate with techno-Orientalism," Chris Goto-Jones is another recent scholar to emphasize the technological embededdness of these Orientalist practices in contemporary video games. See "Playing with Being in Digital Asia," 41.

42 Chun, "Othering Space," 250. For a related take on techno-Orientalism as it has shaped the last two centuries of "Western" artistic production, see R. John Williams's fascinating discussion of the discourse and fantasy of "Asia as techne," wherein modernist and postmodernist writers and artists have been motivated by "a desire to embrace 'Eastern' aesthetics as a means of redeeming 'Western' technoculture," the former being counterintuitively positioned as both "the antidote to and the perfection of machine culture." (Williams, *Buddha in the Machine*, 1).

43 Quoted in Tally, "Fredric Jameson and the Controversy over 'Third-World Literature in the Era of Multinational Capitalism,'" 69; italics in original. It is worth noting that Tally's charge of "prefiguring" takes aim at a broadly intellectual rather than a precisely chronological trajectory, given that Jameson's earliest writings on cognitive mapping actually appeared in 1984, in an article in the *New Left Review*, two years before the "Third-World Literature" article was published in *Social Text*.

44 Ahmad, "Jameson's Rhetoric of Otherness."

45 For a useful account of the relationship between imperialism and cognitive mapping, see also Schenk, "Mental Maps." For a more explicitly redemptive take on Jameson, and the value of cognitive mapping as a tool to apprehend "the persistence of the dialectic within a fully global capitalism given its unique capacity to read space relationally" (as opposed to, say, the "surface reading" trend that emerged in the early 2010s), see Carolyn Lesjak's brilliant "Reading Dialectically," esp. 262–64.

46 Jagoda, *Network Aesthetics*, 26. See also Toscano and Kinkle's wide-ranging reflections on the "aesthetic problem" of cognitive mapping throughout *Cartographies of the Absolute*.

47 The term "cognitive map" was originally coined by American psychologist Edward C. Tolman in 1948.

48 Jameson, *Postmodernism*, 51.

49 Jameson, 51 (quoting Althusser).

50 Jameson, 51.

51 Chun, "Othering Space," 243.

52 Fuller and Jenkins, "Nintendo® and New World Travel Writing," 63.

53 Fuller and Jenkins, 63. See also Shoshana Magnet's compelling discussion of the "Otherizing" gender and racial dynamics maintained through (and in many cases initiated by) the particular physical setting and landscape of the game world,

which she, in a slightly different vein than Wark, refers to as the "gamespace" in which one is "Playing at Colonization."

54 Quoted in Hatakeyama and Kubo, *2000 Pokémon Story*, 421–22.

55 Certainly it's true that, like Nintendo's glocalization efforts to disguise cultural odor, much effort on the part of American software creators and web designers has gone into disguising the fact of the apps' users being tracked—as Wendy Chun puts it, "convincing the user that s/he is not a spectacle, that s/he does not have to become data in order to access data" ("Othering Space," 247).

56 Kline, Dyer-Witheford, and de Peuter, *Digital Play*, 127. See also Dyer-Witheford and de Peuter's brilliant follow-up discussion in *Games of Empire* of video games as a "paradigmatic media of Empire" (xv) vis-à-vis analyses of novel phenomenon through equally novel portmanteaux like "ludocapitalism" and "militainment." This text, and these notions, are discussed in greater detail in chapter 6 of *The Race Card*.

57 "Current Intelligence Study Number 35: The Greater East Asia Co-Prosperity Sphere," CIA Office of Strategic Services, Research and Analysis Branch, August 10, 1945, 3.

58 For a fascinating historical examination of cartographic (and hence self-orienting) practices in Japan, with particularly valuable attention to the distinction between pre– and post–Meiji Restoration maps, see Unno, "Cartography in Japan."

59 Quoted in Lebra, *Japan's Greater East Asia Co-prosperity Sphere*, 75.

60 Quoted in Lebra, 79.

61 "Current Intelligence Study Number 35," 3. The CIA intelligence report referred to this process as "training natives" and to the GEA as "directing local inhabitants [to be] leaders of their people."

62 Although the game describes Pokémon as a series of different "species," they are also broadly categorized according to one of around twenty "types," which are defined as "elemental attributes determining the strengths and weaknesses of each Pokémon and their moves, offsetting each other in rock-paper-scissors relationships." For example, Grass Type Pokémon are weak against Fire Types, Fire Types against Water, and Water against Grass. The strategy underlying gym battles is thus to select six of one's own Pokémon who are not simply the most quantitatively powerful in terms of health and strength, but who collectively constitute the most advantageous racial—or rather, "elemental"—combination of defense and attack against the opposing player's lineup.

63 See also Dower, *War without Mercy*, 240.

64 Dower, 272.

65 In his probing and frequently self-deprecating reflections on postwar shifts in Japanese cultural imagery and aesthetics, internationally renowned Japanese artist Takashi Murakami suggests that in their cuteness (*kawaii*), helplessness, or lethargy (*yurui*), the characters found in anime and games like *Pokémon GO* essentially function as proxies for the Japanese themselves: "Once everything had been blown away in a flash, an infantile and impotent culture gained

strength under the rubric of an unfounded, puppet national infrastructure. What emerged was a culture frozen in its infancy." It is through such creatures, Murakami suggests, that one can grasp the extent to which the radiated afterlife of World War II continues, at least in the mind of many Japanese, to contaminate and stunt the national culture that arose from the ashes: "We Japanese still embody 'Little Boy', nicknamed, like the atomic bomb itself, after a nasty childhood taunt." Taken together, the perpetual state of adolescence in which World War II can be thought to freeze the nation, and the continual state of childhood in which *kawaii* and games ostensibly seek to recapture or reanimate in the present, reorient our perspective on the origins and implications of Pokémon's own dramatization of a much older narrative of territorial expansion in the present. See Murakami, *Little Boy*.

While the traces of Japan's wartime loss can thus be seen at the very heart of the game, attesting to how the legacy of the atomic bombs that brought an official end to the war continues to structure the way Japan views itself and its relationship to "the West," the clockwork consistency with which Japan's proposed World War II history textbook revisions continue to ignite indignance and fury in South Korea and China shows how Japan's early twentieth-century brutalization of its neighbors also radiates and determines the shape of East Asian politics and passions. That is, while we might be tempted to regard the bulbously disproportionate bodies and curiously vivid colors of the Pokémon as visual manifestations of the war's irradiated residues and its tangible effects on Japanese denizens, the sympathy one feels toward them as cute, helpless victims does not change the fact that what one does in playing—what the rules of the game demand that one do—is not heal or cure them, but, as we saw, to capture, domesticate, and ultimately force them to fight for you.

66 Sneider, "Textbooks and Patriotic Education," 36.

67 Quoted in Iwabuchi, *Resilient Borders*, 142. To be clear, such a trend is not unique to Japan, as Joe Jeon reminds us in his work on the uses of CGI in recent South Korean cinema during the "long wake" of the country's IMF crisis. Jeon takes up films like *The Host*, *D-War*, and *HERs*, offering a compelling analysis of the material and allegorical links between (military) hard-power and (cultural) soft-power diplomacy, wherein "forms of aesthetic representation work to the make the conjuncture of finance capital and digital technology visible." See Jeon, "Neoliberal Forms," 88.

68 Iwabuchi, "Pop-Culture Diplomacy in Japan," 420.

69 Chris Goto-Jones has suggested the Cool Japan campaign can also be seen as a form of reverse- or self-Orientalism, "represent[ing] (at least in part) a deliberate attempt to appropriate an emerging techno-Orientalist discourse about Japan ('you Digital Asians!') as a source of empowerment for the Japanese themselves ('we Digital Asians!')" (24). Christine Yano has also described this language as a "wink on pink" (7).

70 Iwabuchi, "How 'Japanese' Is Pokémon?" 61.

71 Allison, "Cuteness as Japan's Millennial Product," 40. Part of why *kawaii* as an aesthetic helps to facilitate, and often goes hand in hand with, glocalized marketing
strategies is that as a visual design principle, it not only tends to reduce the "foreignness" of characters—which frequently take nonhuman, and hence ostensibly
"raceless," forms—but inspires feelings of pity and warmth. The characteristic
"gentleness" (*yasashii*) and vulnerability of cute creatures has been crucial in creating an icon, as Anne Allison observes about Pikachu, "with whom fans would
not so much identify as develop feelings of attachment, nurturance, and intimacy"
(38). Just as linguistic localization allowed a generation of American children in
the 1990s to develop familiarity with the whole genealogy of pocket monsters, the
characters' disarming cuteness—an aesthetic many studies of play in Japan link to
feelings not only of nurturance but of "nostalgia for experiences in a child's past"
(40)—encouraged such a deep attachment to the characters that the news of the
franchise's revival through *Pokémon GO* sent millennials into a frenzy of excitement saturated with sentimentalism. See also Shiokawa, "Cute but Deadly"; and
more recently, Ngai, "Cuteness of the Avant-Garde."

72 See also Larissa Hjorth's discussion of this dynamic as it has played out in a different East Asian context in "Playing at Being Mobile." An important precursor
to these discussions can be found in Brian J. McVeigh's influential discussion of
"techno-cute," particularly as defined in "How Hello Kitty Commodifies the Cute,
Cool and Camp."

73 Jamie Koide, "Why Didn't Japan Include Any Pokémon Character Cameos in
the 2020 Olympic Promo?" *SoraNews24*, August 24, 2016, http://en.rocketnews24
.com.

74 Allison, "Cuteness as Japan's Millennial Product," 35.

75 Kurgan, *Close Up at a Distance*, 17.

76 Mudimbe quoted in Mills, *Racial Contract*, 44.

77 Kurgan, *Close Up at a Distance*, 17.

CHAPTER 6. GAME OVER?

Epigraph. Nyhm, "Ni Hao (A Gold Farmer's Story)," YouTube video, 3:39, August 22,
2007, http://www.youtube.com/watch?v=0dkkf5NEI00.

1 See Castronova, *Exodus to the Virtual World*; and McGonigal, *Reality Is Broken*.

2 Barack Obama, "Remarks by the President on Trade, Beaverton, Oregon," White
House, May 8, 2015, http://obamawhitehouse.archives.gov.

3 Paul Gaita, "Gaming Addiction on the Rise in Asia," *The Fix*, December 16, 2013,
www.thefix.com. Steve Choe and Se Young Kim also discuss this phenomenon
in "Never Stop Playing." For an important discussion of Chinese gold farming in
World of Warcraft as a form of "biopower play" in the age of twenty-first-century
empire, particularly in relation to the shift from "the revolutionary state social-
ism of Mao Tse-tung to the authoritarian state capitalism of Deng Xiaoping," see
chapter 5 of Dyer-Witheford and de Peuter, *Games of Empire*.

4 American Psychiatric Association, *DSM-V*, 796.

5   American Psychiatric Association, 797.

6   Lillie-Blanton, Anthony, and Schuster, "Probing the Meaning of Racial/Ethnic Group Comparisons."

7   Li et al., "Characteristics of Internet Addiction." See also Hayley Tsukayama, "This Dark Side of the Internet Is Costing Young People Their Jobs and Social Lives," *Washington Post*, May 20, 2016.

8   Przybylski, Weinstein, and Murayama, "Internet Gaming Disorder."

9   Przybylski, Weinstein, and Murayama, 230, 235.

10 Julian Dibbell, "The Life of the Chinese Gold Farmer," *New York Times Magazine*, June 17, 2007.

11 Heeks, "Understanding 'Gold Farming.'"

12 Hayot, "Chinese Bodies," 122.

13 Nick Yee, "Yi-Shan-Guan," *Daedalus Project*, January 2, 2006, www.nickyee.com.

14 David Barboza, "Ogre to Slay? Outsource It to Chinese," *New York Times*, December 9, 2005.

15 Cory Doctorow, "Anda's Game," *Salon*, November 15, 2004, www.salon.com.

16 Dibbell, "Life of the Chinese Gold Farmer."

17 Barboza, "Ogre to Slay?"

18 No English translation is provided for the phrase (which means "Wait! Please don't"). Throughout the novel, traditional characters (now used mainly only in Taiwan, Hong Kong, and other overseas Chinese communities) are used to represent Chinese speech, which is strange given that the gold farmers in the story are from mainland China, and would thus almost certainly be using simplified characters (which in this case would read 等一下! 请不要 . . .). The reason for the curious choice of character system (or the identity of the translator) is not made clear.

19 Doctorow and Wang, *In Real Life*, 45. Lucy informs Anda that bots can be identified because, when queried, they either "don't respond or [don't] speak English" (49); in other words, humanity becomes even more fully tied to English-speaking Americans, and nonhumanity (i.e., automated AI) with Asians. Of course, as Anda later learns, the reason gold farmers rarely respond verbally is not because they are bots, but because their "English isn't good enough" (66).

20 Nethaera / Community Manager, "Recent Actions against Botting in WoW," Blizzard World of Warcraft General Discussion Forum, May 19, 2016, http://us.battle.net.

21 Bourdieu, "Forms of Capital," 15.

22 Alexander Galloway offers a compelling critique of this fictional non-correspondence in his essay "Does the Whatever Speak?"

23 Doctorow and Wang, *In Real Life*, 54.

24 Rettberg, "Corporate Ideology in *World of Warcraft*," 20.

25 Yu, *How to Life Safely*, 174.

26 Lye, *America's Asia*, esp. 7.

27 See Nakamura, "Don't Hate the Player"; and Rey, "Gamification and Post-Fordist Capitalism." See also Chan, "Negotiating Intra-Asian Games Networks."

28 Galloway, *Interface Effect*, 136.

29 Bogost, "Gamification Is Bullshit."

30 Lisa Nakamura makes this important point about the connection between female bodies and avatars in "Don't Hate the Player."

31 Doctorow, "Anda's Game."

32 Galloway, *Gaming*, 136.

33 Yee, "Yi-Shan-Guan." The presence, content, and social function of anti-Chinese and anti-Korean racism in online gaming is analyzed at length in groundbreaking essays by Constance Steinkuehler and Douglas Thomas. See Steinkuehler, "Mangle of Play"; and Thomas, "KPK, Inc."

34 Galloway, *Gaming*, 137.

35 Huizinga, *Homo Ludens*, 28.

36 Harper, *Framing the Margins*, 4.

37 Nakamura, *Cybertypes*, xvi.

38 Nakamura, xv.

39 Doctorow and Wang, *In Real Life*, 154.

40 Doctorow and Wang, 133.

41 Allegory literally means "otherspeaking": *allos* (other) + *agoreuein* (to speak in public). One guesses that Galloway's response to such flattening would be that raised by McKenzie Wark in the latter's influential meta-commentary of digital games, *Gamer Theory*, wherein he describes games as "allegorithms" (Galloway's neologism). His definition of allegory as the productive flattening produced by multiple fragmentation is based directly on Walter Benjamin's account as established in *The Origin of German Tragic Drama*, and as such draws on the methodological foundation laid by Julian Stallabrass's illuminating and probing essay "Just Gaming: Allegory and Economy in Computer Games," which regards the avatar or player-character (in his terms, the "alter-ego") as a "fragmented, allegorized and reified self under the conditions of capital" (86) See also Joe Jeon's discussion of how this "retooling of allegory as algorithm" works in other broadly techno-Orientalist settings, such as the digital production of special effects in a recent South Korean film like *HERs*, to effectively capture "the critical capacity of recursion as a lynchpin that connects military, financial, and aesthetic forms" by "spatializing [their] systemic precarity" and revealing the "abstract systemic violence" that takes place in the financialization of daily life, as discussed in chapter 3 of this book (Jeon, "Neoliberal Forms," 100–101).

42 Galloway, *Gaming*, 61.

43 Jameson, *Postmodernism*, 168.

BIBLIOGRAPHY

Aarseth, Espen J. *Cybertext: Perspectives on Ergodic Literature*. Baltimore: Johns Hopkins University Press, 1997.

Ahmad, Aijaz, "Jameson's Rhetoric of Otherness and the 'National Allegory.'" *Social Text* 17 (Autumn 1987): 3–26.

Aksoy, Asu, and Kevin Robins. "Hollywood for the 21st Century: Global Competition for Critical Mass in Image Markets." *Cambridge Journal of Economics* 16, no. 1 (1992): 1–22.

Allison, Anne. "Cuteness as Japan's Millennial Product." In *Pikachu's Global Adventure: The Rise and Fall of Pokémon*, edited by Joseph Jay Tobin, 34–52. Durham, NC: Duke University Press, 2004.

American Psychiatric Association. *Diagnostic and Statistical Manual of Mental Disorders: DSM-5*. 5th ed. Arlington, VA: American Psychiatric Association, 2013.

Baecker, Dirk. "The Form Game." In *Problems of Form*, edited by Dirk Baecker, 99–106. Stanford, CA: Stanford University Press, 1999.

Baerg, Andrew. "Governmentality, Neoliberalism, and the Digital Game." *symplokē* 17, no. 1–2 (2009): 115–27.

Balibar, Etienne. "Is There a 'Neo-Racism'?" In *Race and Racialization: Essential Readings*, edited by Tania Das Gupta, 83–88. Toronto: Canadian Scholars' Press, 2007.

Bascara, Victor. *Model Minority Imperialism*. Minneapolis: University of Minnesota Press, 2006.

Bateson, Gregory. *Steps to an Ecology of Mind: Collected Essays in Anthropology, Psychiatry, Evolution, and Epistemology*. New York: Ballantine Books, 1972.

Baudrillard, Jean. *Seduction*. Translated by Brian Singer. New York: St. Martin's Press, 1990.

Beckett, Henry. "Why Chinese Kids Don't Go Bad: Spare the Rod, Love the Child." *New York Post*, July 11, 1955.

Belletto, Steven. "The Game Theory Narrative and the Myth of the National Security State." *American Quarterly* 61, no. 2 (2009): 333–57.

Bogost, Ian. "Gamification Is Bullshit." In *The Gameful World: Approaches, Issues, Applications*, edited by Steffen P. Walz and Sebastian Deterding, 65–80. Cambridge, MA: MIT Press, 2015.

———. *Persuasive Games: The Expressive Power of Videogames*. Cambridge, MA: MIT Press, 2007.

———. *Unit Operations: An Approach to Videogame Criticism*. Cambridge, MA: MIT Press, 2008.

Booker, M. Keith. *Monsters, Mushroom Clouds, and the Cold War: American Science Fiction and the Roots of Postmodernism, 1946–1964.* Westport, CT: Greenwood Press, 2001.

Bourdieu, Pierre. "The Forms of Capital." In *Handbook of Theory and Research for the Sociology of Education,* edited by John Richardson, 241–58. New York: Greenwood Press, 1986.

Brooks, Cleanth. "The Formalist Critics." *Kenyon Review* 13, no.1 (Winter 1951): 72–81.

Brown, Garrett. *How to Win at Poker; or, The Autocrat of the Poker Table.* Denver: Smith-Brooks, 1899.

Brown, Simon, and Stilman Fletcher, eds. *The New England Farmer; Devoted to Agriculture, Horticulture, and Their Kindred Arts and Sciences.* Boston: R. P. Eaton & Co., 1870.

Burckhardt, Jacob. *The Greeks and Greek Civilization.* Edited by Oswyn Murray, translated by Sheila Stern. New York: Macmillan, 1999.

Cagle, Jeremey E. "Elegant Complexity: The Presence of Cold War Game Theory in Postmodern American Fiction." PhD diss., University of South Carolina, 2010.

Caillois, Roger. "Circular Time, Rectilinear Time." Translated by Nora McKeon. *Diogenes* 11, no. 42 (1963): 1–13.

———. *Man, Play, and Games.* Translated by Meyer Barash. 1958. Reprint, Urbana: University of Illinois Press, 2001.

Capron, E. S. *History of California, from Its Discovery to the Present Time: Comprising Also a Full Description of Its Climate, Surface, Soil, Rivers, Towns, Beasts, Birds, Fishes, State of Its Society, Agriculture, Commerce, Mines, Mining, &c., with a Journal of the Voyage from New York, via Nicaragua, to San Francisco, and Back, via Panama.* Boston: J. P. Jewett, 1854.

Castronova, Edward. *Exodus to the Virtual World: How Online Fun Is Changing Reality.* New York: Palgrave Macmillan, 2008.

Chan, Dean. "Negotiating Intra-Asian Games Networks: On Cultural Proximity, East Asian Games Design, and Chinese Farmers." *Fibreculture Journal* 8 (2006). http://eight.fibreculturejournal.org.

Chan, Jeffery Paul, Frank Chin, Lawson Fusao Inada, and Shawn Wong, eds. *The Big Aiiieeeee! An Anthology of Chinese American and Japanese American Literature.* New York: Meridan, 1991.

Chang, Edmond Y. "Queergaming." In *Queer Game Studies,* edited by Bonnie Ruberg and Adrienne Shaw, 15–23. Minneapolis: University of Minnesota Press, 2017.

Chang, Joan Chiung-huei. "Social Stratification and Plantation Mentality: Reading Milton Murayama." *Concentric: Literary and Cultural Studies* 30, no. 2 (2004): 155–72.

Chapleau, Joseph Adolphe, and John Hamilton Gray, eds. *Report of the Canada Royal Commission on Chinese Immigration.* Ottawa: Royal Commission on Chinese Immigration, 1885. Government of Canada Publications.

Chen, Christopher. "The Limit Point of Capitalist Equality: Notes toward an Abolitionist Antiracism." *Endnotes* 3 (2013): http://endnotes.org.uk.

Chen, Xiaomei. *Occidentalism: A Theory of Counter-Discourse in Post-Mao China*. New York: Oxford University Press, 1995.

Cheng, John. Review of *Techno-Orientalism: Imagining Asia in Speculative Fiction, History, and Media*, edited by David S. Roh, Betsy Huang, and Greta A. Niu. *Journal of Asian American Studies* 18 (October 2015): 382–84.

Cheung, King-Kok. *Articulate Silences: Hisaye Yamamoto, Maxine Hong Kingston, Joy Kogawa*. Ithaca, NY: Cornell University Press, 1993.

Chiang, Mark. *The Cultural Capital of Asian American Studies: Autonomy and Representation in the University*. New York: New York University Press, 2009.

Chin, Frank. "Come All Ye Asian American Writers of the Real and the Fake." In *The Big Aiiieeeee! An Anthology of Chinese American and Japanese American Literature*, edited by Jeffery Paul Chan, Frank Chin, Lawson Fusao Inada, and Shawn Wong, 1–92. New York: Meridan, 1991.

Choe, Steve, and Se Young Kim. "Never Stop Playing: *StarCraft* and Asian Gamer Death." In *Techno-Orientalism: Imagining Asia in Speculative Fiction, History, and Media*, edited by David S. Roh, Betsy Huang, and Greta A. Niu, 113–24. New Brunswick, NJ: Rutgers University Press, 2015.

Chow, Rey. *The Protestant Ethnic and the Spirit of Capitalism*. New York: Columbia University Press, 2002.

Chua, Amy. *Battle Hymn of the Tiger Mother*. New York: Penguin, 2011.

Chuh, Kandice. *Imagine Otherwise: On Asian Americanist Critique*. Durham, NC: Duke University Press, 2003.

Chun, Wendy Hui Kyong. "Othering Space." In *The Visual Culture Reader*, edited by Nicholas Mirzoeff, 243–54. London: Routledge, 2002.

Chun, Wendy Hui Kyong. *Control and Freedom: Power and Paranoia in the Age of Fiber Optics*. Cambridge, MA: MIT Press, 2008.

———. "Introduction: Race and/as Technology; or, How to Do Things to Race." *Camera Obscura* 24, no. 70 (2009): 7–35.

———. "Othering Space." In *The Visual Culture Reader*, edited by Nicholas Mirzoeff, 243–54. London: Routledge, 2002.

Clark, Luke, et al. "Gambling Near-Misses Enhance Motivation to Gamble and Recruit Win-Related Brain Circuitry." *Neuron* 61, no. 3 (2009): 481–90.

Consalvo, Mia. *Cheating: Gaining Advantage in Videogames*. Cambridge, MA: MIT Press, 2009.

Costikyan, Greg. *Uncertainty in Games*. Cambridge, MA: MIT Press, 2013.

Crow, Charles L., and Hisaye Yamamoto. "A *MELUS* Interview: Hisaye Yamamoto." *MELUS* 14, no. 1 (Spring 1987): 73–84.

Culin, Stewart. *The Gambling Games of the Chinese in America*. Philadelphia: University of Pennsylvania Press, 1891.

Daase, Christopher, and Oliver Kessler. "Knowns and Unknowns in the 'War on Terror': Uncertainty and the Political Construction of Danger." *Security Dialogue* 38, no. 4 (December 2007): 411–34.

Danius, Sara, Stefan Jonsson, and Gayatri Chakravorty Spivak. "An Interview with Gayatri Chakravorty Spivak." *boundary 2* 20, no. 2 (1993): 24–50.

Day, Iyko. *Alien Capital: Asian Racialization and the Logic of Settler Colonial Capitalism.* Durham, NC: Duke University Press, 2016.

Dennis, Rutledge M. "Social Darwinism, Scientific Racism, and the Metaphysics of Race." *Journal of Negro Education* 64, no. 3 (1995): 243–52.

Derrida, Jacques. "Structure, Sign, and Play in the Discourse of the Human Sciences." In *A Postmodern Reader*, edited by Joseph Natoli and Linda Hutcheon, 223–42. Albany: State University of New York Press, 1993.

Deterding, Sebastian, Dan Dixon, Rilla Khaled, and Lennart Nacke. "From Game Design Elements to Gamefulness: Defining Gamification." In *MindTrek '11 Proceedings of the 15th International Academic MindTrek Conference: Envisioning Future Media Environments*, 9–15. New York: AMS, 2011.

DeWitt, John L. *Japanese Evacuation from the West Coast, 1942: Final Report.* Washington, DC: Government Publishing Office, 1943.

Doctorow, Cory, and Jen Wang. *In Real Life.* New York: First Second, 2014.

Dower, John W. *War without Mercy: Race and Power in the Pacific War.* New York: Pantheon Books, 1986.

Duckett, Margaret. "Plain Language from Bret Harte." *Nineteenth-Century Fiction* 11, no. 4 (1957): 241–60.

Dyer-Witheford, Nick, and Greig de Peuter. *Games of Empire: Global Capitalism and Video Games.* Minneapolis: University of Minnesota Press, 2009.

Ehrmann, Jacques. "*Homo Ludens* Revisited." *Yale French Studies* 41 (1968): 31–57.

Everett, Anna. *Digital Diaspora: A Race for Cyberspace.* Albany: State University of New York Press, 2009.

———. "Foreword." In *Gaming Representation: Race, Gender, and Sexuality in Video Games*, edited by Jennifer Malkowski and TreaAndrea M. Russworm, ix–xvi. Bloomington: Indiana University Press, 2017.

Fabian, Ann. *Card Sharps, Dream Books, and Bucket Shops: Gambling in Nineteenth-Century America.* Ithaca, NY: Cornell University Press, 1990.

Fan, Christopher T. "Techno-Orientalism with Chinese Characteristics: Maureen F. McHugh's *China Mountain Zhang.*" *Journal of Transnational American Studies* 6, no. 1 (2015): 1–33, eScholarship.

Fickle, Tara. "American Rules and Chinese Faces: The Games of Amy Tan's *The Joy Luck Club.*" *MELUS* 39, no. 3 (2014): 68–88.

———. "English before Engrish: Asian American Poetry's Unruly Tongue." *Journal of Comparative Literature Studies* 51, no. 1 (2014): 78–105.

———. "Family Business." *Journal of Asian American Studies* 22 (forthcoming).

Fong, Timothy W. "The Vulnerable Faces of Pathological Gambling." *Psychiatry* 2, no. 4 (2005): 34–42.

Foster, Thomas. "Faceblindness, Visual Pleasure, and Racial Recognition: Ethnicity and Technicity in Ted Chiang's 'Liking What You See: A Documentary.'" *Camera Obscura: Feminism, Culture, and Media Studies* 24, no. 1 (2009): 135–75.

Frasca, Gonzalo. "Simulation versus Narration: Introduction to Ludology." In *The Video Game Theory Reader*, edited by Mark J. P. Wolf and Bernard Perron, 221–37. New York: Routledge, 2003.

Fuller, Mary, and Henry Jenkins. "Nintendo® and New World Travel Writing: A Dialogue." In *Cybersociety: Computer-Mediated Communication and Community*, edited by Steven G. Jones, 57–72. Thousand Oaks, CA: Sage Publications, 1995.

Galloway, Alexander R. "Does the Whatever Speak?" In *Race after the Internet*, edited by Lisa Nakamura and Peter Chow-White, 111–27. Hoboken, NJ: Taylor and Francis, 2013.

———. *Gaming: Essays on Algorithmic Culture*. Minneapolis: University of Minnesota Press, 2006.

———. *The Interface Effect*. Cambridge, UK: Polity, 2012.

Gelber, Steven M. *Hobbies: Leisure and the Culture of Work in America*. New York: Columbia University Press, 2010.

Gladwell, Malcolm. *Outliers: The Story of Success*. New York: Back Bay Books, 2011.

Gleason, William A. *The Leisure Ethic: Work and Play in American Literature, 1840–1940*. Stanford, CA: Stanford University Press, 1999.

Goffman, Erving. *Encounters: Two Studies in the Sociology of Interaction*. Indianapolis: Bobbs-Merrill, 1961.

———. *Interaction Ritual: Essays on Face-to-Face Behavior*. New York: Pantheon Books, 1967.

Goto-Jones, Chris. "Playing with Being in Digital Asia: Gamic Orientalism and the Virtual Dōjō." *Asiascape: Digital Asia* 2 (2015): 20–56.

Gould, Stephen Jay. "The Geometer of Race." *Discover* 15, no. 11 (1994): 65–69.

Grausam, Daniel. *On Endings: American Postmodern Fiction and the Cold War*. Charlottesville: University of Virginia Press, 2011.

Gray, Kishonna L. *Race, Gender, and Deviance in Xbox Live: Theoretical Perspectives from the Virtual Margins*. New York: Routledge, 2014.

Gu, Hongming. "A Great Sinologue." In *The Spirit of the Chinese People*, 138–46. Guilin Shi: Guangxi Shi Fan Da Xue Chu Ban She, 2001.

Harper, Phillip Brian. *Framing the Margins: The Social Logic of Postmodern Culture*. New York: Oxford University Press, 1994.

Hatakeyama, Kenji, and Masakazu Kubo. *2000 Pokémon Story*. Tokyo: Nikkei BP, 2000.

Hayles, N. Katherine. *How We Became Posthuman: Virtual Bodies in Cybernetics, Literature, and Informatics*. Chicago: University of Chicago Press, 2008.

———. "Print Is Flat, Code Is Deep: The Importance of Media-Specific Analysis." *Poetics Today* 25, no. 1 (2004): 67–90.

Hayot, Eric. "Chinese Bodies, Chinese Futures." *Representations* 99 (2007): 99–129.

Heeks, Richard. "Understanding 'Gold Farming' and Real-Money Trading as the Intersection of Real and Virtual Economies." *Journal of Virtual Worlds Research* 2 (2010): 1–27.

Hilferding, Rudolf. *Finance Capital: A Study of the Latest Phase of Capitalist Development*. New York: Routledge, 1985.

Hirabayashi, Lane Ryo. "Wakako Yamauchi's 'The Sensei': Exploring the Ethos of Japanese American Resettlement." *Journal of American Ethnic History* 29, no. 2 (2010): 55–61.

Hjorth, Larissa. "Playing at Being Mobile: Gaming and Cute Culture in South Korea." *Fibreculture* 8 (2006). http://eight.fibreculturejournal.org.

Hoberek, Andrew. *The Twilight of the Middle Class: Post–World War II American Fiction and White-Collar Work*. Princeton, NJ: Princeton University Press, 2005.

Höglund, Johan. "Electronic Empire: Orientalism Revisited in the Military Shooter." *Game Studies* 8, no. 1 (2008). http://gamestudies.org.

HoSang, Daniel, Oneka LaBennett, and Laura Pulido, eds. *Racial Formation in the Twenty-First Century*. Berkeley: University of California Press, 2012.

Hoskins, Colin, and Rolf Mirus. "Reasons for the US Dominance of the International Trade in Television Programmes." *Media, Culture & Society* 10, no. 4 (1988): 499–504.

Hsu, Madeline Y. *Dreaming of Gold, Dreaming of Home: Transnationalism and Migration Between the United States and South China, 1882–1943*. Stanford, CA: Stanford University Press, 2000.

Huizinga, Johan. *Homo Ludens: A Study of the Play-Element in Culture*. Translated by R. F. C. Hull. New York: Routledge, 1949.

Hune, Shirley. "Politics of Chinese Exclusion: Legislative-Executive Conflict, 1876–1882." *Amerasia Journal* 9, no. 1 (1982): 5–27.

Iwabuchi, Koichi. "How 'Japanese' Is Pokémon?" In *Pikachu's Global Adventure: The Rise and Fall of Pokémon*, edited by Joseph Jay Tobin, 53–79. Durham, NC: Duke University Press, 2004.

——. "Pop-Culture Diplomacy in Japan: Soft Power, Nation Branding and the Question of 'International Cultural Exchange.'" *International Journal of Cultural Policy* 21, no. 4 (2015): 419–32.

——. *Resilient Borders and Cultural Diversity: Internationalism, Brand Nationalism, and Multiculturalism in Japan*. Lanham, MD: Lexington Books, 2016.

Jagoda, Patrick. *Network Aesthetics*. Chicago: University of Chicago Press, 2016.

Jameson, Fredric. "Cognitive Mapping." In *Marxism and the Interpretation of Culture*, edited by Cary Nelson and Lawrence Grossberg, 347–60. Urbana: University of Illinois Press, 1988.

——. *Postmodernism; or, The Cultural Logic of Late Capitalism*. Durham, NC: Duke University Press, 1991.

Jenkins, Henry. "Game Design as Narrative Architecture." *In First Person: New Media as Story, Performance, and Game*, edited by Pat Harrigan and Noah Wardrip-Fruin, 118–30. Cambridge, MA: MIT Press, 2004.

Jeon, Joseph Jonghyun. "Neoliberal Forms: CGI, Algorithm, and Hegemony in Korea's IMF Cinema." *Representations* 126, no. 1 (Spring 2014): 85–111.

Joseph, Miranda. *Debt to Society: Accounting for Life under Capitalism*. Minneapolis: University of Minnesota Press, 2014.

Juul, Jesper. "Introduction to Game Time / Time to Play: An Examination of Game Temporality." In *First Person: New Media as Story, Performance and Game*, edited by Noah Wardrip-Fruin and Pat Harrigan, 131–42. Cambridge, MA: MIT Press, 2004.

Kafai, Yasmin B., Carrie Heeter, Jill Denner, and Jennifer Y. Sun, eds. *Beyond Barbie and Mortal Kombat: New Perspectives on Gender and Gaming*. Cambridge, MA: MIT Press, 2008.

Kanazawa, Mark. "Immigration, Exclusion, and Taxation: Anti-Chinese Legislation in Gold Rush California." *Journal of Economic History* 65, no. 3 (2005): 779–805.

Kim, Claire Jean. "The Racial Triangulation of Asian Americans." *Politics & Society* 27, no. 1 (1999): 105–38.

Kim, Daniel Y. "Once More, with Feeling: Cold War Masculinity and the Sentiment of Patriotism in John Okada's *No-No Boy*." *Criticism* 47, no. 1 (2005): 65–83.

Kim, Jodi. *Ends of Empire: Asian American Critique and the Cold War*. Minneapolis: University of Minnesota Press, 2010.

Kingston, Maxine Hong. *The Woman Warrior: Memoirs of a Girlhood among Ghosts*. 1976. Reprint, New York: Random House, 1989.

Kline, Stephen, Nick Dyer-Witheford, and Greig de Peuter. *Digital Play: The Interaction of Technology, Culture, and Marketing*. Montreal: McGill-Queen's University Press, 2014.

Koshy, Susan. "Neoliberal Family Matters," *American Literary History* 25, no. 2 (2013): 344–80.

Krenn, Michael L. *The Color of Empire: Race and American Foreign Relations*. Washington, DC: Potomac Books, 2006.

Kurgan, Laura. *Close Up at a Distance: Mapping, Technology, and Politics*. New York: Zone Books, 2013.

Lazzarato, Maurizio. *The Making of the Indebted Man: An Essay on the Neoliberal Condition*. Cambridge, MA: Semiotext(e), 2012.

Lears, Jackson. *Something for Nothing: Luck in America*. New York: Viking, 2003.

Lebra, Joyce. *Japan's Greater East Asia Co-prosperity Sphere in World War II: Selected Readings and Documents*. New York: Oxford University Press, 1975.

Lee, Christopher. *The Semblance of Identity: Aesthetic Mediation in Asian American Literature*. Stanford, CA: Stanford University Press, 2012.

Lee, Rachel C., and Sau-ling Cynthia Wong, eds. *Asian America.net: Ethnicity, Nationalism, and Cyberspace*. New York: Routledge, 2003.

Leonard, David J. "Not a Hater, Just Keepin' It Real: The Importance of Race- and Gender-Based Game Studies." *Games and Culture* 1, no. 1 (2006): 83–88.

———. *Playing While White: Privilege and Power on and off the Field*. Seattle: University of Washington Press, 2017.

Lesjak, Carolyn. "Reading Dialectically." *Criticism* 55, no. 2 (Spring 2013): 233–77.

Levinovitz, Alan. "Towards a Theory of Toys and Toy-Play." *Human Studies* 40, no. 2 (2017): 267–84.

Li, Wen, Jennifer E. O'Brien, Susan M. Snyder, and Matthew O. Howard. "Characteristics of Internet Addiction/Pathological Internet Use in U.S. University Students: A Qualitative-Method Investigation," *PloS ONE* 10, no. 2 (2015): e0117372.

Lillie-Blanton, Marsha, James C. Anthony, and Charles R. Schuster. "Probing the Meaning of Racial/Ethnic Group Comparisons in Crack Cocaine Smoking." *JAMA* 269, no. 8 (1993): 993–97.

Ling, Jinqi. *Narrating Nationalisms: Ideology and Form in Asian American Literature*. New York: Oxford University Press, 1998.

———. "Race, Power, and Cultural Politics in John Okada's *No-No Boy*." *American Literature* 67, no. 2 (1995): 359–81.

Lowenthal, Leo. *Literature and Mass Culture*. New Brunswick, NJ: Transaction Books, 1984.

Luhmann, Niklas. *Observations on Modernity*. Stanford, CA: Stanford University Press, 1998.

Lye, Colleen. *America's Asia: Racial Form and American Literature, 1893–1945*. Princeton, NJ: Princeton University Press, 2005.

———. "Racial Form." *Representations* 104, no. 1 (2008): 92–101.

———. "Unmarked Character and the 'Rise of Asia': Ed Park's *Personal Days*." *Verge: Studies in Global Asias* 1, no. 1 (2015): 230–54.

Magnet, Shoshana. "Playing at Colonization: Interpreting Imaginary Landscapes in the Video Game Tropico," *Journal of Communication Inquiry* 30 (2006): 142–62.

Malkowski, Jennifer, and TreaAndrea M. Russworm, eds. *Gaming Representation: Race, Gender, and Sexuality in Video Games*. Bloomington: Indiana University Press, 2017.

Mangan, James Anthony. *The Games Ethic and Imperialism: Aspects of the Diffusion of an Ideal*. Harmondsworth, UK: Viking, 1986.

Marks, Jonathan. "Long Shadow of Linnaeus's Human Taxonomy," *Nature* 447, no. 7140 (2007): 28.

Martin, Paul. "Race, Colonial History and National Identity: *Resident Evil 5* as a Japanese Game." *Games and Culture* 13, no. 6 (2016): 1–19.

Martin, Randy. *An Empire of Indifference: American War and the Financial Logic of Risk Management*. Durham, NC: Duke University Press, 2007.

Mason, Jeffrey D. *Melodrama and the Myth of America*. Bloomington: Indiana University Press, 1993.

McCain, Roger A. *Game Theory and Public Policy*. Cheltenham, UK: Edward Elgar, 2009.

McClanahan, Annie. *Dead Pledges: Debt, Crisis, and Twenty-First-Century Culture*. Stanford, CA: Stanford University Press, 2018.

McGonigal, Jane. *Reality Is Broken: Why Games Make Us Better and How They Can Change the World*. New York: Penguin, 2011.

McVeigh, Brian J. "How Hello Kitty Commodifies the Cute, Cool and Camp: 'Consumutopia' versus 'Control' in Japan." *Journal of Material Culture* 5, no. 2 (2000): 225–45.

Melamed, Jodi. *Represent and Destroy: Rationalizing Violence in the New Racial Capitalism*. Minneapolis: University of Minnesota Press, 2011.

Michaels, Walter Benn. "Model Minorities and the Minority Model: The Neoliberal Novel." In *The Cambridge History of the American Novel*, edited by Leonard Cassuto, Clare Virginia Eby, and Benjamin Reiss, 1016–30. Cambridge, UK: Cambridge University Press, 2011.

———. *The Trouble with Diversity: How We Learned to Love Identity and Ignore Inequality*. New York: Metropolitan Books, 2006.

Mills, C. Wright. *White Collar: The American Middle Classes*. New York: Oxford University Press, 1951.

Mills, Charles W. *The Racial Contract*. Ithaca, NY: Cornell University Press, 1997.

Monk, Leland. *Standard Deviations: Chance and the Modern British Novel*. Stanford, CA: Stanford University Press, 1993.

Morgenstern, Oskar. "Theory of Games." *Scientific American* 180, no. 5 (1949): 22–25.

Morley, David, and Kevin Robins. *Spaces of Identity: Global Media, Electronic Landscapes, and Cultural Boundaries*. New York: Routledge, 1995.

Morton, Suzanne. *At Odds: Gambling and Canadians, 1919–1969*. Toronto: University of Toronto Press, 2016.

Moulthrop, Stuart. "Preface." In *Disappearance*, by Michael Joyce, xix–xxvii. New York: Steerage, 2012.

Mukherjee, Souvik. "Playing Subaltern: Video Games and Postcolonialism." *Games and Culture* 13, no. 5 (2018): 504–20.

Mullen, Harryette. *The Cracks between What We Are and What We Are Supposed to Be: Essays and Interviews*. Tuscaloosa: University Alabama Press, 2012.

Muller, Eric L. *American Inquisition: The Hunt for Japanese American Disloyalty in World War II*. Chapel Hill: University of North Carolina Press, 2007.

Murakami, Takashi. *Little Boy: The Arts of Japan's Exploding Subculture*. New Haven, CT: Yale University Press, 2005.

Murayama, Milton. *All I Asking for Is My Body*. San Francisco: Supa Press, 1975.

Murray, Soraya. "The Work of Postcolonial Game Studies in the Play of Culture." *Open Library of Humanities* 4, no. 1 (2018): 13.

Myer, Dillon S. *Uprooted Americans*. Tucson: University of Arizona Press, 1971.

Nakamura, Hiroshi. *Treadmill: A Documentary Novel*. Buffalo, NY: Mosaic Press, 1996.

Nakamura, Lisa. "Afterword: Racism, Sexism, and Gaming's Cruel Optimism." In *Gaming Representation: Race, Gender, and Sexuality in Video Games*, edited by Jennifer Malkowski and TreaAndrea M. Russworm. Bloomington: Indiana University Press, 2017.

———. *Cybertypes: Race, Ethnicity, and Identity on the Internet*. New York: Routledge, 2002.

———. *Digitizing Race: Visual Cultures of the Internet*. Minneapolis: University of Minnesota Press, 2008.

———. "Don't Hate the Player, Hate the Game: The Racialization of Labor in World of Warcraft." *Critical Studies in Media Communication* 26, no. 2 (2009): 128–44.

———. "'It's a Nigger in Here! Kill the Nigger!': User-Generated Media Campaigns against Racism, Sexism, and Homophobia in Digital Games." In *The International Encyclopedia of Media Studies*, edited by Angharad N. Valdivia, 2–15. Malden, MA: Wiley-Blackwell, 2013.

Nakamura, Lisa, and Peter Chow-White, eds. *Race after the Internet*. Hoboken, NJ: Taylor and Francis, 2013.

Ngai, Sianne. "The Cuteness of the Avant-Garde." *Critical Inquiry* 31, no. 4 (2005): 811–47.

Nguyen, Viet Thanh. *Race and Resistance: Literature and Politics in Asian America*. New York: Oxford University Press, 2002.

Noble, Safiya Umoja. *Algorithms of Oppression: How Search Engines Reinforce Racism*. New York: New York University Press, 2018.

Okada, John. *No-No Boy*. 1957. Reprint, Seattle: University of Washington Press, 1981.

Okihiro, Gary Y. *Margins and Mainstreams: Asians in American History and Culture*. 1994. Reprint, Seattle: University of Washington Press, 2014.

Omi, Michael, and Howard Winant. *Racial Formation in the United States: From the 1960s to the 1990s*. New York: Routledge, 1994.

Oriard, Michael. *Sporting with the Gods: The Rhetoric of Play and Game in American Culture*. Cambridge, UK: Cambridge University Press, 1991.

Osborn, William, Sylvia Watanabe, and Wakako Yamauchi. "A *MELUS* Interview: Wakako Yamauchi." *MELUS* 23, no. 2 (Summer 1998): 101–10.

Palumbo-Liu, David. *Asian/American: Historical Crossings of a Racial Frontier*. Stanford, CA: Stanford University Press, 2000.

Parker, E. H. "Notes." *China Review; or, Notes and Queries on the Far East* 22 (1897): 739–42.

Patterson, Christopher B. "Asian Americans and Digital Games." In *Oxford Research Encyclopedia of Asian American Literature and Culture*, edited by Josephine Lee, Floyd Cheung, Jennifer Ho, Anita Mannur, and Cathy Schlund-Vials. New York: Oxford University Press, 2018. http://oxfordre.com.

Petersen, William. *Japanese Americans: Oppression and Success*. New York: Random House, 1971.

Phan, Hoang Gia. "'A Race So Different': Chinese Exclusion, the *Slaughterhouse Cases*, and *Plessy v. Ferguson*." *Labor History* 45, no. 2 (2004): 133–63.

Phillips, Amanda. "(Queer) Algorithmic Ecology: The Great Opening Up of Nature to All Mobs." In *Understanding* Minecraft: *Essays on Play, Community, and Possibilities*, edited by Nate Garrelts. Jefferson, NC: McFarland, 2014.

Piette, Adam. *The Literary Cold War, 1945–Vietnam*. Edinburgh: Edinburgh University Press, 2009.

Poundstone, William. *Prisoner's Dilemma*. New York: Doubleday, 1992.

Przybylski, Andrew K., Netta Weinstein, and Kou Murayama. "Internet Gaming Disorder: Investigating the Clinical Relevance of a New Phenomenon." *American Journal of Psychiatry* 174 (2017): 230–35.

Reichmuth, Philipp, and Stefan Werning. "Pixel Pashas, Digital Djinns." *ISIM* 18 (2006): 2.

Report of the Joint Special Committee to Investigate Chinese Immigration. Washington, DC: Government Publishing Office, 1877. Internet Archive.

Rettberg, Scott. "Corporate Ideology in *World of Warcraft*." In *Digital Culture, Play, and Identity: A World of Warcraft Reader*, edited by Hilde G. Corneliussen, Jill Walker Rettberg, and T. L. Taylor, 19–38. Cambridge, MA: MIT Press.

Rey, P. J. "Gamification and Post-Fordist Capitalism." In *The Gameful World: Approaches, Issues, Applications*, edited by Steffen P. Walz and Sebastian Deterding, 277–96. Cambridge, MA: MIT Press, 2015.

Rivera, Takeo. "Do Asians Dream of Electric Shrieks? Techno-Orientalism and Erotohistoriographic Masochism in Eidos Montreal's *Deus Ex: Human Revolution*." *Amerasia Journal* 40, no. 2 (2014): 67–86.

———. "Orientalist Biopower in *World of Warcraft: Mists of Pandaria*." In *The Routledge Companion to Asian American Media*, edited by Lori Lopez and Vincent Pham. New York: Routledge, 2017. www.routledgehandbooks.com.

Robertson, Roland. "Glocalization: Time-Space and Homogeneity-Heterogeneity." In *Global Modernities*, edited by Mike Featherstone, Scott Lash, and Roland Robertson, 35–53. London: Sage Publications, 1995.

Roh, David S., Betsy Huang, and Greta A. Niu, eds. *Techno-Orientalism: Imagining Asia in Speculative Fiction, History, and Media*. New Brunswick, NJ: Rutgers University Press, 2015.

Said, Edward W. *Orientalism*. 1979. Reprint, New York: Vintage Books, 1994.

Salen, Katie, and Eric Zimmerman, eds. *The Game Design Reader: A Rules of Play Anthology*. Cambridge, MA: MIT Press, 2006.

Scharnhorst, Gary. "'Ways That Are Dark': Appropriations of Bret Harte's 'Plain Language from Truthful James.'" *Nineteenth-Century Literature* 51, no. 3 (1996): 377–99.

Schiller, J. C. Friedrich von. *On the Aesthetic Education of Man, in a Series of Letters*. New Haven, CT: Yale University Press, 1954.

Seligman, Scott D. *Tong Wars: The Untold Story of Vice, Money, and Murder in New York's Chinatown*. New York: Viking, 2016.

Seltzer, Mark. *The Official World*. Durham, NC: Duke University Press, 2016.

———. "Parlor Games: The Apriorization of the Media." *Critical Inquiry* 52, no. 1 (2009): 100–133.

Shaw, Adrienne. *Gaming at the Edge: Sexuality and Gender at the Margins of Gamer Culture*. Minneapolis: University of Minnesota Press, 2015.

Schenk, Frithjof Benjamin. "Mental Maps: The Cognitive Mapping of the Continent as an Object of Research of European History." *European History Online*, published by the Leibniz Institute of European History, July 8, 2013. www.ieg-ego.eu.

Shiokawa, Kanako. "Cute but Deadly: Women and Violence in Japanese Comics." In *Themes and Issues in Asian Cartooning: Cute, Cheap, Mad, and Sexy*, edited by John A. Lent, 93–125. Bowling Green, OH: Bowling Green State University Popular Press, 1999.

Shiu, Anthony Sze-Fai. "What Yellowface Hides: Video Games, Whiteness, and the American Racial Order." *Journal of Popular Culture* 39, no. 1 (2006): 109–25.

Simmel, Georg. *The Sociology of Georg Simmel*. Translated by K. H. Wolff. Glencoe, IL: Free Press, 1950.

Šisler, Vit. "Digital Arabs: Representation in Video Games." *European Journal of Cultural Studies* 11, no. 2 (2008): 203–19.

Sneider, Daniel. "Textbooks and Patriotic Education: Wartime Memory Formation in China and Japan." *Asia-Pacific Review* 20, no. 1 (2013): 35–54.

So, Christine. *Economic Citizens: A Narrative of Asian American Visibility*. Philadelphia: Temple University Press, 2008.

Sohn, Stephen. "Introduction: Alien/Asian: Imagining the Racialized Future." *MELUS* 33, no. 4 (2008): 5–22.

Stabile, Carol. "'I Will Own You': Accountability in Massively Multiplayer Online Games." *Television and New Media* 15, no. 1 (2014): 43–57.

Stallabras, Julian. "Just Gaming: Allegory and Economy in Computer Games." *New Left Review* 198 (1993): 83–106.

Stefans, Brian Kim. *Word Toys: Poetry and Technics*. Tuscaloosa: University of Alabama Press, 2017.

Steinkuehler, Constance. "The Mangle of Play." *Games and Culture* 1, no. 3 (2006): 199–213.

Sumida, Stephen H. *And the View from the Shore: Literary Traditions of Hawai'i*. Seattle: University of Washington Press, 1991.

Sung, Betty Lee. *Mountain of Gold: The Story of the Chinese in America*. New York: Macmillan, 1967.

Sutton-Smith, Brian. *The Ambiguity of Play*. Cambridge, MA: Harvard University Press, 1997.

Suzuki, Bob. "Education and the Socialization of Asian Americans: A Revisionist Analysis of the 'Model Minority' Thesis." *Amerasia* 4, no. 2 (1977): 23–51.

Tally, Robert T., Jr. "Fredric Jameson and the Controversy over 'Third-World Literature in the Era of Multinational Capitalism.'" *Global South Studies: A Collective Publication with The Global South*, November 9, 2017. http://globalsouthstudies.as.virginia.edu.

Tan, Amy. *The Joy Luck Club*. New York: G. P. Putnam's Sons, 1989.

Taylor, Tina L. *Play between Worlds: Exploring Online Game Culture*. Cambridge, MA: MIT Press, 2009.

Tenen, Dennis. *Plain Text: The Poetics of Computation*. Stanford, CA: Stanford University Press, 2017.

Thomas, Douglas. "KPK, Inc.: Race, Nation, and Emergent Culture in Online Games." In *Learning Race and Ethnicity: Youth and Digital Media*, edited by Anna Everett, 155–74. Cambridge, MA: MIT Press, 2008.

Tobin, Joseph Jay, ed. *Pikachu's Global Adventure: The Rise and Fall of Pokémon*. Durham, NC: Duke University Press, 2004.

Toscano, Alberto, and Jeff Kinkle. *Cartographies of the Absolute*. Lanham, MD: John Hunt Publishing, 2015.

Tuan, Mia. *Forever Foreigners or Honorary Whites? The Asian Ethnic Experience Today.* New Brunswick, NJ: Rutgers University Press, 1998.

Tulloch, Sara. *Oxford Dictionary of New Words.* Oxford, UK: Oxford University Press, 1991.

Ueno, Toshiya. "Techno-Orientalism and Media-Tribalism: On Japanese Animation and Rave Culture." *Third Text* 13, no. 47 (1999): 95–106.

Unno, Kazutaka. "Cartography in Japan." In *The History of Cartography: Cartography in the Traditional East and Southeast Asian Societies*, edited by J. B. Harley and David Woodward, vol. 2, book 2, 346–447. Chicago: University of Chicago Press, 1994.

Victoria, Brian Daizen. *Zen at War.* Lanham, MD: Rowman & Littlefield, 2006.

Von Neumann, John. "On the Theory of Games of Strategy." *Contributions to the Theory of Games* 4 (1959): 13–42.

Von Neumann, John, and Oskar Morgenstern. *Theory of Games and Economic Behavior.* 1947. Reprint, Princeton, NJ: Princeton University Press, 2004.

Vukovich, Daniel. *China and Orientalism: Western Knowledge Production and the PRC.* New York: Routledge, 2013.

Wark, McKenzie. *Gamer Theory.* Cambridge, MA: Harvard University Press, 2007.

War Relocation Authority. *WRA: A Story of Human Conservation.* Washington, DC: Government Publishing Office, 1946. Internet Archive.

Weglyn, Michi Nishiura. *Years of Infamy: The Untold Story of America's Concentration Camps.* Seattle: University of Washington Press, 1996.

Williams, J. D. *The Compleat Strategyst, Being a Primer on the Theory of Games of Strategy.* 1954. Reprint, New York: Dover Books, 1986.

Williams, R. John. *The Buddha in the Machine: Art, Technology, and the Meeting of East and West.* New Haven, CT: Yale University Press, 2014.

Wimsatt, W. K., Jr., and Monroe C. Beardsley. "The Intentional Fallacy." In *The Verbal Icon: Studies in the Meaning of Poetry*, 2–18. Lexington: University Press of Kentucky, 1954.

Wittgenstein, Ludwig. *Philosophical Investigations. New York: Macmillan, 1953.*

Wong, Jade Snow. *Fifth Chinese Daughter.* 1950. Reprint, Seattle: University of Washington Press, 1990.

Wong, Sau-ling Cynthia. *Reading Asian American Literature: From Necessity to Extravagance.* Princeton, NJ: Princeton University Press, 1993.

Wood, Denis, and John Fels. *The Power of Maps.* New York: Guilford Press, 1992.

Wu, Ellen D. *The Color of Success: Asian Americans and the Origins of the Model Minority.* Princeton, NJ: Princeton University Press, 2014.

Wu, Frank H. *Yellow: Race in America beyond Black and White.* New York: Basic Books, 2002.

Yamamoto, Hisaye. "Seventeen Syllables." Edited by King-Kok Cheung. New Brunswick, NJ: Rutgers University Press, 1994.

Yamauchi, Wakako. *Songs My Mother Taught Me: Stories, Plays, and Memoir.* Edited by Garrett Hongo. New York: Feminist Press at the City University of New York, 1994.

Yang, Gene, and Thien Pham. *Level Up.* New York: First Second Books, 2011.

Yano, Christine Reiko. *Pink Globalization: Hello Kitty's Trek across the Pacific.* Durham, NC: Duke University Press, 2013.

Yogi, Stan. "'You Had to Be One or the Other': Oppositions and Reconciliations in John Okada's *No-No Boy.*" *MELUS* 21, no. 2 (1996): 63–77.

Yu, Charles. *How to Live Safely in a Science Fictional Universe.* New York: Pantheon Books, 2010.

Zorbas, Elaine. *Banished and Embraced: The Chinese in Fiddletown and the Mother Lode.* Plymouth, CA: Mythos Press, 2015.

INDEX

"Abe Mario," 169–71, *170*
academics, race and, 83, 90
addiction: gambling, 33–34, 98, 101–2;
    internet, 23, 178, 179, 197; Internet
    Gaming Disorder, 179–81; race and,
    180; substance, 179–80
aesthetics, 225n42; as creativity, 39; cyber-
    punk aesthetics, 205n20; history and,
    175; play and, 223n9; of *Pokémon GO*,
    226n65; representation, 227n67
affirmative action, 80
African Americans, 18–19, 38
agon (competition), 25, 45, 114, 119–21, 131,
    132, 133, 134, 135
agonism, 119–21, 220n18
Ah Sin, 43, *44*, 46, 69, 183
Aiiieeeee! (Chan et al.), 12–13, 75, 100
Akil, Omari, 1–2
alea (chance), 25, 45, 114, 131, *132*, 133, 134, 135
alienation, 92
Allegories of Control (Galloway), 196
allegory, race as, 196, 230n41
All I Asking for Is My Body (Murayama),
    62, 66–70, 103
Amazon, 189
America is in the Heart (Bulosan), 213n54
American dream, 68, 70, 82–83, 94, 107
Americanness, 91
"Anda's Game," 184–86, *185*, 189, 191–92,
    194, *195*, 229nn18–19
And the View from the Shore (Sumida),
    212n52
Anglophone literature, 19
anti-Chinese movement, 44, 46

anti-Japanese journalism, 210n4
Apple Maps, *157*
apps, geospatial data and, 142
AR. *See* augmented reality
art, 206n43
artistic license, 206n35
Asian Americans: Asian nationals and,
    27; assimilation, 21; family life, 85, 92;
    gambling and, 38, 97–98; identity, 13,
    212n46; Internet Gaming Disorder
    and, 180; labor, 3, 15, 22, 149–50; in
    literature, 12, 18, 97, 206n35; loyalty, 98;
    mental health, 85; model minority and,
    83; perception of, 15; representation, 13,
    21, 206n35, 207n55; risk-taking and, 87;
    as role models, 95; self-conception of,
    98; stereotypes of, 4, 15, 89–90; studies,
    8–9; success story, 81–82, 91; technol-
    ogy and, 8; video games and, 203n5
Asian gamer death, 9
Asian invasion, 162
assimilation, 89
assumptions, games and, 144
atomic bomb, 226n65
augmented reality (AR): marketing and,
    157–58; in *Pokémon GO*, 1, 6, 124, 153,
    153, 154, 156, 159, 173
authenticity, 12, 126
autocorrect, 26
avant-garde poets, 206n43
avatars, 2, 184, 193–94, 230n30

banking emergency, 106
Bateson, Gregory, 15–16

Battle Hymn of the Tiger Mother (Chua), 16–17

Baudelaire, Charles, 113

A Beautiful Mind, 62–63

Benjamin, Walter, 215n31, 230n41

biology: of gambling, 85–86; race and, 127–28, 204n18

Blade Runner, 9

Blizzard (company), 186

bluffing, 45, 50, 52

Bob Santo (fictional character), 59–60, 211n33

Bourdieu, Pierre, 13, 86, 187

boxing, 51, 68

branding, 24, 162, 167, 169, 174

bridge, 50, 57, 211n24

Brown, Garret, 33

Bulosan, Carlos, 213n54

Burckhardt, Jacob, 119

Caillois, Roger, 11, 25, 45, 113–18, 124–30, 134, 137, 143, 219n8, 219n14

California, 35

capitalism, 35, 86, 106, 159–60

cartography. *See* mapping

casinos, Las Vegas, 92–93, 97

celebrity, race and, 81–82, 214n15

CGI, 227n67

chance, 24, 25, 45, 79, 132, 207n51. See also *alea*; gambling; games of chance

characters, 18–21. *See also* avatars

cheap labor, 22–23, 37, 43, 184, 210n35; Chinese labor and, 44–46; games of chance and, 39–40; immigration and, 40

cheating, 45, 46, 81, 186

Chiang, Mark, 13

childhood, 129, 161, 226n65

child labor, 194

Chin, Frank, 74–75

China, 224n39; gambling in, 84; parenting in, 16–17; play in, 122; time in, 134–35; trade in, 181

Chinatown, 35, 95, 209n6

"Chinatown Offers Us a Lesson," 95

Chinese Americans: family life, 95–97, 96; gambling of, 33–36, 208n2, 209n6; labor, 95–97, 96, 216n55, 217n59

Chinese-English Dictionary (Giles), 129–30

Chinese Exclusion Act, 33–34

Chinese immigrants, 33, 37–38, 40–41

Chinese labor, 95–97, 96, 182–84, 216n55, 217n59; cheap labor and, 44–46; criminalization of, 38; non-coerced status of, 42; slavery and, 209n23

Chinese question, 34

"Chinpokomon," 171, *172*, 173

Chua, Amy, 16–17

circular indictment, 6–7

circular time, 134, 135–36

citizenship, 34, 70, 71, 89, 193, 217n61

civil rights, 54–55, 81

class, 8, 79–81, 188

Class Craft, 124

Coca-Cola, 147

cognitive mapping, 157, 159–60, 161, 225n45

Cold War, 23, 53; culture, 50, 54, 213n67; game theory, 62; media, 94; model minority and, 88–89

colonization, 162, 225n53

colorblindness, 6, 192–93

commodity white face, 145, 150–51

communication, war and, 54

competition, 25, 42, 45, 84, 86, 128, 132, 209n24. See also *agon*

The Compleat Strategyst (Williams), 63–64

computer games, 215n31. *See also* video games

computer gaming, race and, 4

conflict, globalization of, 53

Confucianism, 103–4

conscience, 65

consumerism and consumption, 85, 177

contests, 120

course of actions, in game theory, 65

cowardice, 68
craps, 34, 51, 69, 208n56
cross-cultural conflicts, 207n55
crossword puzzles, 128
crowdsourcing, 63
Culin, Stewart, 41–42
cultural exchange, 168
cultural odor, 147
cultural unconscious, 158
cultural values, 67, 145
culture, 203n4; class and, 80–81; defini-
    tion of, 219n14; Eurocentric, 115–16;
    gambling and, 97–98; games and,
    129–30; of Hawaii, 69; model minor-
    ity and, 118–19; nationalism and, 168;
    play and, 114–16, 118–19, 124, 127,
    219n14, 220n18; reality and, 115; rules
    and, 20–21; structures of, 219n8; video
    games and, 20
cuteness, 150, 171, 174, 226n65, 228n71
cyberpunk aesthetics, 205n20
cyberspace, 161, 182, 193
cybertypes, 194

debt, economy and, 106
deception, 50, 69
decision making, 52, 56, 63
defection, game theory and, 60
dehumanization, 53–54, 69
democracy, 22, 93, 212n52
Derrida, Jacques, 136
deterministic causality, 207n51
DeWitt, John L., 47, 66, 72, 211n27
Diagnostic and Statistical Manual of
    Mental Disorders (DSM-V), 179–81
dice, 22, 208n56; chirality of, 208n56
Dick, Philip K., 52, 75
dilemma tale, 63, 65–66
Diogenes, 117, 134, 135
A Discourse on Inequality (Rousseau), 60
domesticity, race and, 95
Donkey Kong, 150
Doraemon, 168

The Dream Adventure (Caillois), 117
drugs, 180
DSM-V. See Diagnostic and Statistical
    Manual of Mental Disorders

East Asia, 118–21
economy, 178; debt and, 106; ethics and,
    106; exploitation and, 195–96; as game,
    86; inequality and, 80; internment and,
    106; plantation, 62; race and, 8
education, race and, 88
elections, gambling and, 36
electronic frontier, 161
email, 141, 222n1
Emi (fictional character), 72–74, 213n67,
    213n69
emotion, uncertainty and, 65
empathy, gambling and, 215n31
employment, white-collar, 87
Enlightenment, 204n18
equality, 6
equal opportunity, 8, 80, 86
e-racing, 203n4
escape, games as, 10
eSports, 4
essentialism, 12–14, 132
ethics, 22, 106
ethnocentrism, 119, 125, 143, 145, 149, 166,
    173, 219n14
euchre, 43, 46, 122, 183, 210n34
EverQuest, 187
evolution, 120, 127–28
exceptionalism, 89
exotic representation, 9
experiments, 52
exploitation, 189, 190, 192, 193, 195–96

fair play, 8, 22, 46, 49, 182, 192
fate, 106, 135
fatefulness, 92
Faulkner, William, 19
fiction, modern, 74–76
Fifth Chinese Daughter (Wong, J.), 20

filial piety, loyalty and, 67
finance, 88, 230n41
first-order observations, 55
Fitbit, 124, 189
flower cards, 218n73
folkloric tradition, game theory and, 63–64
foreignness, 34
foreign policy, 23, 50
form games, 206n43
Fortune, 63
free content, 143
freemium games, 144, 189
freeplay, 206n43
free wage labor, 45
frugality, 86

Galloway, Alexander, 125–26, 189–90, 192, 196
Gamblers Unions, 35, 209n6
gambling, 3, 22; abolition of, 215n45; addiction, 33–34, 98, 101–2; American dream and, 94; Asian Americans and, 38, 97–98; Benjamin on, 215n31; biology of, 85–86; in California, 35; in China, 84; in Chinatown, 95; of Chinese, 33–36, 208n2, 209n6; Chinese immigrants and, 40; competition and, 42; criminalization of, 36; culture and, 97–98; debates, 37, 38; disorders, 98; domestication of, 92; elections and, 36; empathy and, 215n31; games, 84; generations and, 95, 215n45; as hobby, 95; houses, 35; immigration and, 85–86, 94; laws, 209n8; losses, 42; model minority and, 92, 106; morality and, 36, 37; narrative, 25; as occupation, 38; Pegúy on, 79; politics and, 98; race and, 97–98, 220n22; romanticization of, 92; stereotypes of, 22–23; U.S. and, 37, 84; wages and, 42; work and, 86–87, 105; yellow peril and, 85–86; youth disgusted with, 215n45

The Gambling Games of the Chinese in America (Culin), 41–42
Gameboy, 150, 224n32
game consoles, 10, 205n24. *See also* video games
Gamer Theory (Wark), 5, 125, 204n10, 230n41
games, 206n43; assumptions and, 144; categories of, 114, 131, *132*; culture and, 5, 129–30; definition of, 11, 39; economy as, 86; as escapes, 10; evolution of, 120; freemium, 144, 189; gambling, 84; honesty and, 45; labor and, 39, 45, 214n20; licenses, 15; literary representation of, 207n51; markets and, 190; nations and, 197; nongame and, 125; perception of, 7; pleasure of, 214n20; politics and, 26; race and, 20, 122; racism and, 230n33; realism in, 125–26; reality and, 125–26; of representation, 12–15, 206n35, 207n55; responsibilities and, 180; rules of, 133; social attitudes about, 10; sociology of, 127, 131, 132–33; stories and, 19; technology and, 10, 15; time in reality and time in, 221n36; as whole world, 221n36; across the world, 208n56; world and, 144. *See also* video games
games of chance, 80, 107, 215n31; cheap labor and, 39–40; labor and, 39–40; social mobility and, 79; yellow peril and, 88–89. *See also* gambling
Games of Empire, 226n56
gamespace, 5, 23
game studies, 11; African Americans and, 38; blind spot in, 125, 131, 144; contemporary, 136; representation in, 203n3
game theory, 137, 144; Cold War, 62; course of actions in, 65; defection and, 60; folkloric tradition and, 63–64; human behavior and, 52; literature and, 75; morality in, 65; narrative, 50; rationality and, 53; second-order observations and, 55; in U.S., 53

gamification, 177; definition of, 190; as exploitation, 190; of race, ludo-Orientalism and, 1–8; race and, 27, 204n18
Gaming Representation, 5
GEA. *See* Greater East Asia Co-Prosperity Sphere
Geary bill, 33
gender, 61, 62, 95, 194. *See also* women
generations, gambling and, 95, 215n45
genetics, 219n14
genre problem, 17
geocentric identity, 158
George Motoyama (fictional character), 61–62
geospatial data, 142
Giles, Herbert, 129–30
globalization, 3, 53, 181, 182
glocalization, 151–55, 157, 173–74, 224n32, 226n55, 233n222
God, 106
Goffman, Erving, 79, 92, 103, 187
Golden Gate Bridge, 47
gold farming, 23, 181–83, 186, 187–97, 195, 228n3
gold mining. *See* Chinese labor
Gold Mountain, 83, 215n21
gold rush, 35
Google, 189; consumer base of, 141; Earth, 141; Gmail, 141, 222n1; Maps, 138–45, 141, 142, 155, 156, 157, 162; MentalPlex, 139, 222n1; Niantic and, 142; Pokémon Challenge, 139–42, 153, 222n4; social hegemony of, 222n5
GPS technology, 6, 138, 141, 145, 156–57, 161
Grand Theft Auto, 2, 15
Granet, Marcel, 120
Gray, Giles, 42
Great Depression, 95
Greater East Asia Co-Prosperity Sphere (GEA), 164–65, 166–67
The Greeks and Greek Civilization (Burckhardt), 119
Gretzky, Wayne, 87

groupthink, 68
guilt, 65

HabitRPG, 124
Half-Real (Juul), 125
Hanke, John, 141, 153–54
hard work, 86
Harper, Philip Brian, 193
Harte, Bret, 23, 43–46, 44, 69, 92, 104, 122, 183
Hawaii, 62, 69
Hayles, N. Katherine, 26
"The Heathen Chinee," 23, 40, 43–46, 44, 182–84, 210nn34–35
Heller, Joseph, 52, 75
Hello Kitty, 145, 168
heredity, 187
higher education, 90, 177–78
historical instrumentalism, 16
historical revisionism, 71
history, 10, 117, 169, 175
hobby: gambling as, 95; models, 95–97, 96, 216n55, 217n59
Homo Ludens (Huizinga), 25, 113, 117, 122, 123, 145–46
Homo sapiens, 132–33
honesty, games and, 45
Hong Kong, 129
honor, 45
hope, 87
How to Win at Poker (Brown), 33
How We Became Posthuman (Hayles), 26
Huizinga, Johan, 11, 25, 113–18, 120, 122, 124, 126, 137, 143, 145–46, 193, 219n8, 219n14
human agency, 53, 56
human behavior, 52, 53–54
human differences, 159
humanism, 51–56, 63
human typologies, 9

Ichiro Yamada (fictional character), 59–60, 70–75, 211n33, 213n62, 213n67, 213n69
ideals, 22

identity, 10, 24; Asian Americans, 13, 212n46; avatars and, 193–94; formation, racial, 51; geocentric, 158; geographic, 136; maps and, 156; of minorities, 207n51; race and, 51, 80, 193; of reality, 197; space and, 7; U.S., 33; in video games, 203n3; Western, 196

ilinx (vertigo), 11, 114, 131, *132*, 133

The Image of the City (Lynch), 160

imagination, 114, 188

imaginative geography, 122–23, 126, 153–67

IMF crisis, 227n67

immigration, 62, 217n61; cheap labor and, 40; gambling and, 85–86, 94; narratives, 86; neurology of, 85–86; social mobility and, 24–25

imperialism, 219n14; cognitive mapping and, 161, 225n45; mapping and, 193; ontological, 158; *Pokémon GO* and, 167–68

Inada, Lawson Fusao, 74–75

individuality, 68

industriousness, 103–4

inequality, 6, 26, 80, 107, 116, 190

Ingress, 124, 154, *155*, 224n29, 224n32

In Real Life (Wang), 184–86, *185*, 194, *195*, 229nn18–19

insanity, 73

instructability, 47, 50, 51, 56–62

intentional fallacy, 76

intentionalism, 76

intentionality, 55

internet addiction. *See* addiction

Internet Gaming Disorder, 179–81

internment: camps, Las Vegas and, 99–103; economy and, 106; fatalism and, 104; female characters in literature about, 74; financial loss from, 88; injustice of, 89; justification of, 48–49, 56, 67; literary depiction of, 51; loyalty and, 49; racism and, 54; segregation and, 59; transnational dimensions of, 212n46

invisibles, 19

Iraq, invasion of, 76

irrationality, 61, 70–74, 79

Ishihara, Tsunekazu, 153–54

Ivy League schools, 83

Iwata, Satoru, 153–54

Jameson, Frederic, 159–60, 196, 225n43

Japan: commodity white face in, 150–51; "Cool Japan" campaign, 168–69, 227n69; mapping in, 166, 226n58; nationalism of, 102, 168; patriarchy in, 68; *Pokémon GO* and, 145, 223n10; propaganda of, 163–66, *164–65*; video games in, 148–50, 223n18

Japanese Americans: Cub Scouts, *91*; loyalty of, 65–66, 211n23; propaganda about, *48*; values of, 104

Les jeux et les hommes (Caillois). *See* "Man, Play, and Games"

Jiro Nishikawa (fictional character), 62

jokers, 210n34

The Joy Luck Club (Tan), 20–21, 86

justice, 45

Juul, Jasper, 125, 221n36

juvenile delinquency, 89

kawaii (cuteness), 150, 226n65, 228n71. *See also* cuteness

Kenji (fictional character), 72, 74, 213n69

Kingston, Maxine Hong, 16–17, 38, 97, 98

Kiyo Oyama (fictional character), 66–70, 212n52

knowledge, formation of, 203n4

Kubrick, Stanley, 52

Kurisu (character), 59–60

labor, 182; Asian American, 3, 15, 22, 149–50; child, 194; criminalization of Chinese, 38; games and, 39, 45; games of chance and, 39–40; gaming and, 214n20; leisure and, 190; micro, 192; organizations, 43; play and, 189; "playbor," 189–90; unpaid, 192; values and, 35; yellow peril and, 216n55. *See also* cheap labor; Chinese labor

"The Lady, or the Tiger?," 73, 75

language games, 206n43

Las Vegas, 99–103

"Las Vegas Charley," 98–106, 218n73

legislation, 25, 34

legitimacy, representation and, 13

leisure, 15, 190

level playing field, 8, 187

Level Up (Yang and Pham), 17–18, *18*

Levinas, Emmanuel, 158

Lévi-Strauss, Claude, 136

life expectancy, 88

liminality, 19, 72, 213n62

linguistics, 152–53, 228n71

Linnaeus, Carl, 131–32

literature, 25; African American, 18–19; Anglophone, 19; Asian American, 12, 18, 97, 206n35; games in, 207n51; game theory and, 75; about internment, female characters in, 74; internment depiction in, 51; politics and, 76; racialization and, 207n51

lotteries, 35, 79–80, 84, 215n45

loyalty, 23–24; Asian American, 98; competing, 74; filial piety and, 67; gender and, 61; hearings, 58; instructability and, 56–62; internment and, 49; of Japanese Americans, 65–66, 211n23; marriage and, 62; national, 56, 61, 67; oath, 71; questionnaire, 57–59, 60, 70–71, 94, 211n24, 211n27, 213n60; race and, 48, 66–67, 210n4; war and, 54

luck, 80, 207n51

ludo-Orientalism, 21, 121, 125, 193; gamification of race and, 1–8; model minority and, 82–83; *Pokémon GO* and, 145; rules of, 178; techno-Orientalism and, 8–12, 205n20; theoretical potential of, 25

ludus (as discipline), 128–31, *132*, 134, 135

Lynch, Kevin, 160

magic circle, 15–18, 27, 39, 143–44, 187; ordinary life and, 118; play as, 113, 123; rules of, 123

mahjong, 208n56

Man, Play, and Games (Caillois), 25, 113–14, 117, 126–28, 130–31, 133–35, 145–46

manifest destiny, 94, 129, 161, 167

mapping: cognitive, 157, 159–60, 161, 225n45; glocalization and, 173–74; identity and, 156; imaginative geography and, 157; imperialism and, 193; in Japan, 166, 226n58; play and, 138, 175; *Pokémon GO* and, 173–74; social, 1; technology, 156–57

marketing, 145, 157–58, 168

markets, games and, 190

marriage, 61–62

mathematics, 23

McClendon, Brian, 139

McDonald's, 142

media, 12, 81, 94

memorization, 178

mental health, 85

MentalPlex, 139, 221n1

meritocracy, 5–6, 187

meta-communicative messages, 16

Michaels, Walter Benn, 80

Middleton, Thomas, 19

migration, 158

military, 50, 88, 227n67

Mills, C. Wright, 39, 79, 86

mimicry (simulation), 11, 114, 131, *132*, 133

mining camps, 37, 131

minorities: classification of, 81; identity of, 207n51; *Pokémon GO* and, 3; social mobility of, 180

mixed societies, 134

modalization, 26

model minority, 5–6, 81; Asian Americans and, 83; Cold War, 88–89; criticism of, 83, 90; culture and, 118–19; gambling and, 92, 106; image, 105; imagination and, 188; ludo-Orientalism and, 82–83;

model minority (*cont.*)
 myth of, 83–85, 105; narrative of, 82, 85; racism and, 82; stereotypes, 85, 215n45, 220n22; success and, 82, 91–92; yellow peril and, 4, 41, 83, 88, 106, 114, 220n22
models (toys), 95–97, *96*, 216n55, 217n59
modern fiction, 74–76
modernity, 115, 158
modernization, 182
modern life, irrationality of, 79
Montesquieu, 117
morality, 36, 37, 65, 92
Morgenstern, Oskar, 50–52
mothers, 95
Mr. Noguchi (fictional character), 58, 61, 66, 71
Mr. Snook (fictional character), 67
Mrs. Yamada (fictional character), 72–74, 213n63, 213n69
Mr. Takemoto (fictional character), 66, 70, 74
mukokuseki (lacking cultural markers), 150
Murakami, Takashi, 226n65
Murayama, Milton, 62, 66–69, 212n52
Myer, Dillon, 47–48, 52
My Location, 156, *157*

Nakamura, Hiroshi, 50, 56–61, 65–66, 211n24
Nakamura, Lisa, 214n20
narcissism, 173
narrative, 17, 82, 85, 86, 137
Nash, John, 62–63
national belonging, 56
national imagination, 12
nationalism, 102, 168
nationality, 145
national loyalty, 61
national security, 88
nation making, 197
nations, games and, 197
"Negro question," 34

neoliberalism, 6, 80, 106
neurology, of immigration, 85–86
Niantic, 141, 142, 153, 154
Nietzsche, Friedrich, 87
"Ni Hao (A Gold Farmer's Story)," 177
A 1942 Declaration for Greater East Asian Co-operation, 163–66, *164–65*
Nintendo, 147, 150, 154, 161, 162, 226n55
Nomura, Tatsuo, 139
nongame, game and, 125
No-No Boy (Okada), 17, 70–75, 103, 213n60, 213n67, 213n69
non-playing characters, 18–21
nostalgia, 173, 228n71
nuclear conflict, U.S.-Soviet, 50
Nyarth (fictional character), 152
Nye, Bill, 43, 44, 46, 182–83, 186

Obama, Barack, 178, 196
obscenity, 192
Occidental dream, 121–37
odds. *See* chance
The Official World (Seltzer), 26
Okada, John, 17, 70, 71, 73n60, 75, 103, 213n67
Olympics, 168, 169
online gaming community, 9
operating system, 21–27
opium, 37
ordinary life, magic circle and, 118
Orient: definition of, 116; in game studies, 122, 129, 159. *See also* ludo-Orientalism; Orientalism
Orientalism, 4, 119, 137; definition of, 117, 135; GPS technology and, 156–57; as imaginative geography, 122–23, 126; *Pokémon GO* and, 146; stereotypes, 122; technology and, 158. *See also* ludo-Orientalism; techno-Orientalism
Orientalism (Said), 116
The Origin of German Tragic Drama (Benjamin), 230n41

Otherness, 3, 192–93
otherspeaking, 230n41

paidia (child), 128–30, 134
Palumbo-Liu, David, 81
parenting, 16–17, 171
parlor games, 5, 19, 79, 113
patriarchy, 68
payoffs, 84
Pearl Harbor, 23, 47, 54, 56, 66, 69,
  147, 171
Pegúy, Charles, 79
Pham, Thien, 17–18, *18*
philosophy, 117
"The Philosophy of Toys," 113
physical intimacy, 20
Pikachu (fictional character), 2, 152, 171,
  228n71
"Plain Language from Truthful James."
  See "The Heathen Chinee"
plantation economy, 62
play, 2; aesthetic, 223n9; in China, 122;
  corruption of, 118; culture and, 114–16,
  118–19, 124, 127, 219n14, 220n18; definition of, 113, 123, 126; labor and, 189; as
  magic circle, 113; mapping and, 138,
  175; power and, 217n65; production
  and, 181–82; race and, 11, 121; reality
  and, 123–24, 138; real life and, 15–16, 23,
  25; seriousness and, 118; smartphones
  and, 141–42; sociology of, 119; universality of, 118–19, 121, 223n9; work and,
  23, 83, 192
"playbor," 145, 189–90
player action, 128
player choices, 188
players, Western, 189
pleasure, of gaming, 214nf20
Pokédex, 161
Pokémania, 146
Pokémon, 146, 147, 148, 162
Pokémon Challenge, 139–42, 153
Pokémon character names, 152–53, 224n26

Pokémon franchise, 23, 144, 149
Pokémon GO: aesthetics of, 226n65;
  AR technology in, 1, 6, 124, 153, *153*,
  154, 156, 159, 173; character types in,
  226n62; circular indictment and, 6–7;
  colonization and, 162; cultural imagery
  in, 226n65; data collection from,
  142–43, 146, 162, 189; global interest in,
  146, 171; glocalization and, 157, 224n32;
  Google Maps and, 138–45, *155*, 156, 162;
  GPS technology and, 6, 156; gyms, 162,
  163, 167, 226n62; *Homo Ludens* and,
  145–46; ideology of, 175; imperialism
  and, 167–68; *Ingress* and, 154, 224n29,
  224n32; interface, 160–61; Japan and,
  145, 223n10; ludo-Orientalism and, 145;
  mainstream appeal of, 154; *Man, Play,
  and Games* and, 145–46; mapping and,
  173–74; marketing, 149, 161; McDonald's and, 142; minorities and, 3; Orientalism and, 146; origin of, 138–44; Pearl
  Harbor and, 147; Pokémon franchise
  and, 149; PokéStops, 162; politics and,
  149; race and, 2, 7, 20, 24, 226n62;
  sentimentality in, 228n71; trainer, 167;
  U.S.-Japan antagonism and, 147–48;
  white privilege and, 2
Pokémon TV, 151–52
poker, 33–34, 45, 50, 52
police, 215n45
politics, 6, 14–15, 26, 76, 98, 148–49
popular culture, 225n41
The Portal of the Mystery of Hope (Pegúy),
  79
Postmodernism (Jameson), 160
Poundstone, William, 63–65
poverty, 101
power, 145, 217n65
primitivism, 116, 219n14
Prisoner's Dilemma (Poundstone), 63
privilege, 2, 17
problem box (puzzle box), 64, 212n42
production, 177, 181–82

professional game tournaments, 4
propaganda, *48*, 163–66, *164–65*, 173
property rights, 89
prostitution, 37, 191
Protestant work ethic, 39, 79, 104
psychological incompatibility, 129
public assistance, 88
puerilism, 122, 221n36
puzzle box. *See* problem box

race, 188; academic success and, 83, 90;
    addiction and, 180; as allegory, 196,
    230n41; of avatars, 2; binary of, 196,
    230n41; biology and, 127–28, 204n18;
    capitalism and, 106; celebrity and,
    81–82, 214n15; chance and, 24; class
    and, 80; classification of, 11–12; com-
    puter gaming and, 4; determinism
    and, 83; domesticity and, 95; economy
    and, 8; education and, 88; equality and,
    107; gambling and, 97–98, 220n22;
    games and, 20, 122; gamification and,
    27, 204n18; identity and, 51, 80, 193;
    ideologies of, 24; inequality and, 190;
    instructability and, 51; invention of,
    204n18; legislation and, 34; loyalty
    and, 48, 66–67, 210n4; making, 197;
    play and, 11, 121; Pokémon and, 146;
    Pokémon GO and, 2, 7, 20, 24, 226n62;
    relations, 6, 38, 204n18; representa-
    tion and, 12, 14; social conditions and,
    87–88; social meaning of, 2; space and,
    1, 7; stigma of, 88; success and, 83–84,
    107; in video games, 203n3
race card term, 14
racialization, 7, 177, 207n51
racialized trauma, 20
racial scapegoating, 188
racial stratification, 209n8
racial taxonomy, 132–33
racism, 5, 12, 54, 82, 127–28, 230n33
RAND (corporation), 54–55, 64
rationality, 53, 70–74, 135

The Raw and the Cooked (Lévi-Strauss),
    136
realism, 125–26, 203n3
reality, 175; as broken, 177; culture and,
    115; games and, 125–26; identity of, 197;
    narrative and, 17; play and, 123–24,
    138; rules of, 123. *See also* augmented
    reality
real life, play and, 15–16, 23, 25
rebranding, 167–74
relocation, 50, 61
repatriation, 62
representation: aesthetic, 227n67; Asian
    Americans, 13, 21, 206n35, 207n55;
    dehumanization of, 53–54; exotic, 9;
    fake, 206n35; game of, 12–15, 206n35;
    in game studies, 203n3; of human
    behavior, 53–54; imagination and, 114;
    legitimacy and, 13; media, 81; politics
    and, 14–15; privilege and, 17; race and,
    12, 14
Resident Evil, 159
responsibilities, games and, 180
risk-taking, 24, 87
rituals, 120
room escape, 212n42
rote learning, 178
roulette, 86
Rousseau, Jean-Jacques, 60
rules, 10; culture and, 20–21; of games,
    133; of irrelevance, 187; of ludo-
    Orientalism, 178; of magic circle, 123;
    of reality, 123
Rumsfeld, Donald, 76

Said, Edward, 116, 118, 121, 122–23, 130, 157
San Francisco Illustrated Wasp, 35–36
satellite technology, 171
scapegoating, 188
Schiller, Friedrich, 2
science fiction, 8
scientific racism, 127–28
Scrabble, 95

second-order observations, game theory and, 55
segregation, internment and, 59
self, 116, 134
self-expression, 39
Seltzer, Mark, 26, 70
"The Sensei," 98–100, 103, 105
sentimentality, 213n67, 228n71
seriousness, play and, 118
sex, 95
sexism, 5
sexuality, 73–74
shame, 74
sic bo, 208n56
Silicon Valley, 148
simulation. *See* mimicry
skin color, 191–92
slavery, 34, 40, 45, 209n23
sleight of hand, 69
smartphones, 141–42, *153*
social attitudes, about games, 10
social conditions, race and, 87–88
social dynamics, in U.S., 36
social engineering, of race relations, 6, 204n18
socially marginalized groups, 193
social mapping, 1
social meaning, of race, 2
social mobility, 24–25, 79, 107, 180
social pathology, 89
social relations, 90
social systems, 26
sociology, 118, 127, 131–33
South Park, 171, *172*, *173*
space, 1, 7
spatial dislocation, 3
spending money, 84
StarCraft, 4, 179
stereotypes, 12, 83; of Asian Americans, 4, 15, 89–90; of Asians, 4; of gambling, 22–23; model minority, 85, 215n45; 220n22; Orientalism, 122; in video games, 2; yellow peril, 83

Stimson, Henry, 49
stories, games and, 19
strategy, 52
structuralism, 136
"Structure, Sign, and Play," 136
subprime mortgage crisis, 106
success, 81–84, 91–92, 107
Sumida, Stephen, 212n52
Super Mario Bros., 150, 169–70, *170*
survival, 206n43
Suzuki, Peter, 51, 56–57
sweatshops, 191–93
Systema Naturae (Linnaeus), 132

Tadao Oyama (fictional character), 61
Tajiri, Satoshi, 147–48, 152
Tan, Amy, 20–21, 86
tax, 37
taxation, 178
technology: Asians and, 8; gaming, 10, 15; GPS, 6, 138, 141, 145, 156–57, 161; mapping, 156–57; Orientalism and, 158; satellite, 171. *See also* augmented reality
technonormativity, 4
techno-Orientalism, 225nn41–43, 227n69, 230n41; imaginative geography as new, 153–67; ludo-Orientalism and, 8–12, 205n20; origin of term, 158; yellow peril and, 205n20
temporality, 135
Teru Noguchi (fictional character), 57–59, 61–62, 65
A Theory of Games and Economic Behavior (Von Neumann and Morgenstern), 51–52
"Third World Literature in the Era of Multinational Capitalism," 159–60, 225n43
time, 134–35, 221n36
Tobin, Joseph, 151
Tosh (fictional character), 67–69
tourism, 168
trade, 182, 196

trauma, 20
Treadmill (Nakamura, H.), 51, 56–62, 65–66, 71, 75
Tripmaster Monkey (Kingston), 38

Ultima Online, 187
uncertainty, emotion and, 65
United States (U.S.): foreign policy, 23; gambling and, 37, 84; as gamespace, 23; game theory in, 53; identity, 33; social dynamics in, 36; work in, 86–87; World War II and, 56
updates, 26
urbanization, 219n14
U.S. *See* United States
U.S.-China interdependency, 205n20
U.S.-Japan, *Pokémon GO* and antagonism of, 147–48
U.S.-Soviet nuclear conflict, 50

valorization, 10
values, 22, 35, 67, 94, 104
vertigo. See *ilinx*
video games: Asians and, 203n5; culture and, 20; embedded mechanics of, 10; exotic representation in, 9; history and, 169; identity in, 203n3; in Japan, 148–50, 223n18; parlor games and, 5; politics and, 148–49; procedural logic of, 7; race in, 203n3; realism in, 125; rebranding and, 169; room escape, 212n42; stereotypes in, 2; wealth in, 188
vidushaka (court jester), 117
violence, 230n41
virtual currency, 22
virtual escapism, 9
Von Neumann, John, 50–52, 59, 63, 70

wages, 40–42
"Waiting for the Signal from Home," 48
wan (play), 129–30, 135
Wang, Jen, 184, *185*, 194, *195*
war, 54, 226n65

Wark, McKenzie, 5, 125, 204n10, 230n41
War Relocation Authority, 47, 51
Warren, Earl, 47–48
The Wasp. See San Francisco Illustrated Wasp
wealth, in video games, 188
Western civilization, 116
Western garb, 93
Western self, 116
"Where the Action Is," 79
white face, 145, 150–51
whiteness, 97
white privilege, 2
"Why Chinese Kids Don't Go Bad," 215n45
Wi-Fi, 138
Williams, J. D., 63–64
The Woman Warrior (Kingston), 16–17, 97, 98, 217n61
women, 61, 194
Women Beware Women (Middleton), 19
Wong, Jade Snow, 17, 20
Wong, Sau-ling, 223n9
word processing software, 19
work, 23, 83, 86–87, 105, 192. *See also* labor
world, game and, 144
World of Warcraft, 22, 113, 177, 181, 183, 184, 186, 187–88, 205n22, 228n3
worldviews, 175
World War II, 23, 24, 56, 170, 226n65

Yahtzee, 208n56
Yamamoto, Hisaye, 98–99
Yamauchi, Wakako, 98–101, 217n71, 217n78
Yang, Gene, 17–18, *18*
yellow peril: cheating and, 81; era, 85, 215n45; gambling and, 85–86; games of chance and, 88–89; gold farming and, 181–87; labor and, 216n55; model minority and, 4, 41, 83, 88, 106, 114, 220n22; new, 181–87; stereotypes, 83; techno-Orientalism and, 205n20
Yelp, 138, 189

ABOUT THE AUTHOR

Tara Fickle is Assistant Professor of English at the University of Oregon and an affiliated faculty in Ethnic Studies, the Center for Asian and Pacific Studies, and the New Media & Culture certificate. She has published articles on contemporary American fiction, Asian American cultural politics, and game theory in journals including *Modern Fiction Studies*, *Comparative Literature Studies*, and *MELUS*.

Printed and bound by CPI Group (UK) Ltd, Croydon, CR0 4YY

09/06/2025

14685825-0001